New Economic Windows

Massimo Salzano • Alan Kirman (Eds.)

Economics:
Complex Windows

 Springer

Massimo Salzano
Dipartimento di Scienze Economiche e Statistiche,
Università di Salerno, Italy

Alan Kirman
GREQAM/EHESS, Université d'Aix-Marseille III, France

The publication of this book has been made possible thanks to the financial support of the European Union-HPCF-CT-1999-91, the MIUR-FIRB RBAU01B49F, the Università degli Studi di Salerno and the Regione Campania

Library of Congress Control Number: 2004110092

ISBN 88-470-0279-6 Springer Milan Berlin Heidelberg New York

Springer is a part of Springer Science+Business Media

springeronline.com

© Springer-Verlag Italia 2005

Printed in Italy

Cover design: Simona Colombo, Milano
Cover figure: © www.pixed2000.org from a formula by Damien M. Jones
Typeset by the authors and edited by Antonio Abatemarco, Salerno, using a Springer Macro package
Printing and binding: Staroffset, Cernusco S/N (MI)

Printed on acid-free paper

y20

Main Book Title: _____

Preface

"In some ways, the effect of achieving understanding is to reverse completely our initial attitude of mind. For everyone starts (as we have said) by being perplexed by some fact or other: for instance... the fact that the diagonal of a square is incommensurable with the side. Anyone who has not yet seen why the side and the diagonal have no common unit regards this as quite extraordinary. But one ends up in the opposite frame of mind... for nothing would so much flabbergast a mathematician as if the diagonal and side of a square were to become commensurable". [Aristotele]

This is the first volume of a new series entitled "New Economic Windows". Each volume in the series will, we hope, provide pointers towards a better understanding of the nature of economic phenomena and help to "reverse our initial state of mind" as economists. As H. Simon observed, Economics must be considered a "hard", (in the sense of difficult rather than precise), science. As he cogently argued, the problems dealt with are so complex they "cannot simply be reduced to analytically solvable models or decomposed into separate sub processes".[1] In this he was following on from Einstein who, many years earlier, when asked why he had not turned his attention to economics said that he found it too difficult a subject to handle scientifically.

One of the major problems is that evoked by Aristotele. We have become locked into a particular way of thinking and of framing economic problems. Our aim is to help to change the way in which we view economic questions by exploiting the new methods and tools stemming from the so-called "complexity approach" to science. These have mainly been developed for the analysis of natural systems, both in physics and biology but many examples of their application in economics have already been proposed in the literature.

The history of intellectual thought shows how new and innovative ideas, even

---

[1] F. Schweitzer (2002): Editor's Introduction; www.WorldSciNet.com/acs/acs.html.

though these may later be proved to be sound, often find it difficult to penetrate standard approaches and seem to be unable to stimulate new work in the same direction. Their first appearances are usually ephemeral and have little impact. If ants left pheromone traces that evaporated quickly, individuals would not be able to find their way to food and to organize themselves. The same applies to new concepts. Later these ideas appear in isolated articles dispersed in journals and books. How these isolated contributions arrive suddenly at the critical mass necessary to generate a school of thought might be referred to as the problem the "emergence of emergence".

In economics, in particular, the time seems to be ripe for such an "emergence".[2] Therefore, in this series, we would like to present a number of new contributions which will help to consolidate the place of complexity in economics. This is a more optimistic view than that expressed by Max Planck when he said, "New Ideas do not grow up because those who believed in the old ones are converted to them but rather because those people die and are replaced by younger more open-minded individuals capable of adopting the new vision".

The aim of this first volume is not, of course, to give a "definitive view" of complexity in economics, but to use some of its concepts to open some "windows" on economics questions. The overall goal will be to give some indications as to why and how the complexity approach to economic now seems sufficiently mature to allow us to use it to progress beyond traditional (neoclassical) economic modelling.

The term "complexity" is itself difficult to define and several meanings have been attributed to the term. Sometimes the simple application of deterministic chaos theory is referred to as complex, some consider the interrelation among constituent parts of a system as an important aspect of complexity analysis, others emphasize the presence of "emergence" In this book we will mainly follow the latter approach. A definition of what makes something complex, given by one of the authors in this book is "the fact that available knowledge stored in well established models is not sufficient to reliably predict the emergence, and one must integrate the deductive chains with extra information which introduces a historical [swarm, structural, psychological, or other self-organizing] flavour into the scientific procedure".[3] Put alternatively, breaking down the analysis of an economic system into analytically tractable sub-models may not enable us to account for certain aggregate phenomena. Indeed, the difference between the aggregate and its components lies at the heart of the complexity approach.

But here we should pause a moment and ask why economists are so attached to the idea of reducing economic phenomena to simple analytically solvable

---

[2] See S. Johnson (2001): Emergence. P. 56 Italian Edition.
[3] See Arecchi's contribution to this volume.

models. There is no doubt that the influence of Debreu and the axiomatization of the economic theory that we inherited from the marginalists has a lot to do with it. By reducing this theory to its basic essentials, and spelling out its basic assumptions we had the illusion of making our discipline more scientific. This, for some, provided an answer to a question that has been raised by a bevy of authors as to whether or not economics is a science. Of course, the fact of the matter is that this is the question that the many heterodox approaches in economics, address to mainstream (neoclassical) theory. The basis ingredients of the Neoclassical approach are well known, a well-defined notion of: general equilibrium; non evolutionary (if any) dynamics; well defined preferences, perfect rationality embodied in the principle of optimising behaviour (implying that the individual maximize their expected utility); non increasing returns guaranteeing the convesity of production sets; this in turn together with the convexity of preferences justifies formally the marginalist approach,the use of the representative agent in analysing aggregate behaviour;and so on. These, are of course, exactly the hypothesis at which critics of the neoclassical approach direct their objections.

It would be fair to say that conventional economic modelling follows the paradigm that we inherited from nineteenth century physics, in particular, and which still has an influence on conventional science, and on the ideas that also form a major part of our intellectual culture.

The complexity approach is a more holistic mode of thought and concerns the various different properties of systems[4] that are present at different levels of aggregation and in different contexts.

The complexity approach invokes philosophical ideas that differ from more conventional thinking. The most significant of these relates to self-organisation itself. In this respect at least, traditional (neoclassical) and complex economic modelling are in strong contrast.

A natural question at this point, is as to whether it is necessary to change the basic framework and to introduce new forms of analysis into economic theory. Many authors have tried to modify the basic traditional neoclassical

---

[4] Claire Lucas provides us with a list that is useful as a reference point. She emphasises the following:: a) Uncontrolled - Autonomous agents; b) Nonlinear; c) Emergence ; d) Co-evolution; e) Attractors; f) Non-Equilibrium or dissipative; g) Heterogeneous in space and time; h) Non-Uniform (different rules or local laws); i) Phase Changes (power law distributions); j) Unpredictability - Sensitivity to initial conditions (chaos); k) Instability (punctuated equilibria); l) Mutability (dynamic state space); m) Self-Reproduction (growth); n) Self-Modification (redesign); o) Undefined Values (constructivist semantics); p) Fuzzy Functions (probabilistic correlation). Of course, not all these features need be present in all systems, but the most complex cases should include them.) For an overview of the philosophical implications of complex systems thought see: Chris Lucas: Complexity Philosophy as a Computing Paradigm: clucas@calresco.org.

structure. Like most economists they were aware that the assumptions were highly unrealistic, but at the same time they were unwilling to change their reference paradigm. This presented a nimber of technical challenges for the traditional model , but, in the end, may have revealed its limits rather than its capacity to explain real economic problems.

For example, some researchers consider that the problem of mainstream economics has been its failure to deal adequately with the "heterogeneity of agents". This is too simplistic since general equilibrium theory allows for agents having very diverse preferences and incomes. It is only when this heterogeneity exists at the individual level and individuals are allowed to interact directly with each other and to influence each others' choices and preferences that the history of the process starts to unfold and that we see clearly the "emergence" of certain features of the economic system.[5] Other examples of efforts to modify the standard framework include the relaxing of the concept of perfect rationality to allow for the fact that individuals may have asymmetric information for example. Yet one surely needs to go beyond this and allow for having only local knowledge and furthermore that this varies according to his or her history. Then we get a little closer to a more realistic representation of reality and our models start to reveal "emergent" phenomena. Of course, we should not lose sight of the fact that the very existence of rationality lies at the heart of the difference between economic and natural systems.

Economics has made extensive use of metaphors derived from other disciplines. Neoclassical Economics was based heavily on nineteenth century classical physics and indeed some authors, such as Mirowski have convincingly argued that this was much more than a metaphor.[6] Evolutionary Economics, on the other hand used biological metaphors extensively. Other disciplines use economic concepts and metaphors. Darwin was influenced by Malthus' ideas and the literature on "optimal foraging" in entomology makes almost slavish use of marginalist ideas.[7]

A crucial question here is whether the importing of ideas from other disciplines involves the mere use of metaphors or whether there is a real modification of the analytical structure of the discipline. To answer this question when looking at the many tools deriving from physics and biology that have been incorporated into economics, one is obliged to compare the analytical structure of the original disciplines with that of economics.

In the case of physics and economics the answer is quite clear, as Mirowski

---

[5] See: Kirman (1999) Introduction to "Beyond the representative agent" Kirman, Gallegati (Eds.) Edward Elgar.

[6] See P. Mirowski (1991), More heat than light: Economics as Social Physics, Physics as Nature's Economics; Cambridge University Press.

[7] See e.g. Stephens D.W. and J.R. Krebbs, (1986), "Foraging Theory", Princeton University Press, Princeton N.J.

points out and as Walras openly admitted economics imported the structure of of classical mechanics, "lock stock and barrel". However, in the case of biology the answer is much more ambiguous.[8]

In every case in which tools are transferred from one discipline to another the main question seems to be to evaluate what the differences in the structures are and then, how to satisfactorily adapt, if necessary, the original tools to the new discipline.

A clear example of this type of problem is that of incorporating individual rationality (perfect, bounded, local, or whatever) into the analysis of social networks Another is that of dealing with the multi-dimensionality of economic choices or decision processes when using ideas from artificial intelligence.[9]

Again problems are posed since one of the characteristics of economic systems that strongly differentiate them from inanimate systems is the quality and quantity of data and the ability to undertake experiments.

Again "econophysics", has emphasized the importance of the power law distribution which is considered a universal invariant that applies also to economic reality. The fact that this can be of use to economics is beyond question, but differences exist between power laws and other similar forms of distributions which have already been developed and tested in economics. Furthermore the models which generate power laws frequently take little account of the rationality of the agents involved and are somewhat mechanical in nature. This fact has stimulated a considerable volume of work on alternative kinds of distribution.

The contributions presented here reflect these sorts of consideration and look at economic questions both from a complex point of view and from a variety of disciplinary backgrounds.

The disciplines represented include: Physics, Biology, Mathematics, Statistics-econometrics, Statistical Mechanics and, last but not least, Economics. Most of the contributions are new. Some have been selected from papers presented at the I International Conference "New Economic Windows" held in Salerno - Italy. Of course, the current selection does not cover all the topics involved in "economic complexity", but only a rather narrow range. Papers dealing with purely formal methods or those dealing with very general aspects of complexity in economic systems have, for example, not been selected.

Naturally, given the wide range of questions, it was not possible to consider

---

[8] See e.g. A. Kirman, "La Pense Evolutioniste dans la Thorie conomique Noclassique", in Philosophiques revue de la Socit de Philosophie du Qubec Vol XXV No 2 pp220-237, 1999.

[9] See: Nowak, A. and Vallacher, R.: 1998, Dynamical social psychology, Guilford Press; Albert, R. and Barabasi, A.: 2002, Reviews of Modern Physics 74(1), 47; Cohen, R., Rozenfeld, A., Schwartz, N., ben Avraham, D. and Havlin, S.: 2003, Lecture Notes in Physics 625, (23).

all of them in one single book or even to give simple examples of all the important questions raised.

The choice that has been made is to offer a balanced selection of both general and analytical methodological papers and applied papers. Applied papers were chosen on two grounds, the sector with which they deal and and the tools and methodology that they employ. We tried to cater to a range of complex methodologies and tools, each of which seemed appropriate for analysing its particular economic question. In a sense therefore, this book itself opens a "window" on "complexity in Economics".

The chapters are grouped into 3 different sections: methodological contributions; tools - techniques, and finally empirical studies.

Without abusing our basic metaphor we can say that each chapter opens a new window on its subject and expands our view of the latter. If we then take the overall view that the book reveals it is that a promising avenue for Economics is to look at the economy as a complex system. The different chapters of this book together demonstrate the existence of a well structured approach that will allow us to move on from the restrictive framework of the neoclassical approach. This will allow a shift of perspective in economics. In fact, the essays offer compelling evidence both as to the importance of this analytical approach for the study of the economy and as to the relevance of its potential results. We hope that this will stimulate a discussion on economic methodology which goes beyond the usual arcane debate as to the relative merits of this or that paradigm from the past.

In the first section, that concerned with methodology, there is a particular focus on the underlying logic of the complex approach and its application to economics. This topic has recently attracted considerable research interest since the differences between the neoclassical and the complexity approach to Economics is often not clearly spelled out.

In his work Arecchi describes the concept of "complexity and emergence" and provides clear definitions of these terms. He focuses on determining how much of what we say stems from a cultural bias, and how much is derived from hard facts and grounded on an ontology. He discusses "why among many peculiarities (saliences) we prefer to focus our attention on some ones (pregnancies)"; how, "we select the relevant words (names) depending on their relation with an ontology (things)". Then, he introduces a separation between purely mental situations (closed systems) and what we in fact come across daily (open systems). In so doing he echoes many great economists from the past such as Pareto, Hicks and Koopmans who all were very conscious that the basic assumptions of our science are derived from introspection rather than observation.

Brock and Colander start from the consideration that the majority of economists are applied economists who are used to applying the "received economic wisdom embodied in a set of canonical models" to specific cases. However, they have in fact contributed, almost unconsciously, to "a broader shift away from Solow's holy trinity, rationality-equilibrium-greed that is occurring in modern economics" of which complexity work is a part. Thus, the authors highlight the discord between the welfare theory we teach, and the actual practice of applied policy economics, in the hope that researchers will become more conscious of it and make a more conscious effort to develop a rather different welfare framework suggested by recent works, which consider the economy as a complex system. Four types of changes in applied policy that can follow from this complexity foundation are discussed. Perhaps most importantly, given the emergent aggregate properties of complex systems the authors suggest that more careful attention should e paid to the design of institutions.

Day concentrates his interest on the impact that history can have on the present and on the evolution of structures and how this impact can be revealed if the correct tools are used. Even if it is tempting to presume that the "long ago past" has "little relevance for the present", he concludes "nothing could be further from the truth". The paper describes and applies a multiple phase theory of macroeconomic evolution that is able to explain certain salient, qualitative attributes of very long run historical records.
Indeed, given the ability of the theory to explain the past and certain important events such as the sudden collapse of certain economic systems, we should draw some implications which might help us better understand the present and enable us to take measures to mitigate such collapses in the future.

In his work Keen deals with the theory of the firm, and explains, in his view, "Why Economics Must Abandon its Theory of the Firm". He focuses on two main questions: the notion of a marginal revenue function, and the idea of perfect competition. He says that: "There are simple, intuitive explanations of why the conventional theory of the firm is erroneous". The marginal revenue curve exists regardless of how many firms there are in industry, and the mantra that a firm maximizes profit by equating marginal cost and marginal revenue is wrong in multi-firm industries. The only feasible defence for perfect competition comes from game theory.

The second section, tools and techniques, deals mainly with the problem of how to adapt tools and techniques derived from other disciplines to some of the specific characteristics of economics. Differences and similarities between economics and these other disciplines are considered.

Zbilut looks at one of the main differences between economics and physics which resides the characteristics of the data on which empirical researches must rely.
Whereas the physical sciences can generate reasonably long stationary data, economic sciences necessarily depend upon data collected from imperfectly

controlled sources. In addition, a considerable amount of noise is often present in economic data. Much effort has been devoted to modelling economic time series in the context of nonlinear chaotic dynamics. Unfortunately, these attempts have not been characterized by unequivocal results. Some of the difficulties have been attributed to the characteristics of the algorithms used to quantify chaotic invariants (dimensions, entropies, and Lyapunov exponents) but, as is well-known, more traditional methods (FFTs) have also encountered difficulties. To overcome the latter the use of "Recurrence Quantification Analysis" is proposed. This tool has some characteristics that could help to identify economic chaotic dynamics in economic time series, if it exists.

D'Apuzzo looks, from a mathematical point of view, at the "evaluation of the alternatives" which is a crucial point in a decision making process.
Usually, for every alternative the Decision Maker has at his disposal n estimates that can be either degrees of satisfaction of the alternative to n criteria, or the judgements of n experts, or evaluations of n possible consequences of the alternative. In any event, before making a choice, the Decision Maker has to translate the n local estimates into a real number representing the global evaluation of the alternative; so he needs an aggregation operator. The question is: what operator? In this evaluation the "Quasilinear Aggregation Operators and Preference Functionals" could be of help. In some situations, for example paradoxical cases, the usual description based on a single functional is not sufficient. Certain behaviour of decision maker, like most of the subjects in Kahneman and Tversky's experiments, and those related to Allais paradoxes, cannot be modelled by applying just one functional for every choice situation:since the functional representing the preference depends on the gambling schemas.

Buendia, in his chapter, focuses on the important topic of increasing returns. He integrates them in a general model of business competition that provides tools and insights concerning the size distribution of firms and skewedness of industrial structures but this model alone is incapable of explaining some important possibilities of increasing return. Then, in a second step, he incorporates in the general model a whole set of strong and important increasing return mechanisms, namely, reputation effects, network externalities and infrastructure effects and he concentrates on the theoretical process through which this general model of business competition will gradually reveal the central role of increasing return mechanisms.

Finally, section three, that which contains empirical contributions, deals with many examples of application in different areas of economics. These contributions are ranked according to the level of "complexity" of the approach used. Therefore, the following approximate order has been followed: the limits of general equilibrium in dealing with heterogeneous agents, the connection between the fiscal and financial sectors as an element that must be considered for explaining the dynamic behaviour of aggregate data (multi-dimensionality), the dynamics of group formation, and the multi-dimensionality of choices.

Abatemarco presents an analysis of the main Italian stock-market index (Mibtel) in order to point out the relevance of the interrelations between public and financial sectors, in contrast with the main approach in the traditional economic literature.

He considers that analyses of structural instabilities in the financial market necessarily require a quali-quantitative approach, as this specific market is closely interrelated with other economic sectors, like the public one (multi-dimensionality of economic phenomena).

In this context, the fiscal variable, traditionally neglected in financial market analysis, seems to be a good explanatory variable for understanding financial market behaviour. In fact, it seems able to determine radical changes in individual choices.

In "Heterogeneity in General Equilibrium: The Battle of Coalitions" Busato and Chiarini address some of the failures of the general equilibrium model in dealing with phenomena present in real-world economies.

The paper introduces a decentralized process and agents' heterogeneity in a dynamic general equilibrium model. With agents' heterogeneity the equilibrium laws of motion appear not only as functions of aggregate variables, but also as functions of the distributions of these variables across different types of agents. Often, this requires iteration of the problem also at the individual level. The use of "rules of thumb" among the feasible decision rules allows for the introduction of two types of agents: sophisticated and unsophisticated. This is similar to the hypothesis made in work on volatility in financial markets in which different percentages of fundamentalist and chartist are considered.

Two Coalitions are considered: one on the labor side (Consumer-Worker and a Consumer-Unemployed), and the other on the firm side (Consumer-Shareholder, and a Delegated Manager). While incorporation of these features force the model's equilibrium to be Pareto suboptimal, it may improve the model's ability to replicate adequately a set of stylized facts about business cycles and, moreover, the sub optimality of the equilibrium affords a necessary rationale for countercyclical policy intervention studies. The authors address some features of the European labor market: such as union wage setting and unemployment benefits.

In their work D. Delli Gatti, C. Di Guilmi, E. Gaffeo, M. Gallegati, G. Giulioni, and A. Palestrini look at possible inconsistencies between power laws and the well established, in the industrial economics field, Gibrat's law.

Since the pioneering work of Gibrat (1931), it has been clear that - given the "law of proportional effect" (LPE) - the distribution of firms' sizes must be right skew ("Gibrat's law" in its weak form), and such distribution must be log-normal (strong form of "Gibrat's law").

As is well known, this is connected with the rate of growth, and the log-normal was not the only asymptotic distribution consistent with Gibrat's law. In fact, minor modifications in the random growth model at the basis of Gibrat's law - for instance, allowing growth rates to be independent on average - result in a skewed distribution of firms' size of the Yule or of the Pareto (or "power law") types. Some new empirical evidence is presented.

Yegorov studies the dynamics of group formation - especially the emergence of firms and countries under the hypothesis of a possibility of surplus creation in particular pairs - given that different shapes of production function are possible.
He focuses on the fact that the traditional concept of equilibrium in economics often lacks the property of dynamic sustainability, in the sense that there might be no process leading to its emergence. He thus returns to the long debate on stability in economics. In contrast, equilibria in physics and other natural sciences emerge as natural outcomes of some dynamics and bear the property of stability with respect to small perturbations. The paper tries to fill this gap by considering the analogy and difference with physics. The analogy is that all these structures are composed of elements (atoms in physics and agents in economics) and are relatively stable. The difference is that atoms are irrational and obey the laws of nature while agents are fully or partly rational and maximize some internal objectives. The gap can be closed by imposing some information structure, and the principle of local interaction in economics. These make it possible to derive structures similar to physics. For simplicity, competition of only two technologies is studied, but some results can be generalized. He describes the procedure of group emergence as a process similar to chemical reaction or crystallization. The elements of these self-organized groups formally obey economic laws, but the dynamics of the process depends on the shape of production technologies.

Erez, Hohnisch, and Solomon aim at formulating a general framework for modelling economic systems, where each agent is characterized by a vector of variables (multi-dimensionality of decision process).
They present the theoretical landscape, a first step towards this general framework and its possible ramifications. Their contribution starts from the consideration that for Statistical Economics (a term coined by Grandmont 1992), to benefit from the vast knowledge accumulated in Statistical Mechanics, it is crucial to establish which structures are shared by physical and economic systems, and which are intrinsically different. Both objects of interest involve local interactions of both the attractive and repulsive type. The locality of the interactions raises the issue of the structure of the underlying network. In fact, economic dynamics involve social networks, for which a regular graph topology, often adequate in the physical world, does not seem to be so in economics. Scale-free graphs and many layers each with a particular graph structure would be a better way in which to analyse the way in which agent

in could interact in different graphs. Moreover, social networks formalize communication links rather than physical proximity as in Physics. The work presented is strictly connected to, and implicitly suggests some lines of possible enhancement of the recently developed agent-based economic models where the connections/interactions between the agents were usually represented by a single network.

In conclusions we hope that all of these contributions will give us a better idea of where we are in economics and, more importantly, where we are going.

Alan Kirman
Massimo Salzano

August, 2004

Contents

Part III Empirical Works

List of Contributors

Antonio Abatemarco
University of Salerno,
Department
of Economics and Statistics, Salerno,
Italy.

Tito F. Arecchi
University of Florence,
Department of
Physics, Florence, Italy.

William A. Brock
University of Wisconsin,
Department
of Economics, Madison, USA.

Fernando Buendia
University of the Americas-Puebla
Business School,
Business Administration Depart-
ment, Puebla,
Mexico.

Francesco Busato
Columbia University, Department of
Economics, New York, USA.

Bruno Chiarini
University of Naples "Parthenope",
Istituto di Studi Economici, Naples,
Italy.

David Colander
Middlebury College,
Department of
Economics, Middlebury, USA.

Livia D'Apuzzo
University of Naples "Federico II",
Department of Architecture, Naples,
Italy.

Richard H. Day
University of Southern California,
Department of Economics, Los
Angeles, USA.

Domenico Delli Gatti
University "Cattolica del Sacro
Cuore", Institute of Quantitative
Methods and Economic Theory,
Milan, Italy.

Corrado Di Guilmi
Università Politecnica delle
Marche, Department of Economics,
Ancona, Italy.

Tom Erez
Hebrew University,
Racah Institute of
Physics, Jerusalem, Israel.

Edoardo Gaffeo
University of Trento, Department of
Economics and CEEL, Trento, Italy.

Mauro Gallegati
Università Politecnica delle
Marche, Department of Economics,
Ancona, Italy.

Gianfranco Giulioni
Università Politecnica delle
Marche, Department of Economics,
Ancona, Italy.

Martin Hohnisch
University of Bonn, Department of
Economics, Bonn, Germany.

Steve Keen
University of Western Sydney,
Department of
Economics and Finance, Sydney,
Australia.

Alan Kirman
Université dAix-Marseille III,
Greqam/Ehess, Marseille, France.

Antonio Palestrini
Università Politecnica delle
Marche, Department of Economics,
Ancona, Italy.

Massimo Salzano
University of Salerno,
Department of
Economics and Statistics, Salerno,
Italy.

Sorin Solomon
Hebrew University,
Racah Institute of
Physics, Jerusalem, Israel.

Yuri Yegorov
Central European University,
Department
of Economics, Budapest, Hungary.

Joseph P. Zbilut
Rush Medical College,
Department of
Molecular Biophysics and Physiology,
Chicago, USA.

Part I

Methodological Works

Complexity and Emergence of Meaning: Toward a Semiophysics

F.T. Arecchi*

1 Introduction

In a debate on "Complexity and emergence", we should first of all provide clear definitions for these terms, in order to ascertain how much of what we say depends on our cultural bias, is an artifact of our linguistic tools, and how much corresponds to hard facts, to our embedding in an open environment, whose features, even though actively elaborated by our semantic memory, can not be taken as sheer "autopoiesis", but are grounded on an ontology.

This inquiry is done from the point of view of a physicist who has been active for decades in investigating the formation of collective or coherent processes out of a large amount of otherwise separate individuals, pointing out the critical appearance (emergence) of new world configurations and the elements of novelty of this emergence, which make this phenomenon complex. By complex we do not mean the trivial fact that the computational cost of their description is high (in such a case I would rather call them complicate) but the fact that available knowledge stored in well established models is not sufficient to predict reliably the emergence, and one must integrate the deductive chains with extra information which introduces a historical flavour into the scientific procedure.

This presentation is organized as follows.

In a first part we discuss the sources of wonder, what Plato called the origin of science, that is, why among many peculiarities (saliences) we prefer to focus our attention on some ones (pregnancies) (Sec. 2). Then we explore how, as we organize our knowledge into a scientific language, we select the relevant words (names) depending on their relation with an ontology (things) (Sec. 3).

* This paper has been published with the permission of E. Agazzi and L. Monte-cucco: "Complexity and Emergence", E. Agazzi and L. Montecucco Eds., World Scientific, Singapore, 2002, pp.115-146.

In a second part we try to put order into the debated issue of complexity, introducing a fundamental separation between some purely mental situations without any realistic counterpart (closed systems) and what we in fact come across everyday (open systems) (secs. 4 and 5).

As for the Reference list, I have often replaced the specific mention of an article or a book by a Web site, where one can conveniently browse for a more satisfactory answer. I think that time is ripe to consider this reference tool as a standard one.

2 Salience vs pregnancy

The world around us is full of salient features, that is, sharp gradients which denote the transition from one domain to another one. Salience can be captured automatically by a scanning detector equipped to grasp differential features. Saliences have a geometric (space-wise) and dynamic (time-wise) flavor. They correspond to objective features: what Thomas Aquinas called "ispositio rei" and more recently A.Reinach (a follower of Husserl) called "Sachverhalt" (Smith).

We might say that saliences uncover an ontology (Poli), however, in order to classify a set of features and organize them through mutual relations, we need to assign selection criteria.

These descriptive criteria have guided the construction of sectorial ontologies in many AI (Artificial Intellicence) areas (Guarino).

Hence the problem arises: are there individual objects, or instead any world organization is an arbitrary cut that we operate by picking up some saliences and disregarding other ones?

Historically the modern European culture, in line with its Greek - Jewish roots, had chosen the first side of this dilemma; however the contact with Eastern philosophies, through Schopenhauer and Mach, introduced a "conventionalism" or linguistic relativism, whereby one could build different, uncorrelated, ontologies depending on the points of view from where saliences were selected (Feyerabend 1975, Capra 1975).

The recent emphasis on "regional ontologies", focused on particular saliences and whence on particular classes of objects, is a modern technical limitation. A philosopher of science (Agazzi 1974) would rather say that selecting a point of view gives rise to a particular science, focusing on some truths different from other ones. Yet there is a hard aspect of saliences, that is, they uncover facts having their own existence, and not just dependent on our cultural artifacts.

In line with Gestalt psychology, René Thom has introduced "pregnancy" to denote a subset of saliences which are relevant for the individual observer (Thom 1988).

In the case of animals, pregnancy is related to vital needs (search of food, escaping from predators, sexual appeal). Some of these needs may be genetically imprinted (Lorenz), some others are the result of cultural influences. This latter case is particularly important for human beings. In this regard, it is fundamental the contribution of J. Piaget called "Genetic epistemology". As one explores the formation of logical structures in children, one realizes that they derive from actions on the objects, not from the objects themselves; in other words, the formation of logical structures is grounded on the coordination of actions, not necessarily on language. In fact, language is one of the possible semiotic functions; the other ones, as gestures, or imitation, or drawing, are forms of expression independent from language, as carefully studied in the case of deaf-mutes (Evans 1973).

Anyway, against relativism, Thom insists on the objective character of the prominent saliences, which he classifies in terms of differential geometry (Thom 1975).

A very convincing dynamical formulation of the emergence of a new feature, or the disappearance of an old one, as a "control parameter" is changed, is given by 1937 Landau's theory of phase transitions (Landau and Lifshift 1980). We present the argument in the updated 1973 formulation called "Synergetic" by Haken (Haken 1983) and initially motivated by a new astonishing phenomenon as the laser threshold, namely, the onset of a collective coherent emission of light out of billion of atoms, which below that threshold instead contribute individual, unrelated (so called spontaneous) emission acts, as it occurs in a conventional light source.

Let me anticipate something I'll discuss in greater detail in Sec. 3. Assume from the time being that we succeeded in describing the world as a finite set of N features, each one characterized by its own measured value $x_i (i = 1 \, to \, N)$, x_i being a real number, which in principle can take any value in the real domain $(-\infty, \infty)$ even though boundary constraints might confine it to a finite segment L_i.

A complete description of a state of facts (a "*dispositio rei*") is given by the N-dimensional vector

$$\underline{x} \equiv (x_1, x_2, ..., x_i, ..., x_N) \tag{1}$$

The general evolution of the dynamical system $\underline{x}$ is given by a set of N rate equations for all the first time derivatives $\dot{x}_i = dx_i/dt$. We summarize the evolution via the vector equation

$$\dot{\underline{x}} = \underline{f}(\underline{x}, \mu) \tag{2}$$

where the function $\underline{f}$ is an N-dimensional vector function depending upon the instantaneous $\underline{x}$ values as well as on a set of external (control) parameters μ.[1]

---

[1] A pedagogical example, Newton's law $F = ma$, relating the acceleration $\alpha = d\nu/dt$ (rate of change of the velocity ν) to the force $F(q)$ depending upon the positions q, can be expressed as a 2-dimensional relation between position and velocity $\dot{q} = \nu$ as well as acceleration and force $(\dot{\nu} = \frac{1}{m}F(q))$. In this case $\underline{x}(x_1, x_2) \equiv (q, \nu)$.

Solution of Eq. (2) with suitable initial conditions provides a trajectory $\underline{x}(t)$ which describes the time evolution of the system. We consider as ontologically relevant those features which are *stable*, that is, which persist in time even in presence of perturbations. To explore stability, we perturb each valuable x_i by a small quantity ξ_i, and test whether each perturbation ξ_i tends to disappear or to grow up catastrophically.

However complicated is the nonlinear function $\underline{f}$, the local perturbation of (2) provides for ξ_i simple exponential solutions versus time of the type

$$\xi_i(t) = \xi_i \mu e^{-\lambda_i t} \tag{3}$$

The λ_i can be evaluated from the functional shape of Eq. (2). Each perturbation ξ_i shrinks or grows in course of time depending on whether the corresponding stability exponent λ_i to positive or negative.[2] Now, as we adjust from outside one of the control parameters μ, there may be a critical value μ_c where one of the λ_i crosses zero (goes from + to -) whereas all the other $\lambda_j (j \neq i)$ remain positive. We call λ_u the exponent changing sign (u stays for "unstable mode") and λ_s all the others (s stay for stable) (fig. 1). Around μ_c, the perturbation $\xi_u(t) \approx e^{-\lambda_u t} \approx e^0$ tends to be long lived, which

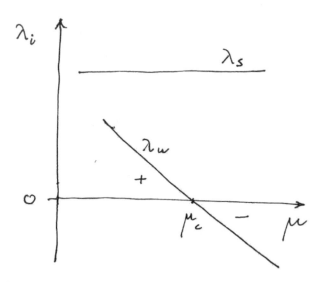

Fig. 1. When the control parameter crosses the value μ_c, the eigenvalues λ_s remain positive, whereas the eigenvalue λ_u goes from positive to negative.

---

[2] Technically, λ_i are the eigenvalues of the matrix J. For simplicity we assume that J is already in diagonal form.

means that the variable x_u has rather slow variations with respect to all the others, that we cluster into the subset x_s which varies rapidly. Hence we can split the dynamics (2) into two subdynamics, one 1-dimensional (u) and the other (N-1) - dimensional (s), that is, rewrite Eq. (2) as

$$\dot{x}_u = f_u(x_u, x_s, \mu)$$
$$\dot{x}_s = f_s(x_u, x_s, \mu)$$

(4)

The second one being fast, the time derivative $\dot{x}_s$ rapidly goes to zero, and we can consider the algebraic set of equations $f_s = 0$ as a good physical approximation. The solution yields x_s as a function of the slow variable x_u

$$x_s = g(xu)$$

(5)

We say that x_s are "slaved" to x_u. Replacing (5) into the first of (4) we have a closed equation for x_u

$$\dot{x}_u = f_u(x_u, g(x_u), \mu)$$

(6)

First of all, a closed equation means a self consistent description, not depending upon the preliminary assignment of x_s. This gives an ontological robustness to x_u; its slow dependence means that it represents a long lasting feature and its self consistent evolution law Eq. (6) means that we can forget about x_s and speak of x_u alone. Furthermore as μ crosses μ_c, a previous stable value x_u is destabilized. A growing ξ_u means that eventually the linear perturbation is no longer good, and the nonlinear system saturates at a new value x_u (fig. 2). Such is the case of the laser going from below to above threshold; such is the case of a thermodynamic equilibrium system going e.g. from gas to liquid or from disordered to ordered as the temperature at which it is set (here represented by μ) is changed. To summarize, we have isolated from the general dynamics (2) some critical points (bifurcations: see the shape of fig. 2) where new salient features emerge. The local description is rather accessible, even though the general nonlinear dynamics f may be rather nasty.

Told in this way, the scientific program seems converging towards firm answers, as compared to the shaky arguments of philosophers. However it was based on a preliminary assumption, that there was a "natural" way of assigning the x_i. In the next Section we explore how to extract the x_i from observations.

3 Names and things

To avoid subjective biases, one should replace definitions in everyday language by quantitative assessments. This is done by isolating something which can be represented in a metrical space as a number, and speaking of a larger or smaller degree of it, of the distance between two values etc., by referring to the corresponding numbers.

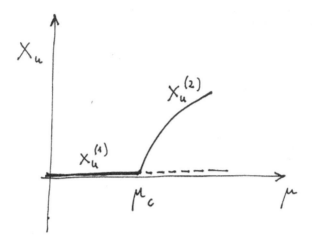

Fig. 2. The horizontal branch x_u becomes unstable at μ_c and a new stable branch x_u emerges from the bifurcation point.

In modern science this attitude was consecrated by G. Galilei in his 1610 letter to Marc Welser (Galilei 1932), where he says: "*don't try to grasp the "essence" (i.e. don't try to define the "nature" of things) but stick to some quantitative affections*".

For instance, in the case of apples, rather than arguing on the nature of apples, make comparisons among them, based on quantitative measures of "affections" as flavour, colour, shape, size, taste. I have listed five qualities for each of which we know how to introduce a meter and hence set a metrical space. At Galilei's time, there was a distinction between primary (measurable) and secondary (subjective) qualities. Nowadays, we know how to objectify and measure secondary quality as flavour or taste, thus, that old distinction is no longer relevant.

Two different attitudes may be adopted, namely,

i) *Phenomenology*: once apples are characterized by a sufficient group of parameters, all apples will be a suitable intersection of the flavour axis, the colour axis etc. in a multidimensional space; such a description is complete (all apples will be included) and unambiguous (two different apples will not overlap in such a multidimensional space, that is, they differ by at least one of their representative numbers).

ii) *Reductionism*: split the apple into small pieces, and these again into smaller ones, until you reach a set of elementary components (the biomolecules) out of which, with a wise dosage of the elements of the set, one can reconstruct (synthesize) all kinds of apples. This procedure is lengthier than phenomenology, but it is universal; out of a set of components one can also synthesize oranges, dogs etc. Moreover it looks objective; if we come across intelligent beings from elsewhere, we don't know if our selected affections are relevant for them, but surely they know how to split the apple into components and catch each component's dynamics. When the only known interaction law (2) was Newton's, this approach seemed the ultimate one; thus Newtonianism was considered as the new revolutionary approach upon which to build any world view. An Italian writer of XVIII century,F.Algarotti, wrote in this regard a booklet "Il Newtonianesimo per le dame" ("Newtonianism for ladies") which was the first manifesto of the woman liberation movement, translated into most European languages.

Both approaches can be formalized. A familiar example of a formal theory is Euclid's geometry. Once a set of components has been defined and their mutual relations stated, via a group of axioms, all possible consequences are deducible as theorems, which provide by necessity all explanations as well as predictions on the future behavior.

In phenomenology, we have many sciences, in reductionism, we have a single fundamental science, that of the elementary components, out of which we can extract all relevant levels of organization.

Such an approach has been abundantly criticized (Anderson 1972, Arecchi 1992, 1995, Arecchi and Farini 1996). The main criticism is that the nonlinear dynamics of microscopic components undergoes multiple bifurcations, of the kind of fig. 2, as a control parameter is varied in order to build up a macroscopic object; thus the construction from scratch of a large size system is by no means unique, and the multiple outcomes are a token of *complexity*, as discussed in Sec. 5.

Since however this essay points at a more fundamental approach to our cognitive acts, for the time being we list current approaches without criticism, just to introduce the technical language and get acquainted with the corresponding problems.

Reductionism does not mean to refer always to Democritus' atoms (nowadays, we would say to leptons and quarks), but to stop at a suitable level where the elementary components are sufficiently characterized. Such are the biomelecules for living beings.

For all practical purposes, the biologists need the descriptive properties of the biomolecules, plus some knowledge of the nearest lower level, that of atomic physics. Think e.g. of the role of $Na^+, K^+ and Ca^{2+}$ ion conductances in neurophysiology or of the devastating effect of some atoms as thallium or plutonium on enzymatic processes, or the balance of hydrogen bonds and van der Waals bonds in stabilizing protein folding.

Thus biochemistry is founded on atomic physics but it does not require nuclear or subnuclear physics. Similarly, atomic physics requires only nuclear physics but not further levels below, and so on.

However, there is no fundamental level which acts as the ultimate explanatory layer.

In fact, recently the problem has been addressed whether a formal description of the state of an elementary particle is sufficient to build a faithful replica of it elsewhere (the so called teleportation problem (Bennett 1987)). As described in Appendix I, a formal description within the current language of quantum mechanics is not sufficient to provide full recovery of the particle. One must add some non formalizable piece of information. Just like interacting with a baby or somebody of different language; nominal definitions are not enough, the dictionary must be integrated by "ostensive definitions", just putting your finger on the object.

We now discuss how the set (1) of relevant variables and the law of motion (2) are established in the two cases apriori (or reductionistic) and aposteriori, or phenomenological.

3.1 Apriori

This approach started with Newton and has continued up to the present search for a unified theory of all fundamental interactions. It consists in counting the particles in the universe attributing to each one 6 numbers, 3 coordinates in Euclidean space and 3 momenta (or more simply in the non relativistic limits, 3 velocity components).

Quantum mechanics added more specifications for internal degrees of freedom, such as "spin" and electrical charge, both for leptons and quarks, plus "strangeness", "charm" and some other properties for quarks. The numbers corresponding to these internal degrees of freedom do not span over all real, but are confined to a small set of possible values. Most often, they correspond to dichotomous variables with just two values, conventionally denoted as 0 and 1. Anyway, each x_i is a group of 6 real numbers for a classical particle, plus a few other discrete numbers for quantum particles.

The coupling function f of Eq. (2) implies mutual relations. Initially, the single universal one was considered Newton's gravitational interactions. Later, Maxwell electromagnetic theory became the prototype of any field theory. Here, the coupling is no longer between particles but each particle feels forces corresponding to a new entity, the local electromagnetic-field at its position. Viceversa, the fields are generated by moving charged particles. Thus the particle-particle interactions are mediated by the fields; in field dynamics we speak no longer of "action at distance".

In electromagnetic theory one adds a new set x_i of consisting of the 6 components of the electric and magnetic field at each point in space. In this case we have a continuous field problem, since the position is not a discrete set of numbers, but varies with continuity. We write $x(r)$ where r denotes the position coordinates in a 3 dimensional space; here r is made of three real numbers and we write this as $r \in \Re^3$ (r belongs to the 3 dimensional real space).

The continuum problem has haunted modern physics since its start, and clever devices to deal with it have been produced. However in most cases the continuous fabric of space can be discretized as a lattice of points at finite distances from each other.

I illustrate this trick with reference to a time dependent signal $x(t)$ observed over a finite time interval T; it depends on all the real values taken by t in the segment T. Outside T the signal is not defined, thus we can arbitrarily assume that it repeats periodically with period T, without affecting the values within the observation interval. This means that its information is contained in a discrete Fourier series of pairs of real numbers A_n, φ_n sampled at a frequency $n\frac{1}{T}$ which is the $n\text{-}th$ harmonic of the fundamental repetition frequency $1/T$, that is

$$x(t) = \sum_{n\cong 1}^{\infty} A_n \cos\left(n\frac{2\pi}{T} + \varphi_n\right) \qquad (7)$$

Thus, the finite interval T limitation has simplified the mathematical description of the signal from continuum to discrete. We do indeed probe with continuity each real t, but we synthesize the signal by summing up at each point a discrete set of sinusoids. If furthermore we consider that any detection or signal processing device is a low pass filter with a finite frequency window B (i.e., it responds only to frequencies up to B), then we can truncate the sum (7) up to a maximum value $n_{max} = B \cdot T$ and the signal information of $x(t)$ over T is contained in n_{max} sinusoids. Since however for each frequency we have an amplitude A_n and a phase φ_n, the set of numbers which fully specify our signal is twice $B \cdot T$, that is,

$$N = 2BT \qquad (8)$$

This important sampling theorem, stated by RADAR investigators during World War II (Shannon 1949), sets the resolution limit for an observation with bandwidth B lasting for a time T. To acquire more information, one must either increase B or T. In a similar way, a visual system (the eye, or a telecamera) frames a finite two-dimensional domain of sizes L_1, L_2 with bandwidths and B_1 and B_2 . Thus the number of relevant picture elements (pixels) of a two dimensional image is given by

$$N = 4B_1 B_2 L_1 L_2 \qquad (9)$$

The sampling theorem has induced the strong belief that any cognitive process deals with a finite number of elements, and furthermore that the universe is described by a finite, though very large, number of degrees of freedom.

The mathematics of XVIII century physics has been expressed in terms of ODE's (ordinary differential equations) for the continuous variation of a variable x_i as a continuous time t flows. If infinitesimally close space points have to be coupled, then we express the co-presence of space derivatives together with time derivatives by PDE's (partial differential equations). If time is discretized by sampling it at final distances, then the ODE's are replaced by iteration maps, whereby the value of x at the discrete time $n + 1$ depends upon the value of x at the previous time n, that is,

$$x_{n+1} = f(x_n; \mu) \tag{10}$$

If also the space can be discretized as a lattice of disjoint points denoted by discrete indices i, j, than the space derivatives reduce to coupling the iteration maps at different points, as (CML= coupled map lattice)

$$x_{n+1}(i) = f(x_n(i), x_n(i+1); x_n(i-1), ...) \tag{11}$$

Eventually, if also the variable x is bound to assume a finite set of values, in the limit binary values (0,1), than we have a CAM (cellular automaton machine) consisting of a network of points each represented by a binary variable which updates at discrete times depending on the values of the neighboring points or "cells" (Wolfram 1984). We summarize in Table 1 the different types of mathematically modeling the evolution of a physical system.

Table I

State Variable	Time Variable	Space Variable	
C	C	C	PDE
C	C	D	ODE
C	D	D	CML
D	D	D	CAM

C = Continuos, D= Discrete

CAM techniques have been very powerful in dealing with model problems, from biology (genetics, population dynamics, immune system) to sociology (traffic problems, econophysics) and meteorology. They have become the basis of a finitistic ideology, whereby the universe can be seen as a large CAM (Toffoli 1998).
However a fundamental limitation to this ideology arises from quantum non commutativity of pairs of complementary observables, as we'll discuss in Sec.6.

3.2 Aposteriori

New classes of phenomena are disclosed by the exploitation of innovative sophisticated systems of investigation, e.g. recording long time series in financial trading or in car traffic, imaging techniques in brain investigation, automatic machines for sequencing DNA. It is very difficult to fit this new phenomena into a Newtonian frame. A component description is hopeless and one wants to approach the problem directly, without prejudices.
Suppose that, by salience considerations, we have focused our attention on a time dependent quantity $u(t)$. Salience means that $u(t)$ displays a patterned behavior, that is, it is strongly correlated with its values at later times. Take $u(t)$ as the deviation from an average value, then its time average is zero, that

is, $u(t)$ looks as a sequence of $+/-$ values. Consider the product of two u's at different times. If they are unrelated, then also the average product of them, called correlation function $C(t, t')$, is zero.

A nonzero $C(t, t')$ is a signature of salience. Karhunen (1946) and Loève (1955) introduced independently the following retrieval method that we call KL [Karhunen,Loeve] and whose technical details are given in Appendix II. If $\theta_n(t)(N = 1, 2, ..., L)$ are the L most prominent characteristic functions (called eigenfunctions) which retrieve the correlation $C(t, t')$ and if l is a small number, then we can accurately reconstruct the signal as a weighted sum of L functions as follows:

$$u(t) = \sum_{n=1}^{L} \alpha_n \theta_n(t) \tag{12}$$

If the signal depends on space rather than time, then we grasp the salient features of a given space pattern. Each of these saliences in general is spread over the whole domain. A relevant example in the convective motion of a fluid was given by Ciliberto and Nicolaenko (1991), where the three main "modes" of behavior ($L = 3$) are distributed over the whole fluid cell.

The opposite limit occurs when saliences are strongly localized. Think e.g. of the face elements (nose, eyes, mouth shape) upon which identikits of criminals are built in police investigation. In such a case, KL would be inconvenient, since it requires a large L to converge toward a localized feature. Here the successful phenomenological approach is just the opposite of KL. It consists in reconstructing a pattern, e.g. a face, by a small series of "prototypes". This approach is used in many machine vision programs (?).

4 Closed versus open systems

I have discussed elsewhere (Arecchi 1995) the failure of what Anderson called the "constructionist" program (Anderson 1972). Trying to build a structured system out of its elementary components does not provide a univocal outcome.

Indeed the components interact via a nonlinear law as Eq.(2) and the emergence of a new stable structure starting from an initial condition P_0 requires the appropriate tuning of the control parameters. Such a tuning provides in general more than one new stable state.(Fig.3) The emerging states $2, 2'$ are equivalent, thus, as μ is tuned to μ_{C1}, the system has equal probability of emerging in the state 2 or $2'$, unless we break the symmetry of the bifurcation by the application of an external field (fig.3b), which makes the two stable states non equivalent, and hence one of the two (the upper one in the figure) chosen with higher probability. The number of equivalent outcomes increases exponentially with the order of the bifurcation: 2 at μ_{C1}, 4 at μ_{C2} and so on. Hence, a reductionistic program based on the dynamical description of the components does not provide a unique outcome. We must assign some extra

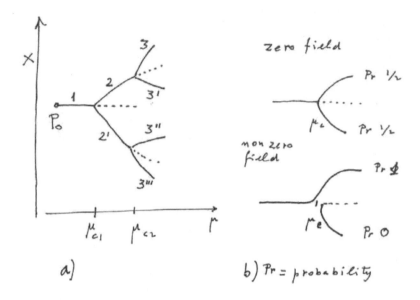

Fig. 3. :(a) Example of bifurcation diagram. The dynamical variable x (order parameter) varies vertically, the control parameter μ varies horizontally. Solid (dashed) lines represent stable (unstable) steady states as the control parameter is changed. (b) Upper: symmetric bifurcation with equal probabilities for the two stable branches. Lower: asymmetric bifurcation in presence of an external field. If the gap introduced by the field between upper and lower branch is wider than the range of thermal fluctuations at the transition point, then the upper (lower) branch has probability 1 (0).

information consisting of possible external fields, which specify univocally the final state.

But external fields are beyond the information provided by the dynamical properties of the components.

We must then distinguish between *closed* and *open* systems. The first ones are surrounded by walls which provide precise boundary conditions. Their evolution yields multiple outcomes so that we predict "potentialities", never the "actual" system that is observed.

In the case of open systems we must augment our description including the values of the external fields which select a unique outcome at each bifurcation. In general we don't know how to do that apriori; we can rather proceed backward to an historical reconstruction of external contributions which have obliged our open system to evolve from an initial to a final state. Notice that the setting of μ on the horizontal axis is at our will for a closed system, whereas in an open system it has a proper evolution in time that we do not control. Thus a bifurcation tree as fig. 3 looks as an evolutionary tree, usually plotted in biology as a function of time.

We might think that a metalevel description could treat the overall situation (set of components plus external process) as a closed system. In fact, we would transfer the ambiguities at the metalevel, and to recover uniqueness the metalevel must be affected by its own external forces and so on. In other words, by successive layers we deal with an "onion" structure.

A global description of the whole cosmic onion as a closed system is the dream of theoretical physics. A TOE (theory of everything) would be an equation as (2) where $\underline{x}$ are now all the degrees of freedom of the universe $\underline{f}$ and is the unified mathematical formulation that one day will be reached among electroweak, strong and gravitational interactions. In such a situation there would be *nothing* left out, thus new must itself be a function of $\underline{x}$ and hence Eq. (2) of TOE would be *closed*, with no external control parameters.

In fact, this is in principle impossible. Any foreseeable nominal description (that is, expressed by precise numbers) is incomplete even for a single particle, as discussed in Appendix I. Therefore we must split the vector x_{tot} of all the degrees of freedom of the universe into an observable set x_0 and a complementary set $\bar{x}$ which escapes our description. Our relevant physical equation refers only to the observed part x_0. Thus Eq. (2) must be re-written as

$$\dot{x}_0 = \underline{f}(x_0, \mu(x_0, \bar{x})) \tag{13}$$

This way of writing shows that the $\bar{x}$ dependence of μ excludes the above equation from being a closed one.

5 Complication versus complexity

5.1 Complexity of symbolic sequences

In computer science, we define the complexity of a word (symbol sequence) as some indicator of the cost implied in generating that sequence (Hopcroft and Ullman 1979). There is a "space" cost (length of the instruction stored in the computer memory) and a "time" cost (the CPU time for generating the final result out of some initial instruction).

A space complexity called AIC (Algorithmic Information Complexity) (Kolmogorov 1965, Chaitin 1966) is defined as the length in bit of the minimal instruction which generates the wanted sequence. This indicator is *maximum* for a random number, since there is no compressed algorithm (that is, shorter than the number itself) to construct a random number.

A time complexity called "logical depth" (Bennett 1987) is defined as the CPU time required to generate the sequence out of the *minimal* instruction. It is minimal for a random number, indeed, once the instruction has stored all the digits, just command: PRINT IT.

Of course, for simple dynamical systems as a pendulum or the Newtonian two-body problem, both complexities are minimal.

While AIC refers to the process of building a single item, logical depth corresponds to finding the properties of all possible outputs from a known source. In fact, the exact specification of the final outcome is beyond the ambition of the natural scientist, whose goal is more modest. It may be condensed in the two following items:

i) to transmit some information, coded in a symbol sequence, to a receiver, possibly economizing with respect to the actual string length, that is, making good use of the redundancies (this requires a preliminary study of the language style);

ii) to predict a given span of future, that is to assign with some likelihood a group of forthcoming symbols.

For this second goal, introduction of a probability measure is crucial (Grassberger 1986, Gell-Mann 1994) in order to design a complexity-machine, able to make the best informational use of a given data set.

Such a machine which should mimic the scientific procedure acts as follows (Crutchfield and Young 1989). Assume that a group of measuring apparatuses have provided the agent A with an information coded as a numerical sequence s (for convenience we use a binary code, so that the length $|s|$ of s is measured in bits). Agent A has a good understanding of what happens if it can transfer to a received B a compact information y upon which B reconstruct the sequence $s' = s$. Of course, y has to be shorter than s otherwise it would be a tautology, which implies no understanding whatsoever. Thus A is obliged to recur to a class of models built in its memory. Suppose it has chosen a model m, then A can simulate the behavior of the observed system and realize that there is an error e between the actual measurement s and its model reconstruction. If B receives both information m and e, then B can reconstruct $s' = s$. The bit length of the transmitted information is

$$|y| = |m| + |e| \tag{14}$$

and it has to be minimized for a successful description.

In this case we call complexity of the explanation the compression ratio

$$C(m, s) = \frac{|y|}{|s|} = \frac{|m| + |e|}{|s|} \tag{15}$$

The value of C is bounded above by 1; it depends upon the choice of the model m. There are two limit cases for which C=1 is the worst. When the model is trivial ($|m| = 0$) the entire information is on the error channel ($|e| = |s|$). When the model is tautological m=s there is no error $e = 0$.

The class of models can be scanned by a Bayes rule (Crutchfield and Young 1989). This is the case of an "expert system" equipped with a class of models, within which the system formulates the best diagnosis by minimizing C.

5.2 A dynamical approach to complexity

As discussed in Sec. 3, the reductionist approach consists of building a hierarchy from large to small and showing how the behaviour of smaller objects should determine that of larger ones. But here a perverse thing occurs. If our words were a global description of the object in *any* situation (as the philosophical "essences" in Galileo) then, of course, knowledge of elementary particles would be sufficient to make predictions on animals and society. In fact, Galileo's self-limitation to some "affections" is sufficient for a limited description of the event, but only from a narrow point of view. Even though we believe that humans are made of atoms, the affections that we measure in atomic physics are insufficient to make predictions on human behaviour.

We call *complexity* the fact that higher levels of organization display features not predictable from the lower ones, as opposed to the previous computer cost of a symbolic task, which we rather call *complication*.

This way, complexity is not a property of things (like being red or hot) but it is a relation with our status of knowledge, and for modern science it emerges from Galileo's self-limitation. Reductionism from large to small was accompanied by a logical reduction of the scientific explanation to a deductive task out of a set of axioms.

In this spirit, a scientific theory is considered as a set of primitive concepts (defined by suitable measuring apparatuses) plus their mutual relations. Concepts and relations are the axioms of the theory. The deduction of all possible consequences (theorems) provides predictions which have to be compared with the observations. If the observations falsify the expectations, then one tries with different axioms.

The deductive process is affected by a Gdel undecidability like any formal theory, in the sense that it is possible to build a well formed statement, but the rules of deduction are unable to decide whether that statement is true or false.

Besides that, a second drawback is represented by *intractability*, that is, by the exponential increase of possible outcomes among which we have to select the final state of a dynamical evolution. As discussed in Sec. 4, during the dynamical evolution of an open system, the control parameters $\{\alpha\}$ may assume different values, hence the cascade of bifurcations provides a large number of final states starting from a unique initial condition.

Thus the reductionist tentative of explaining reality out of its constituents yields an exponentially high number of possible outcomes, when only one is in fact that observed. This means that, while the theory, that is the syntax, would give equal probability to all branches of the tree, in reality we observe an organization process, whereby only one final state has a high probability of occurrence. Hence, whenever we are in presence of organization, that is of a unique final state, this means that at each bifurcation vertex the symmetry was broken by an external agent which forces a unique outcome, as shown in Fig. 3.

We can thus summarize the logical construction (to rephrase Carnap (Carnap 1967)) of a large system out of its components as follows:

i) A set of control parameters is responsible for successive bifurcations leading to an exponentially high number of final outcomes. If the system is "closed" to outside disturbances, then all outcomes have comparable probabilities and we call complexity the impossibility of predicting which one is the state we are going to observe.

ii) For a system of finite size embedded in an environment, there is a set of external forces applied at each bifurcation point, which break the symmetries, biasing toward a specific choice and eventually leading to a unique final state.

We are in presence of a conflict between (i) "syntax" represented by the set of rules (axioms) and (ii) "semantics" represented by the intervening external agents. The syntax provides many possible outcomes. But if the system is open, then it organizes to a unique final outcome. Once the syntax is known, the final result is therefore an acknowledgement that the set of external events must have occurred, that they have made the evolution meaningful (whence "semantics").

We define "certitude" the correct application of the rules, and "truth" the adaptation to the reality. However, due to the freedom we have in formulating theoretical conjectures, the same final outcome would be reached by a different set of rules, corresponding to a different syntactic tree. In such a case, retracing back the new tree of bifurcations, we would reconstruct a different set of external agents. Thus, it seems that truth, is language dependent!

Furthermore, this freedom in choosing the rules (the syntax) means that we can even find a set of axioms which succeeds in predicting the correct final state without external perturbations. This is indeed the pretension of the so called "autopoiesis", or "self-organization" (Krohn et al. 1990).

From a cognitive point of view, a selforganized theory can thought of as a "petitio principi", a tricky formulation tailored for a specific purpose and not applicable to different situations. Rather than explicitly detailing the elements of environment which break the symmetry, the supporter of the selforganized theory has already exploited at a pre-formalized level a detailed knowledge of the process in planning appropriate axioms.

An "ad-hoc" model may fit a specific situation, but in general it lacks sufficient breadth to be considered as a general theory. Think e.g. of the Ptolemaic model of the solar system which holds only for an Earth based observer, as compared to the Newtonian one, which holds also for an observer travelling through the solar system.

However, in describing the adaptive strategy of a living species, or a community etc., "self-organization" may be the most successful description. In other words, once the environmental influences have been known, better to incorporate their knowledge into the model, thus assuring the fast convergence to a given goal.

5.3 Complexity differs from complication

When all the rules of a game and all the partners (components) have been introduced, we are in presence of a definite symbolic system. The corresponding problems can be solved at a cost which may increase more than polynomially with the number of partners, e.g. consider the Travelling Salesman problem or TSP. We prefer to call "complication" the difficulty of solution of a problem within a formal system, and use "complexity" to denote any cognitive task in front of an open system. In such a case, a cognitive machine as an "expert system" is limited to a finite set of models m. Furthermore, it is bound to a precise setting of the measuring apparatuses: take for instance the list of the apple properties listed in Sec. 2. As discussed in Arecchi (2001) this limitation of an expert system is overcome by an adaptive strategy, whereby an agent spans not only the class of available models by a Bayesian strategy, as in the computer based model reasoning peculiar of expert systems (Magnani et al. 1999), but also changes in course of time the type of measures performed, thus reaching a meta-level where that cognitive agent is equivalent to a large class of expert systems.

Notice that "large" can be still finite. In a separate paper on neurophysics I have discussed a fundamental quantum relation for time dependent processes, which excludes finitism and therefore draws a sharp boundary between cognitive tasks and the operations of the Turing machine (Turing 1950).

Appendix I - *Quantum Teleportation*

Teleportation is the name given by science fiction writers to the feat of making an object or person disintegrate in one place while a perfect replica appears somewhere else. How this is accomplished is usually not explained in detail, but the general idea seems to be that the original object is scanned in such a way as to extract all the information from it, then this information is transmitted to the receiving location and used to construct the replica, not necessarily from the actual material of the original, but perhaps from atoms of the same kinds, arranged in exactly the same pattern as the original.

A teleportation machine would be like a fax machine, except that it would work on 3-dimensional objects as well as documents, it would produce an exact copy rather than an approximate facsimile, and it would destroy the original in the process of scanning; the teleporter functions as a super transportation device, not as a perfect replicator.

In 1993 a group of scientists (Bennett et al. 1993) confirmed the intuitions of the majority of science fiction writers by showing that perfect teleportation is indeed possible, but only if the original is destroyed. Meanwhile, other scientists have done the experiments demonstrating teleportation in microscopic objects, such as single atoms or photons.

Until recently, teleportation was not taken seriously, because it was thought to violate the uncertainty principle, which forbids any measuring or scanning process from extracting all the information in an atom or other object. The more accurately an object is scanned, the more it is disturbed by the scanning process, until one reaches a point where the object's original state has been completely disrupted, still without having extracted enough information to make a perfect replica. This sounds like a solid argument against teleportation: if one cannot extract enough information from an object to make a perfect copy, it would seem that a perfect copy cannot be made. But the scientists made an end-run around this logic, using a paradoxical feature of quantum mechanics known as the Einstein-Podolsky-Rosen effect (EPR). In brief, they found a way to scan out part of the information from an object A, which one wishes to teleport, while causing the remaining, unscanned, part of the information to pass, via EPR, into another object C which has never been in contact with A. Later, by applying to C a treatment depending on the scanned-out information, it is possible to maneuver C into exactly the same state as A was in before it was scanned. A itself is no longer in that state, having been thoroughly disrupted by the scanning, so what has been achieved is teleportation, not replication. As Fig. 4(a) suggests, the unscanned part of the information is conveyed from A to C by an intermediary object B, which interacts first with C and then with A. Can it really be correct to say "first with C and then with A"? Surely, in order to convey something from A to C, the delivery vehicle must visit A before C, not the other way around. But there is a subtle, unscannable kind of information that, unlike any material cargo, and even unlike ordinary information, can indeed be delivered in such a backward fashion. This subtle kind of information, also called EPR correlation or "entanglement", has been at least partly understood since the 1930s when it was discussed in a famous paper by Einstein, Podolsky, and Rosen. In the 1960s John Bell showed that a pair of entangled particles, which were once in contact but later move too far apart to interact directly, can exhibit individually random behavior that is too strongly correlated to be explained by classical statistics. Experiments on photons and other particles have repeatedly confirmed this correlation, thereby providing strong evidence for the validity of quantum mechanics, which neatly explains them. Another well-known fact about EPR correlations is that they cannot by themselves deliver a meaningful and controllable message. It was thought that their only usefulness was in proving the validity of quantum mechanics. But now it is known that, through the phenomenon of quantum teleportation, they can deliver exactly that part of the information in an object which is too delicate to be scanned out and delivered by conventional methods.

The Fig. 4 compares conventional facsimile transmission (b) with quantum teleportation (a). In conventional facsimile transmission the original is scanned, extracting partial information about it, but remains more or less intact after the scanning process. The scanned information is sent to the receiving station, where it is imprinted on some raw material (eg paper) to produce an approximate copy of the original. In quantum teleportation two objects B and C are first brought into contact and then separated. Object B is taken to the sending station, while object C is taken to the receiving station.

a)

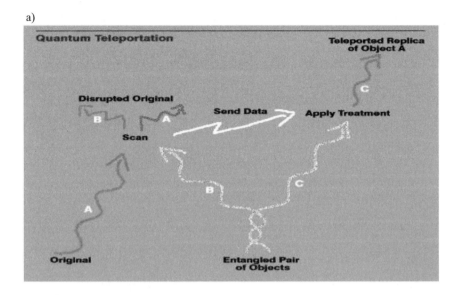

b)

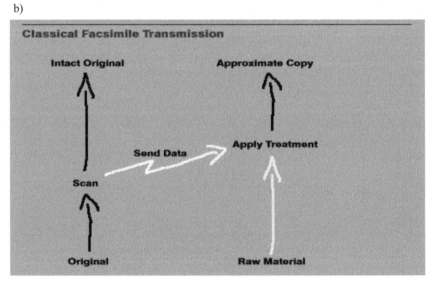

Fig. 4. Teleportation via a pair of EPR particles (a) compared to a classical facsimile transmission (b).

At the sending station object B is scanned together with the original object A which one wishes to teleport, yielding some information and totally disrupting the state of A and B. The scanned information is sent to the receiving station, where it is used to select one of several treatments to be applied to object C, thereby putting C into an exact replica of the former state of A.

Appendix II: *the KL method*
The time average of $u(t)$ is defined as

$$< u(t) >= \lim_{t \to \infty} \frac{1}{t} \sum_{t'} u(t') \tag{16}$$

In a similar way, we define the autocorrelation formation as

$$C(t, t') =< u(t)u(t') > \tag{17}$$

If values of u at different times are uncorrelated, then $C(t, t')$ factors out into the product of the two independent averages $\langle u(t) \rangle \langle u(t') \rangle$, and therefore it is zero.

Consider $C(t, t')$ as a kind of evolution operator from time t to $t' > t$. If we know the exact interval $U(t, t')$ of the equations of motion (2), then the dynamical solution would be

$$x(t) = U(t, t')x(t') \tag{18}$$

and in a trivial way the correlation would amount to

$$C(t, t') = U(t, t') \tag{19}$$

Measuring directly the function C, we consider it as an operator and search for its eigenfunctions $\theta(t)$ through the equation

$$\int C(t, t')\theta^*(t')dt' = \lambda\theta(t) \tag{20}$$

The θ's form a complete orthogonal set, so that any solution $u(t)$ can be expanded as

$$u(t) = \sum_1 \alpha_n\theta_n(t) \ with \ \alpha_n\alpha_m >= \delta_{nm}\lambda_n \tag{21}$$

where the brackets denote a scalar product on the space of the eigenfunctions. In practical situations KL method is convenient when the sum (21) is rapidly converging, and we need only L terms of the sum, where e.g. L=3 or 4.

L is optimized by minimizing the truncation error, that is, the energy (cost function) ε_L corresponding to the time integral of the square of the difference between the actual signal $u(t)$ and its truncated expansion $\sum_1^L \alpha_n\theta_n$.

$$\varepsilon_L \equiv \int_0^T \left[u(t) - \sum_1^L \alpha_n\theta_n(t) \right]^2 dt \to \min \tag{22}$$

References

Agazzi, E.: 1974, *Temi e Problemi di Filosofia della Fisica*, Edizione Abete.

Anderson, P.: 1972, More is different, *Science* **177**, 393–396.

Arecchi, F.: 1992, Models of metaphors in science, *Proceedings of Ponitificial Academy of Sciences, Pulman B. (eds)* .

Arecchi, F.: 1995, Truth and certitude in the scientific language, *Self-Organization of Complex Structures from Individual to Collective Dynamics*, F. Schweitzer, Gordon and Breach.

Arecchi, F.: 2001, Complexity versus complex system: a new approach to scientific discovery, *Nonlin. Dynamics, Psycology, and Life Sciences* **5**(21).

Arecchi, F. and Farini, A.: 1996, *Lexicon of Complexity*, Studio Editoriale Fiorentino.

Bennett, C.: 1987, Dissipation, information, computational complexity and the definition of organization, *in* D. Pines (ed.), *Emerging Syntheses in Science*, Addison Wesley.

Bennett, C., Brassard, G., Crepeau, C., Jozsa, R., Peres, A. and Wootters, W.: 1993, Teleporting an unknown quantum state via dual classical and epr channels, *Phys. Rev. Lett.* **70**, 1895–99.

Capra, F.: 1975, *The Tao of Physics: an Exploration of the Parallels Between Modern Physics and Eastern Mysticism*, The International Bestseller, 3rd Ed. 1991.

Carnap, R.: 1967, *The Logical Construction of the World*, University of California Press.

Chaitin, G.: 1966, On the length of programs for computing binary sequences, *J. Assoc. Comp. Math* **13**, 547–560.

Ciliberto, S. and Nicolaenko, B.: 1991, Estimating the number of degrees of freedom in spatially extended systems, *Europhys. Lett.* **14**, 303.

Crutchfield, J. and Young, K.: 1989, Inferring statistical complexity, *Phys. Rev. Lett.* **63**, 105.

Evans, R.: 1973, *Jean Piaget: the Man and His Ideas*, E.P. Dutton.

Feyerabend, P.: 1975, *Against Methid*, Verso.

Galilei, G.: 1932, Letter to m. welser "on the sun spots", *Opere di G. Galilei*, pp. 187–188.

Gell-Mann, M.: 1994, *The Quark and the Jaguar*, W.H. Freeman.

Grassberger, P.: 1986, Toward a quantitative theory of self-generated complexity, *Int. J. Theor. Phys.* **25**, 907–919.

Haken, H.: 1983, *Synergetics, An Introduction*, 3rd edition, Springer-Verlag.

Hopcroft, J. and Ullman, J.: 1979, *Introduction to Automata Theory, Languages and Computation*, Addison-Wesley.

Karhunen, K.: 1946, Zur spektraltheorie stochasticher prozess, *Ann. Acad. Sci. Fennicae* **37**.

Kolmogorov, A.: 1965, Three approaches to the quantitivative definition of information, *Problems of Information Transmission* **1**, 4–20.

Krohn, W., Kuppers, G. and Nowotny, H.: 1990, Self-organization, portrait of a scientific revolution, *Kluwer Academic Publishers* .

Landau, L. and Lifshift, E.: 1980, Statistical physics, *(3rd edition) Pergamon* .

Loève, M.: 1955, Probability theory, *VanNostrand* .

Magnani, L., Nersessian, N. and Thagard, P.: 1999, *model-Based Reasoning in Scientific Discovery*, Kluwer.

Shannon, C.: 1949, Communication in the presence of noise, *proc. IRE* **37**(1).

Thom, R.: 1975, *Structural Stability and Morphogenesis*, Reading, Mass.

Thom, R.: 1988, *Esquisse d'une sémiophysique*, InterEditions.

Toffoli, T.: 1998, Non-conventional computers, *in* J. WEbster (ed.), *Enc. of El. and Electronic Eng*, J. Wiley and Sons.

Turing, A.: 1950, Computing machinery and intelligence, *Mind* **59**, 433.

Wolfram, S.: 1984, Cellular automata as models of complexity, *Nature* **311**, 419–424.

Complexity, Pedagogy, and the Economics of Muddling Through

W.A. Brock, D. Colander

E 60

All

1 Introduction

Economics has evolved significantly since the 1950s, both in what it covers and the approaches it uses. Whereas the applied policy economics through the 1950s could reasonably be called neoclassical, modern economics has outgrown that classification. Its approach is more eclectic, and its applied policy models are not required to adhere to the assumptions that Solow calls the holy trinity–rationality, equilibrium, and greed. (See Kreps (1997) for a discussion.)

The welfare economics underlying applied policy has not evolved at the same pace. We still teach students, and implicitly base policy discussions on, a welfare economics that evolved out of the neoclassical mold-built on a foundation of Pareto optimality, externalities, and Walrasian general equilibrium. The essence of that welfare economics for pedagogical purposes is captured in Abba Lerner's "economic of control" metaphor. In it economists' underlying general equilibrium model, based on the holy trinity, serves as a map for the economy; the applied policy problem is to get a workable steering wheel on the car, a reasonable driver, and decent linkages. In essence the goal is to design policy, or, in sophisticated presentations, policy rules, to get the car to follow the map. In a nutshell: theory points out the way to go; applied policy deals with getting you there.

In the economics of control vision the Arrow Debreu McKenzie Walrasian general equilibrium model provides the correct set of prices or targets. (In advanced models, the target prices could be specified as dynamic stochastic variables.) The job of applied policy economists is to specify those prices with their model and to design general rules of policy, and policy instruments, to achieve those prices.

Recent work in complexity science, which sees the economy as a complex system such as that found in Arthur et al. (1997) suggests a different welfare framework within which to consider applied policy. This complexity work is part of a broader shift away from the holy trinity that is occurring in modern economics. In applied work, and in some theoretical work, more general assumptions are replacing the more narrowly specified holy trinity assumptions. Specifically, more general forms of purposeful behavior are replacing simple "greed"; cognitive awareness is replacing simple rationality; and sustainability is replacing simple equilibrium. In the complexity approach the economy is thought of as a self-organizing system that structures communication patterns among agents.[1]

The work done at CeNDEF (http://www.fee.uva.nl/cendef) is an example of the approach we have in mind. Researchers there are combining new and old strategies to address fundamental questions. For example their theoretical work is calibrated to reproduce many features of real world data, but is based on heterogeneous agents with differing degrees of rationality, rather than on homogeneous agents. Their choice of assumptions is further governed by experimental and econometric work using field data. They study how changing the degree (e.g., the "dial") of rationality creates dynamical patterns in their artificial economies, which are then compared to dynamical patterns observed in actual economies. They use complexity tools such as bifurcation theory to study these pattern-generating mechanisms analytically as well as computationally.

Viewing the economy as a complex system suggests the need for some modifications in the underlying welfare foundations for applied policy work. The "right price" economic of control view of applied policy does not fit the complexity approach. The complexity approach places more emphasis on the "right price process" rather than the "right price". The complexity approach also differs from earlier approaches that took complexity seriously, such as the "Austrian" approach. That Austrian approach also stressed the "right price process" view of policy, but it was perceived as opposing formal modeling and econometric work. The modern complexity approach is intricately involved in modeling and econometric work. It uses computationally assisted model building, analytics, and econometrics, to move the discussion in a more quantitative direction than that favored by Austrians. It pushes mathematical methods to the limit, using analytical and computational tools such as bifurcation theory, interacting systems theory, and hierarchies of temporal and spatial scales.

Even with these methods the complexity approach does not achieve the understanding needed to base policy on the "right price" view. If the economy is a complex system there is no definitive map for the economy. Novelty may continually develop, making the economy, in a fundamental sense, non-ergodic. When working on microfoundations of complex systems, researchers must pay

---

[1] Defining complexity is too complex a task to deal with here, other than to say that we are here using an inclusive definition that includes a variety of different approaches. For a discussion of the definition of complexity see Brock and Carpenter (2000a) and Arthur et al. (1997).

close attention to issues like temporal and spatial variations in the interconnection structure of the economy and the potential of such issues to create abrupt and "surprising" changes.

When one faces seriously the econometric problems of identifying the "true" causal pathways in a system with important observable and unobservable heterogeneity at various temporal and spatial scales (where "space" is taken in the wide sense) the best policy makers can do is to determine temporary patterns that may allow for exploitable policy opportunities while keeping a careful outlook for the potential of "surprises". To prepare students to deal with the complexity modern researchers are dealing with, we need to teach them a welfare economics that allows for that complexity. We call this modified approach to welfare economics *the economics of muddling through because muddling through* is, in the immediate future, the best one can hope for as a policy objective.

In this paper we offer some initial explorations of how the welfare foundations of economic policy might change if welfare theory started from the premise that the economy is a complex system. Our discussion is directed at non-specialists in complexity. Its purpose is to provide some insight into why the complexity revolution is more than the latest toy of mathematical economists-more than a method of increasing the mathematical complexity of studying economics. It has, we argue, important policy implications that will make a difference in how applied policy economist work, the methods they use, and how they think about their policy work.

Specifically, we discuss four types of changes in applied policy that we believe follow from this complexity foundation. They are:

1. Changes in the degree of certainty with which policy advice is presented.
2. Changes in the methods of examining policy alternatives.
3. Changes in the nature of the policy questions asked.
4. Changes in the nature of the general policy solutions.

Before we explore these we briefly discuss the way in which modern economics uses welfare economics in practice.

2 How Modern Economics uses Welfare Economics in Practice

Modern economics is very much about policy. The majority of economists are applied economists who see their job as taking received economic wisdom embodied in a set of canonical models and applying that wisdom to specific cases. That application is highly empirical, and, by mathematical standards, not very formal, although to a humanist, it certainly looks formal. Solow (1997) has captured the essence of the current approach with his "loose fitting positivism" terminology. He writes:

Today, if you ask a mainstream economist a question about almost any as-
pect of economic life, the response will be: suppose we model that situation
and see what happens.... There are thousands of examples; the point is that
modern mainstream economics consists of little else but examples of this pro-
cess. (p. 43)

The positivism of modern economics is embodied in its focus on empirical
testing and its methodological adherence to the separation of positive and
normative elements. It is "loose fitting" positivism because the actual policy
models used often have only a slight connection to the pure theoretical models that currently form the general equilibrium core of the theory of welfare
economics. The theoretical welfare models provide the framework for thinking about policy, but that framework is not seen as limiting the assumptions
made in the actual applied policy models.

Modern microeconomics uses an eclectic set of models that employ a variety of assumptions and methods. For example, the formal general equilibrium
model provides no learning by doing, or feedback of activity on tastes; it takes
tastes as a primitive. Applied policy models, however, such as those of Frank
(1999), can take tastes as a variable. Another example concerns rationality;
formal general equilibrium models assume strong rationality; many applied
policy models assume bounded rationality when that assumption provides a
better fit with the data. Akerlof (1993)'s cognitive dissonance model of inter-
relationships and Solow (1990)'s sociological model of the labor market are
examples. Yet another example is in finance where psychological assumptions
are replacing strong rationality assumption. This has occurred so much that
Thaler (1999) argues, that soon, "the term 'behavioral finance' will be correctly viewed as a redundant phrase. What other kind of finance is there?"

The "tight fitting positivism" limitations on applied policy modeling, requir-
ing the assumptions of applied policy models to be consistent with the assumptions of the formal general equilibrium core, are gone. In modern applied
policy the choice of assumptions are generally made on empirical grounds: if
it provides a better fit with the data, especially out-of-sample data, while
maintaining a tractable model, it is a better model.

These examples demonstrate a major split that has developed between most
formal general equilibrium models, where assumptions are generally chosen to
create global tractability, and applied policy models, where assumptions are
generally chosen to create a type of local model tractability, but still achieve
an empirical fit with the evidence.

The differing assumptions of core general equilibrium theories and applied
policy models presents a consistency problem for the welfare foundations of
applied economics. Economists' detailed work on welfare theory, and the standard welfare propositions that follow from that work, can serve as a firm basis
of applied policies only for those tight-fitted models that share the assumptions of its formal general equilibrium core. Applied policy models using different assumptions from the formally developed general equilibrium theory

must implicitly make a robustness assumption if the welfare theory associated with that general equilibrium theory is to serve as a backdrop for policy. Loose fitting positivism requires strong robustness assumptions.

The eclectic modeling, applied policy approach has evolved over the last thirty years as micro economists reacted to objections that it was too concerned with pure theory and logical models. It is a pragmatic approach that has been fought by purists, who have pointed out the above-mentioned consistency problem. Purists argue that the eclectic models are ad hoc and unreliable; they argue that all applied work should use the same assumptions as the developed core general equilibrium theory: If you use the welfare theory, you should use the holy trinity of assumptions upon which it is based. The pragmatic approach developed, nonetheless, because of the usefulness of these eclectic, ad hoc models and the generally perceived failure of purists to provide acceptable real-world policy linkages in the absence of such ad hoc models.

For example, consider DeLong's "What's Wrong with Our Bloody Economies?" (http://econ161.berkeley.edu/ created 1/11/98) where he discusses recent financial crises and footloose capital movements. He states: "The root cause of the crises is a sudden change of state in international investors' opinions. Like a herd of not-very-smart cattle, they all were going one way in 1993 or 1996, and then they turned around and are all going the opposite way today...The correct answer....the market was manic....not a cool judgment of changing fundamentals but instead a sudden psychological victory of fear over greed." After a discussion of the enormous benefits of free flowing capital, while mentioning caveats about the problems (like the above) caused by such enormous amounts of footloose capital DeLong suggests we look at three basic policy rules coined by W. Bagehot long ago: (i) Make Lenders of Last Resort available; (ii) Make it painful to be bailed out; (iii) Don't bail anyone out unless they are solvent if there were not a panic.

Whether one agrees with DeLong or not, it is hard to find better guidance than Bagehot's from our conventional textbook general equilibrium model towards a useful policy posture in financial panic management. This is not to say that we cannot model it in intertemporal general equilibrium models. With jump variables (e.g. Turnovsky (1995) one can create patterns that look like "panics" but are, in fact, just rational expectations equilibrium responses to changes in underlying fundamental parameters unobservable to the econometrician. But in financial panic management the abrupt changes in asset prices and the magnitude of financial movements seem difficult to link to any financial rational expectations "jump variable" at the "right" time scale.

Complexity models of financial asset pricing with social interactions (e.g. Brock (1993)) provide a better fit with DeLong and Bahehot's educated common sense policy precepts. They stress the ability of observable and unobservable correlations propagated through the financial community's interaction structure to create not only alternative states but also lightning quick changes of state via a breakdown of the usual smoothing effects of something like a Law of Large Numbers.

Writers like Prigogine have stressed the link between breakdowns of phenomena like Laws of Large Numbers and complexity-type behavior such as bifurcations and emergent structures for years. See for example, his paper in Day and Chen (1993). These abrupt changes can be triggered by minute unobservables undetectable by an observing scientist. Basically this phenomenon happens because a certain infinite series of appropriate "spatial" cross correlations amongst agents fails to converge absolutely in a large system of agents. This type of complexity-based approach to studying asset pricing and trading volume seems to be appropriate in our huge highly interconnected (via "on line" trading engines and news feeds) financial trading system assisted by current electronics.

In our view the problem of current applied theory is not so much that it is ad hoc and does not follow a particular model, e.g. the extended general equilibrium model faithfully. The problem is that it too closely ties its welfare foundation to the current general equilibrium core without modifying that core to include complexity-based features like a temporal/spatial hierarchy of interconnective elements amongst the agents. These elements can create "policy surprises" in the real world that the core is not good at training the analyst to watch out for. To help solve the problem we suggest that loose fitting positivism be replaced by loose fitting pragmatism, based upon a broader complexity view of the economy. Loose fitting pragmatism starts from the proposition that any model is inherently ad hoc, but it attempts to limit that adhocness and take it into account in its policy advice.

Let us now turn to four differences we see following from seeing welfare economics as a type of muddling through, rather than as part of the economics of control.

2.1 Changes in the degree of certainty with which policy advice is presented

Above, we argued that there is often a false sense of connection between the policy advice economists give based on ad hoc models and the underlying welfare economics. In the complexity welfare framework that connection is given up. Pure theory can say very little definitively about complex systems. It may be able to add insights to intuition; it may temporarily provide an acceptable fit upon which one can tentatively base policy. But there always remains an underlying uncertainty-the possibility that the system might change in ways that cannot be currently modeled or created-that must be taken into account in designing policy. In complexity uncertainty is part of the core theory. Currently, in much applied policy work, while uncertainty is recognized, it often is not given much weight. Specifically, we suggest that uncertainty has an important implication for policy design and policy focus, as we will discuss below.

Our argument is not that we have to throw out all current work that is based on the current general equilibrium core. It is simply that standard welfare economics underlying applied policy work gives too much reverence to it. Loose fitting pragmatism allows the Arrow-Debreu-McKenzie Walrasian general equilibrium core to be used, but without the reverence. It is useful in guiding models in those cases where the assumptions provide an acceptable match to reality. But the complexity approach also allows the use of other currently implicit general equilibrium models with different assumptions. In short the general equilibrium cores is seen as a useful, pragmatic model, and not as the single model that defines the core assumptions that must be used. Theoretical researchers are currently working on broadening and modifying the benchmark Arrow Debreu model. But no clearly defined alternatives have been developed, and without a clearly defined alternative, the Arrow Debreu model has remained the benchmark of welfare economics.

Integrating this uncertainty into applied policy will require new techniques such as computational Bayesian techniques and Bayesian Model Averaging (e.g. Geweke (1999), Brock and Durlauf (2000a), Brock and Carpenter (2000b)). Technically, these new techniques allow for the possibility of data to speak to the presence of alternative stable states and to the measure the added impact of this possibility upon the posterior distribution of welfare measures in a dynamical system where alternative stable states are a serious potential possibility.

The advantage of a Bayesian framework is that it produces automatically, as a byproduct, a theory of the burden of proof in the form of a potential precautionary principle in the quantitative form of a Bayesian posterior welfare distribution. For example Pizer (1996) produces a quantitative expression for how much the case for caution in climate change policy is strengthened when uncertainty is taken into account. The uncertainty in the evidence leads to a strengthened case (relative to "best-guess" parameter values) for emission reductions and to an increased preference for flexible regulatory/management modes and gives a quantitative expression for each.

Brock and Durlauf (n.d.) and Brock and Carpenter (2000a) have considered a start on this kind of work in the context of growth econometrics and dynamic management of ecosystems by using formal treatments of model uncertainty in the Bayesian literature. As shown by Brock and Durlauf (n.d.) adjustment for model uncertainty (even when that uncertainty is constrained by theory) as well as Knightian Uncertainty causes an increase in the level of modesty which is probably appropriate when giving advice given our current level of science. It also allows data to speak to theoretical debates in a statistically sensible way by forcing each side to submit a model class that represents their theory to a Bayes type procedure that allows the data to attach posterior odds to the truth of each theory. Computational advances have now allowed such methods to be operationalized. Brock and Carpenter (2000b) use a dynamic treatment where there is the complicating factor of two-way feedback between the management and the model selection and estimation process with the extra complication of possible alternative stable states in the underlying system dynamics.

It is likely that adjustment for uncertainty in the more realistic manner being suggested here will strengthen the case for adaptive management based upon monitoring of "expert leading indicators of systemic health". In ecology this would mean focusing policy analysis on populations of organisms sensitive to changes of relevant state and especially informative organism populations signatory of an impending "poised"-"near bifurcational" state. In economies it might mean focusing policy analysis on certain sociological indicators, such as suicides of youth, surveys and other measures of "wellbeing" as stressed by the hedonic economic psychologists cited in Frank (1999) to estimate when the anomie of a system has increased to a near bifurcation state. It suggests that applied economists should develop continuously updated quantitative value indices of such leading indicators presented in a form for immediate use by policymakers who must face compromise tradeoffs and who must face the decision whether the gains from a policy change are worth the costs of promoting it.

The complexity foundation to welfare economics also has some more general implications for thinking about the advantages of market systems. Specifically, it presents modified welfare foundations for markets than those suggested by standard welfare theory. For example simulations and analytics (cf. SFI II) suggest that, complex systems can self-organize, after application of policy action, in surprising ways in contrast to the predictions of conventional comparative statics exercises. They can also manage quite well–going along as they have gone along with no central controller. In such cases there is a slight status quo (not a perfectly competitive market) bias in the complexity approach because the status quo has, by its existence, shown that it is a feasible solution. Other states may not be (for a discussion see Brock and Colander (2000)).

Whether the status quo is optimal in any sense is a much harder question since many equilibria are possible. Moreover, as we will discuss below, global optimality is reduced in importance when taking a complexity perspective as other attributes, such as resilience and sustainability, are directly considered as policy goals.

2.2 Changes in the methods of modeling policy alternatives

If less certainty were all one could say about the policy implications of complexity, it would not be worth discussing. But approaching policy from a complexity framework does more than simply build in the uncertainty of policy. It suggests significantly different methods be used in designing policy, and in designing policy research. Let us list and briefly discuss some of the most important of these.

More use of nonlinear dynamics and recursive mathematics
The first difference between modeling in the standard approach and modeling in a complexity approach is that complexity approach is the mathematics used.

Complexity focuses more on non-linear dynamics and recursive mathematics than does the standard approach. Non-linear models typically lead to multiple equilibria, sunspot, and path-dependent models involving sudden regime shifts. Thus, these models are more emphasized in the complexity work. Standard applied economics gets to these type of models, but the path is not so direct, and it is only with reluctance (Schumpeter (1954) argued that unique equilibrium models were essential to doing economics as a science).

Consistent with the use of these techniques there would be a stronger focus of theoretical work on model and equilibrium selection mechanisms, as well as broader dynamic concepts of equilibrium (see Blume (1997), Brock and Durlauf (2000a), and Brock and Carpenter (2000b)).

More Focus on computational work

The difference in mathematics used is associated with another important difference in approach. *Researchers using a complexity approach to economics are more willing to use techniques that provide insight into issues but do not lead to full analytic solutions.* The reason standard economics does not use nonlinear mathematics is that such models are generally analytically intractable. Whereas in standard approaches analytic tractability is a key component, in the complexity approach, analytic tractability is not an absolute requirement because now computational advances have been made that allow us to deal with economic models closer to the complex systems that may permeate real economies (Judd 1998).

More use of Simulations and Agent based models

In standard economics, computational methods are used to gain insight into general equilibrium issues (i.e. computable general equilibrium models) The complexity approach suggests a broader role for computational methods. It sees important insights into the problems being gained via simulations and agent-based modeling starting from scratch. In essence one "grows" the economy rather than formally models it. Such agent-based modeling is a quite different approach to thinking about policy. There is increasing interest in agent-based computational economics (ACE), the computational study of economies modeled as evolving systems of autonomous interacting agents (see http://www.econ.iastate.edu/tesfatsi/ace.htm). Agent-based modeling presents a whole new set of problems; solving them is central to the complexity approach to welfare economics, whereas they are tangential to standard welfare economics.

Assumptions are Determined Empirically to Fit the Data

All the above differences are associated with a difference in the way one conceives of designing a model. In the standard approach one designs a model deductively, following core assumptions. The complexity approach eliminates any particular general equilibrium model as the background-coordinating model of the economy and replaces it with a broader set of, often-implicit, general equilibrium models whose assumptions are determined through backward through induction from the assumptions that fit the data in applied policy work. An example here is the work of Brock and Hommes (1998) in their work on alternatives to the efficient market hypothesis. In that work they explore the implications of the heterogeneous market hypothesis.

In the complexity approach both abstract theory and simulation work provide stories that are used to check the compatibility of narrower applied-policy stories that form the basis of applied policy work. In the complexity approach the core general equilibrium model must be designed to be consistent with the applied policy work, not the other way around. For example, if applied policy work suggests that positional consumption goods are important, then we need the core to include assumptions that allow positional consumption. That unknown core should be given as much initial weight in policy choice as is current general equilibrium propositions.

By using the Bayesian Model Averaging tools used in Brock and Durlauf (n.d.), as well as the integration of econometrical and theoretical tools of "Interactions-Based Models" (e.g., Brock and Durlauf (2000a), one could attach posterior odds to modifications of that core, and possibly model dealing with unknown parts of the "true core" by formal treatments of "ambiguity" like Knightian Uncertainty.[2]

Justifying Assumptions

The ability to choose assumptions to fit with applied work's focus on relating theory to data does not provide a free ride. Along with that flexibility comes a set of limitations on assumptions and a reduction in the degree of certainty attached to the model; assumptions cannot be chosen in an ad hoc manner; each must be justified as being appropriate. Justification of ad-hoc assumptions is often missing in current applied work even though the assumptions often differ from general equilibrium assumptions, creating the consistency problem discussed above. The acceptance of the need for justification would make the consistency problem a key issue in discussions of policy models, and hence would represent a major change in how applied-policy work is done.

The new methods discussed above, such as agent based modeling, offer one way of justifying assumptions. There are others, including experimental work–showing that the assumption is consistent with how people actually behave–and importing behavioral assumptions that have been developed by researchers in experimental and behavioral psychology.

Four desirable requirements for assumptions used in policy models include the following:

---

[2] See Brock and Durlauf (n.d.).

(1) *Intuitive plausibility*

In complexity, one does not use induction or deduction; instead one uses a combination of the two—what the pragmatist, Charles Pierce, called abduction. In abduction the best one can do in theory is to tell intuitively plausible stories. Notice that this is a quite different use of intuitive plausibility than that found in the calibration literature. In that literature the assumptions need not be intuitively plausible; the intuitively plausibility focus is on the ability of the calibrated models to reproduce relevant empirical regularities. That requirement still exists but the additional requirement that fits the complexity approach is that the model's assumptions reasonably match the assumed characteristics of the agents in the observable system. Thus, we would argue that representative agent models in macro-economic work do not meet the intuitive plausibility requirement, even if they can be calibrated to the relevant empirical regularities because (i) researchers have essentially harvested already most of the useful macro economic insights available from such models; and (ii) the "Gorman" type conditions for existence of such an "as if" agent, even if extended to some type of large system limit framework, do not seem all that promising to add future value, especially given the large volume of observed trading amongst agents. Heterogeneity and interaction of agents is important on an intuitive level, and thus cannot be ignored.

We do not want to claim too much for this requirement. What is intuitively plausible is clearly an ambiguous criteria, and "intuitively plausible" is more effective at ruling out general models, than it is in choosing among them.

(2) *Empirically relevant*

Science is about efficiently storing and summarizing patterns in data, and putting those patterns together to better understand, and possibly predict, patterns that otherwise would not be observable. Based on arguments such as Friedman's F-twist, standard economics has emphasized the latter part of definition, and has focused on choosing whatever assumptions are necessary to best predict new patterns. Assumptions that predict "best" are the best assumptions. The problem is that empirically determining what predicts best is difficult, if not impossible, which has left standard economics free to use the holy trilogy with the argument that they predict as well as anything else. The complexity approach emphasizes the storing, or summarizing succinctly via devices such as scaling laws, as well as the predicting, aspect of the empirical foundations of science. It begins with determining standard outcomes of complex systems that occur independently of assumptions. Zipf's Law, and other power laws, are examples; complex systems seem to generate certain outcomes that match the size distribution of cities and commodity price series. The existence of such standard outcomes has significant modeling and policy implications. If there are strong self-organization forces that lead to data patterns independent of assumptions made about agents, then those assumptions don't matter and deductive theory is irrelevant.

Most economists working in complexity, including us, take the position that the forces of self-organization are not so overwhelmingly strong that deductive work is irrelevant. Insight into the patterns can be gained by studying the microfoundations of the complex system. The two approaches can complement one another. Agent based complexity models are designed to add further information; they take those predictions that follow independently of assumptions as a baseline prediction, and see what theoretically based models can add to that predictive power. The models are not totally deductive. As discussed above, since the assumptions used in these models generally cannot be judged by their predictive value, they need to reflect observed behavior-what people actually do.

(3) *Logically consistent with the data being modeled*
At this point precisely what simulations are adding to our understanding is a bit unclear. There is much work to be done in determining what inferences can be drawn from simulation work. Will it be limited to general understanding of the process, or will it be more specific? At the stage of development it does seem able to help us establish some minimal restrictions on allowable models. Much of the work in simulations is currently at this stage. For example, Joshua Epstein (1999) has suggested that a minimal requirement of any "macroscopic explanandum" is that it can be generated by agents following the assumptions made in the model. This might be called the computable existence requirement. Work that has explored existence includes Epstein (1996), Arthur et al. (1997) and Axelrod (1997). This existence requirement seems like a natural desideratum of a model. Its converse could also be a strong requirement of a model: If it can be proved that the assumptions of the model cannot generate the empirical results, then the model is unacceptable.

Notice that the simulation has two roles in the complexity approach: (1) as a way of testing assumptions, and (2), as a way of inducing assumptions-growing systems and finding patterns that match patterns in nature consistent with those assumptions. (4) Consistent with the assumed information set of the researcher.

Learning and expectations play key roles in any model of a complex system. Both raise important issues in model symmetry. A desirable requirement in any model is *model symmetry* - the compatibility of the expectations and learning behavior of agents with the underlying foundation of the model. *Strong model symmetry* requires that the assumptions one makes about one's own knowledge of the model are consistent with the assumptions made about the learning behavior and expectations of the agents in the model. Rational expectations models reflect strong model symmetry with an economics of control framework, and is a reasonable requirement for applied policy models in standard welfare economics.

In the complexity approach to welfare economics, rational expectations do not meet the strong model symmetry assumption. Since the complexity approach assumes less than full knowledge on the part of the researcher, to have a model meet the model symmetry assumption requires that we assume less than full knowledge on the part of the agents in the model. Much work remains to be done in determining precisely what set of assumptions that meet strong model symmetry are best, but, as a requirement, it seems highly desirable requirement to place on models. Sargent (1993, 1999) builds models that "back off" from pure rational expectations by replacing rational expectations agents with agents who act like the scientists who study them. These type of models satisfy model symmetry as we use the term above.

One could also imagine building models of the Sargent (1993, 1999) type but where the agents are Bayesian Model Averaging (BMA) types of statisticians rather than the more "frequentist" type statisticians in Sargent's models. An example of BMA work that could be used is in Brock and Durlauf (n.d.). It applies statistical techniques, such as Bayesian Model Averaging, to deal with cases where the model is not known and the data are allowed to convert prior assessments over members of a family of plausible models into posterior assessments. It attempts to incorporate the reporting of "model uncertainty" with "confidence intervals" thereby imbedding uncertainty into policy analysis. It is plausible to believe that agents living in a model are as uncertain about the true model of the economy they are co-creating as are the scientists studying the economy. The principle of model symmetry would argue for assuming that if the scientists are BMA then the agents in the model should also be BMA.

2.3 The nature of the policy goals considered would be broader

Economic applied policy today in large part focuses heavily on allocative efficiency to the exclusion of other goals. In principle, it is recognized that there is more to welfare theory than allocative efficiency, but, in applied policy practice, little concern is actually given to other goals. This focus is a legacy of the economics of control welfare approach that could only come to definitive conclusions for efficiency. The formal limitations of the economics of control welfare framework to applied policy work are well known; to logically derive policy directives from the set of carefully specified initial conditions to policy is difficult, and significant limitations must be placed on the policy directives as to what they mean. It is for that reason that the work focuses on efficiency. Consider VonGraaf (1995)'s conclusion to his celebrated study of welfare economics:

... the possibility of building a useful and interesting theory of welfare economics-i.e. one which consists of something more than the barren formalisms typified by the marginal equivalencies of conventional theory is exceedingly small.

It was criticisms such as Von Graaf's that led economics to stop working on the barren formalisms in their applied work, and to take a looser approach to assumptions made in applied policy.

In complexity welfare economics, the limitations of drawing specific policy conclusions are built into the structure of the initial policy thinking. Since one cannot even come to definitive conclusions about efficiency, it frees economics up to consider a broader range of issues. This does not mean that economics' focus on allocative efficiency would be eliminated; it would just not be the exclusive focus, as it often currently is. For example, one would expect complexity economics to deal much more with moral questions, such as those raised by Sen (2000), the systemic creation of norms and tastes raising positional goods issues such as those raised by Frank, resilience and other systemic-existence issues, such as those raised by the work in ecology. These considerations would be given an equal footing with standard efficiency considerations.

An example of the type of work we have in mind here is that done by the Resilience Network (Rnet), a group of ecologists and economists associated with the Beijer Institute of Sweden. They are unified by exploration of concepts of "resilience" where "resilience" refers to the ability of a system to restore itself when buffeted by shocks or, in the wider sense of the word, maintain its function after shocked. (See Holling (1997a) or Holling et al. (1997)).

The Rnet approach to complexity uses dynamical systems theory and nonlinear control systems theory to study the locating of patterns of spatial and temporal "lumpiness", where "space" is interpreted in a wide sense. (See, for example, Holling (1992)'s paper. This attempt to simplify complexity by application of spectral analysis in time and "space" in order to identify "clumps of high spectral power" is analogous to application of spectral analysis in macroeconomics to locate regions of high spectral power, and is the type of work that must be done if the mathematics of complexity is to affect policy.

The underlying mathematics is complicated, but the results can be reduced to a tool simple enough to be useful to policy makers. For example the log/log space/time scaling plot of Holling et al. (1997) (p. 356), called a Stommel plot, and the adaptive cycle diagram of Holling et al. (1997) (p.389), both could be used to suggest to policy makers how much focus they should give to equilibria shifts.

Pedagogically, this broader view of welfare economics would change the way we present microeconomics. The existence of an externality would not be seen as an immediate call for policy action, since externalities would be seen as contextual to the model one is working with, not something that exists in the world. Indeed, complexity-based thinking with its emphasis on such things as slow moving unobserved variables, and latent self organization potential causing "surprises", most likely would approach policy action on a perceived externality quite gingerly. Similarly, from this broader welfare perspective, the absence of externalities would not be seen as an argument for laissez faire. The complexity-based policy analyst, much like the Rnet analyst, would constantly be on the lookout for unpleasant "surprises" caused not only by observed spillovers left out by markets, but also unobserved slow moving uncosted spillovers that may lead to very unpleasant surprises (e.g. jumps in loss of environmental quality caused by bifurcations). In short, failures of market outcomes, as well as market failures, will be part of the policy analysis.

3 The Nature of the Policy Solutions Would Change

In the economics of control policy solutions involve getting the economy to the "right price". In muddling through, there is no right price; policy solutions involve finding a "right", or at least acceptable, process. This means that policy work is more focused on institutional issues-designing institutions that are generally lead to desirable ends. Examples of right process solutions can be seen in Scott (1998)'s Seeing Like a State. This process view of policy gives one a different perspective on the nature of competition and the desirability of the market than does standard welfare economics. The market is a desirable institution not only because it leads to efficient results, but also because it is resilient; it allows for the change that is necessary in a complex evolving system. But the market that does this is seen as a real world institution, not as an abstract ideal, and arguments as to whether intervention into the market process is or is not desirable would have to be made contextually, in reference to the actual institutions, not theoretically, in reference to a hypothesized state of perfect competition.

The muddling through approach sees the policy process as a complex system in which any researcher is seen as part of the process, not the entire process. Thus, it would not see economists arriving at policy recommendations alone (even in principle); instead it would see economists as part of an integrated regulatory approach that uses economics, but is not fully directed by economics. In this approach economists provide advice both in the form of benefit cost/analysis and mechanism design analysis. This would especially be so on issues where preferences of economics agents are likely to be altered by participation in a mutually respectful interactive educative process like an idealized town meeting "teach-in".

Some policy commentators (e.g. Farber (1999)) argue that components of preferences that are invariant to such mutually educative interactive exchange processes should loom much larger in policy weightings (i.e. almost lexicographical) relative to components of preferences measured by standard economics-based methods such as benefit/cost analysis as conventionally applied. Notice how "complexity-based" our interpretation of Farber is–i.e. his "educative process invariant" components of tastes are "emergent properties" of his idealized interactive political decision process.

The result of taking a complexity approach to policy would be a combining of the expertise of economists, scientists and lawyers and a mixed approach to regulation. That mixed approach would contain elements from measures of willingness to pay, but it would also have measures of "willingness-to vote". It would back away from approaches that only consider benefit/cost analysis, but it also would nonetheless respect the efficiency goals embodied in the benefit/cost movement. It would see the political sphere as a dynamic uniquely deliberative evolver of value systems that have a higher claim for representation in an over-all "value calculus" than private preferences.

This change would lead to some changes in regulatory processes. For example, in environmental regulation we believe there would be more focus on devices such as regulatory tiering, separation of users, "smart markets", and treatment of chunks of the ecosystem as Tieboutian local public goods, as ways of reducing the impact of the "fumbling fist" of the State and, perhaps, reducing some of the public resistance to environmental regulation.

Complexity-based methods, by focusing more on the surprise potential contained in self organization of large complex adaptive systems, would direct policy in a manner that would take care in designing institutions, i.e. changes in the "rules-of-the-game" to avoid rent seeking behavior. It would, as Magee and Brock (1984) try to design economic institutions to reward invisible hand behavior more than invisible foot behavior. It would work hard to avoid wasteful policies put in place by narrow special interest "rent seeking" groups where the benefits to such groups are less than the cost to society as a whole. The reality is that many attempts at institutional design end up generating unpleasant surprises in the form of stimulating the self organization of such "rent seeking" groups. A focus of complexity based policy research would be on ways of structuring incentives for groups of agents to self organize in order to produce useful goods and services for society at large rather than self organizing to extract wealth through the use of the state.

Another change in the type of policy solution would follow from the broadening of the goals discussed above. The greater focus on norm creation would also change the nature of policy solutions considered. For example, reducing positional consumption races caused conspicuous consumption of winners of "winner-take-all" markets which was stressed by Frank and Cook (1995) and amplified by (Frank 1999) would likely be more emphasized. Since the total volume of consumption pressure generated by lower strata of society is so huge (even relative to that of the top strata), this kind of "renorming from the top down" could have enormous impact. This is so because the rarified rich are tiny in population and even their total volume of consumption is small relative to the total volume of consumption of the classes below them.

One can only imagine the alteration of behavior that might take place if the talent of Madison Avenue were applied to educate consumers to generate behavior that minimized the load on the environment. It is easy to imagine the revenues from appropriate externality taxes would be large enough to fund potent ad campaigns.

We fully recognize that care must be taken in making any of these arguments, but the small discussion given to it relative to its potential importance suggests to us that more intensive consideration of such issues by economists would be a worthwhile applied policy investment.

4 Conclusions

Our discussion has been wide-ranging and highly preliminary. We do not want to claim too much for it, of for how any of the propositions offered directly follow from taking a complexity perspective. However, we believe that the topics are important, and are too little discussed by economists. Moreover, we recognize that many of the changes in method currently occurring in the profession, changes which are moving in the muddling through direction, would probably be made even if complexity had never been developed. There is a natural tendency of systems to muddle through and arrive at reasonable approaches on their own, and that has been the case in applied economic research, where the applied work had deviated significantly from its theoretical welfare foundations.

Our hope is that by highlighting the discord between the welfare theory we teach, and the actual practice of applied policy economics, researchers will become more conscious of the pragmatic approach they are taking, and embrace it, and develop it further, rather than reluctantly use it.

Economics often considers itself the queen of the social sciences. Its coronation has been associated with its formal scientific nature, it's consistency of approach, its certainty in its applied policy suggestions, and its empirical nature. Each of those elements is closely tied to the holy trilogy of assumptions, which gives an almost religious nature to the monarchy. It is this connection that accounts for why the core general equilibrium theory has remained the center of welfare economics, even as applied policy work moved away from those assumptions. There was fear that if we give up the holy trilogy we will give up our reign. That need not be true. However, if muddling through is accepted as the best we can do with welfare economics, then the economic profession's claim to being the queen cannot be a religious claim, as the holy trilogy analogy suggests it is by some researchers. Instead it would be a secular claim based on its usefulness in arriving at reasonable and workable policy solutions to the difficult policy problems we face.

References

Akerlof, G.: 1993, The economic consequences of cognitive issonance, *International Library of Critical Writings in Economics*.

Arthur, B., Durlauf, S. and Lane, D.: 1997, *The Economy as an Evolving Complex System II*, Reading Mass Adison-Wesley.

Axelrod, R.: 1997, *The Complexity of Cooperation: Agent-Based Models of Competition and Collaboration*, Princeton University Press, Princeton.

Brock, W.: 1993, Pathways to randomness in the economy: Emergent nonlinearity and chaos in economics and finance, *Estudios Economicos* **8**(1).

Brock, W. and Carpenter, S.: 2000a, *A Theory of Adaptive Management: A Bayesian Model Averaging Approach*, Department of Economics and Limnology, University of Wisconsin, Madison.

Brock, W. and Carpenter, S.: 2000b, *Habitat Change, Harvest and Depensation in Living Resources: Thresholds, Learning and Policy Choice*, Department of Economics and Limnology, University of Wisconsin, Madison.

Brock, W. and Colander, D.: 2000, Complexity and economic policy, *in* Colander (ed.), *The Complexity Vision and the Teaching of Economics*, Edward Elgar.

Brock, W. and Durlauf, S.: 2000a, Interactions-based models handbook of econometrics, *http://www.nber.org* .

Brock, W. and Durlauf, S.: n.d., Growth economics and reality, *World Bank Economic Review, YEAR* = .

Brock, W. and Hommes, C.: 1998, Heterogeneous beliefs and routes to chaos in a simple asset pricing model, *Journal of Economic Dynamics and Control* **22**, 1235–1274.

Day, R. and Chen, P.: 1993, *Nonlinear Dynamics and Evolutionary Economics*, Oxford University Press.

Epstein, J.: 1996, *Growing Artificial Societies: Social Science from the Bottom Up*, Ma. MIT Press, Cambridge.

Farber, D.: 1999, *Eco-Pragmatism: Making Sensible Enviromental Decisions in an Uncertain World*, University of Chicago Press, Chicago.

Frank, R.: 1999, *Luxury Fever: Why Money Fails to Satisfy in an Era of Excess*, University of Chicago Press, Chicago.

Frank, R. and Cook, P.: 1995, *The Winner-Take-All Society*, The Free Press, New York.

Geweke, J.: 1999, Computational experiments and reality, *Department of Economics - The Universities of Iowa and Minnesota* .

Holling, C.: 1992, Cross-scale morphology, geometry, and dynamics of ecosystems, *Ecological Monographs* **62**, 447–502.

Holling, C.: 1997a, Conservation ecology, *http://www.consecol.org* .

Holling, C., Gunderson, L. and Peterson, G.: 1997, Comparing ecological and social systems, *Department of Zoology, University of Florida* .

Judd, K.: 1998, *Numerical Methods in Economics*, MIT Press, Cambridge.

Kreps, D.: 1997, *Economics-The Current Position*, Dedalus, Winter.

Magee, S. and Brock, W.: 1984, The invisible foot, *Neocalssical Political Economy*, Ballinger, Boston.

Pizer, W.: 1996, Modeling long-term policy under uncertainty, *Ph.D. Thesis, Department of Economics, Harvard University* .

Sargent, T.: 1993, *Bounded Rationality in Macroeconomics*, Clarendon Press, Oxford.

Sargent, T.: 1999, *The Conquest of American Inflation*, Princeton University Press.

Scott, J.: 1998, *Seeing like a State: How Certain Schemes to Improve the Human Condition Have Failed*, Yale University Press, Oxford.

Solow, R.: 1990, *The Labor Market as a Social Institution*, Cambrideg Mass and Blackwell.

Solow, R.: 1997, *How Did Economics Get that Way and What Way Did it Get?*, Dedalus, Winter.

Turnovsky, S.: 1995, *Methods of Macroeconomic Dynamics*, MIT Press, Cambridge.

VonGraaf, X.: 1995, *Theoretical Welfare Economics*, Cambridge University Press, Cambridge.

The Multiple Phase Theory of Macroeconomic Evolution

ƎꝹꝺ

R.H. Day

For there are no examples so frequent in history as those of men withdrawing from the community they were bred up in, and setting up new governments in other places; from whence sprang all the petty commonwealths in the beginning of ages, and which always multiplied, as long as there was room enough, till the stronger or more fortunate swallowed the weaker; and those great ones again breaking into pieces, dissolving into lesser dominions, (paraphrased) [John Locke, *Two Treatises on Government* 1690]

... for time does not stop its course for nations any more than for men; they are all advancing towards a goal with which they are unacquainted. [Alexis de Tocquiville, *Democracy in America* 1832]

1 Introduction

In an obscure article first published in 1944, Jan Tinbergen set out to explain in quantitative terms the exponential economic growth trends that had commenced with the Industrial Revolution. The subsequent articles of Nelson, Solow, and Swan, all published in 1956, established macroeconomic growth modelling as a major stream of theoretical and econometric research that has continue unabated through nearly half a century. Current examples of this genre focus on the role of knowledge and human capital.

Facts that have received much less attention from economic theorists are the highly irregular fluctuations of the data around the trend, the collapses or disintegration of whole economic systems and the re-establishment of growth through the adoption of completely new systems of technology and socio-economic organization. The irregularity of growth is reflected in the modern macroeconomic data. To appreciate fully the more dramatic structural changes that have occurred and are occurring, a time perspective is required longer than permitted by the available numerical indexes. Such a time perspective is made possible by the work of historians and archaeologists who have constructed a careful, descriptive record of socioeconomic evolution. According to this record, individual economies emerged, grew to prominence, flourished for a time and then, more often than not, declined (from an archaeological perspective) precipitously. Many disappeared altogether; others transformed themselves into new, quite different forms and continued their expansion. Some appear to have fluctuated erratically for many centuries before making the transition to a different form, while others, after a period of growth and oscillation, seem to have collapsed, reverting to an earlier economic form; then, after perhaps experiencing alternating periods of fortune in that stage, re-entered a more advanced form and resumed an upward trajectory. This paper describes a multiple phase theory of macroeconomic evolution that explains certain salient, qualitative attributes of this very long run historical record.

Because the vast changes under consideration have occurred over the millennia, it is tempting to presume that the long ago past has little relevance for the present. In my own opinion, nothing could be further from the truth. The past provides evidence of fundamental ingredients of socioeconomic structure that would seem to be involved at all times and all places; those fundamental ingredients must be playing a central role in what is going on now. Indeed, given an ability to explain the past in terms of the theory, implications for understanding present and possible future developments can be derived with some confidence.

Section 2 presents the primary concepts involved in the theory. Section 3 briefly describes a model based on the theory and summarizes the properties of numerical "histories" the model can generate. Section 4 then displays a computer generated history that mimics (in broad qualitative terms) the developmental process known to have occurred for the world as a whole. Section 5 concludes the paper with a reflection on the lessons for understanding present and anticipating future developments. The implications for population control, resource conservation, and urban organization are emphasized.

2 Components for a Theory of Macroeconomic Evolution

The class of recursive programming models that I developed to simulate multiproduct output, the expansion and contraction of alternative technologies, and the changing patterns of resource utilization and productivity in various economic sectors forms one approach for modelling economic evolution using microeconomic data.[1] Inspired by scientists who wanted to develop models of

---

[1] I first developed the ideas incorporated here for a course on economic dynamics given at the University of Wisconsin in the early 1970s. Subsequently, I came in contact with Jerry Sablov, then at Harvard, who later organized an advanced sem-

human socioeconomic evolution over its entire history, I decided to work out a much simplified version of that approach that would retain its evolutionary character but which would be re-oriented to mimic the macro patterns of production, population, and technological change over very long periods of time and in terms of the world as a whole.

2.1 The Classical Starting Point

I began with the basic classical economic ingredients.

(i) *Population and the Work Force*
Time is reckoned in the classical unit of a human generation or a quarter century, each period is represented by a population of adults and their children who inherit the adult world in the next generation. Each generation must provide its own capital goods which only last the period. Each family is assumed to allocate one adult equivalent to the household economy and one to the social economy. The social work force is then equivalent to the number of families, x, or to the number of adult females or males.

(ii) *The Family Function*
The number of children who survive (that is, who become adults the next period) depends on the average standard of living as represented by per capita production, the Malthusian form of this *family function* is readily derived from the standard household theory. For all positive incomes it is positive, montonically, non-decreasing, and bounded above.

---

inar at the Center for American Studies in Santa Fe in the fall of 1978 involving archaeologists M. Aldenderfer, L. Cordell, G. Low, C. Renfrew, and E. Zubrow, a mathematician K. Cooke, a philosopher J. Bell, and myself. The goal was to see how the fascinating prehistory of our species that had been so patiently constructed by archaeologists in the preceding hundred years could be understood in formal terms and simulated numerically. It was not until I came across Ester Boserup's Population and Technological Change, quite by serendipity, that I actually set down in writing my theory of macroeconomic evolution and subsequently delivered at the conference on Evolutionary Dynamics and Nonlinear Economics, sponsored by Ilya Prigogine's Center for Statistical Mechanics and the IC2 Institute in Austin. A version, co-authored with a young French mathematician, Jean-Luc Walter, who spent a year visiting USC, was published in the proceedings. See Day and J.-L. (1989). I should also mention the provocative and stimulating interaction with Arthur Iberall's interdisciplinary group with R. Baum and D. Wilkerson (political scientists), A. Moore and D. White (anthropologists), and L. Goldberg (biologist). Although that group was concerned with fundamental concepts of deep physical and social structure, my theory represents a course, macro aggregative representation of some of the ideas discussed there.

(iii) Technology and the Production Function
The production function describes the dependence of potential aggregate output on the work force and on knowledge, the former being treated as a variable (in generational time units), L, and the latter as a parameter, B. According to the usual assumptions, production within a given economy must eventually exhibit diminishing marginal returns to variable factors due to the scarcity of land, water, and other material resources.

(iv) Continuous Productivity Advance
The productivity of labor using a given technology tends to increase faster than can be accounted for by the increase in work force (and capital) alone. The simplest way to accommodate this fact is to assume it occurs at a positive constant rate as has been done in most macroeconomic analyses until very recently, which amounts to assuming that the technology level parameter increases exponentially at a constant rate. Later this assumption will be replaced by a learning by doing formulation.

Using (i)-(iii) and given a small initial population, population and output grow, but ultimately converge to a stationary level. Adding (iv) allows output and population to grow indefinitely. Thus, we have the classical story in its simplest form. It clearly explains one salient characteristic of economic development in the very long run, but provides no insight whatever on the chaotically complex multiple phase evolution that underlies the trend.

2.2 Expanding the Concept of the Macro Economy I

Let us continue by augmenting the classical theory,

(v) A Family Welfare Threshold
A positive standard of living below which no children survive to adulthood exists for physiological reasons alone. Its empirical relevance is evident whenever famine or social conflict become severe, as has been the case repeatedly in the past and is occurring now at several places in the world (Africa, North Korea, circa 1997). A family function with such a threshold can be derived from a reasonable specification of family preferences.[2] It is easy to show that a positive survival threshold, introduced into the classical model, is sufficient to induce fluctuations in output, income, and population numbers: a result

---

[2] See Day, Kim and Macunovich (1989). At high levels of income, birth rates decline. This phenomenon does not change the results of the present analysis in a significant way. However, see Day and Pavlov (2001) who extend the present analysis to include this phenomenon.

explicitly anticipated by Malthus early in the nineteenth century.[3]

(vi) Infrastructure

Organizational structure includes that of households, producers, marketing firms, financial enterprises, and public institutions of various kinds. It provides the coherent framework of rules and procedures within which work can occur. It must be supported by human effort. The humans devoted to this effort form the infrastructure for a given socioeconomic system that mediates the human energy devoted to coordinating production and exchange, to providing social cohesion for effective cooperation, for training and enculturating the work force, and for producing the public goods such as waste disposal and public safety required for the well being of the work force. The knowledge that makes this human infrastructure effective is the *administrative technology*. It must augment the production technology. Given that the social infrastructure requires a significant block of human resources, it follows that for an economy to be feasible with a fixed technology, the population must exceed a given bound which implies that technology is "population linked", as cogently argued by Boserup (1996) in a trenchant note.

Infrastructural institutions reside in both public and private domains. The importance of the latter is sometimes overlooked. Large scale corporations allocate roughly half their expenditures to educational, research, managerial and administrative functions, and roughly half on the production of goods and services. Although some economists would include such things in the category of intermediate goods used in the production process, it is worth distinguishing them because their individual productivity cannot be measured in the usual ways (output per hour expended). Their productivity, like that of the elements of public infrastructure, is only reflected in the productivity of the entire organization. The contribution of individual scientists, teachers, managers, and accountants to the organization's success is impossible to measure except by profit comparisons among similar organizations. A productive public infrastructure will be reflected in some measure of aggregate accomplishment such as political, military or economic dominance, a high level of culture, and a wide distribution of welfare.[4]

For purposes of macroeconomic analysis, details of infrastructure cannot be taken into account any more than can the details of production technology.

---

[3] 3. See Easterlin (1978) on thresholds and Malthus' Principles of Population for the conjecture concerning fluctuations.

[4] Infrastructure has been receiving increasing attention. See North (1981) for very broad aspects and the World Bank (1996) for numerous details. For a suggestive attempt to quantify infrastructural effects on productivity, see the working paper by Charles I. Jenes and Robert Hall, "Measuring the Effects of Infrastructure on Economic Growth," Stanford University.

I, therefore, represent it by a parameter, M, quantifying it by a fixed number of people for a given individual macro economy. That is, each macro economy must have a social infrastructure of size M as a prerequisite for the effective operation of the given production technology.

(vii) Social Space

In addition to the diseconomies implied by resource scarcity, diseconomies also accrue because of the increasing complexity of planning, communicating, and coordinating production as an economy grows. The ability to overcome these diseconomies depends on the social space which the administrative technology "produces". If there is *social slack*, then more people can be easily accommodated within the economy. As social space is "used up", cooperation becomes increasingly difficult, social conflict increases, and productivity declines. These *internal diseconomies* can yield absolutely diminishing returns to population within an economy.

Again, in the interest of macroeconomic simplicity, the social space is represented by a single parameter, N, quantified by the maximum number of people that can coexist in an economy with an infrastructure given by M.

Even in the presence of the diseconomies resulting from declining social slack, a negative sloping segment in the aggregate production function cannot occur if resources are freely disposable. *People*, however, are not freely disposable so that the "free disposal axiom" often involved in economic equilibrium theory is not germane. It could be argued that people would never reproduce to such an extent as to depress absolute production, but this is a view supported more by faith than by facts. Over-population within the context of a given administrative technology seems to have occurred, and very likely is occurring in a number of places so that its analysis would seem relevant indeed. Economists sometimes argue that such problems can easily be solved merely by paying people not to work. Indeed, such a solution has been widely practiced in Western countries. But a part of the effect seems to have been to alienate the unemployed even though they have been enabled to live at greater than survival standards of living. The resulting political and social conflict affects production adversely.

Given ingredients (i)-(vii), a given economy is represented by (a) a family function whose parameters include a maximum (representative) family size, the income elasticity of family size, α, the real cost of raising children to adulthood, q, and a family welfare threshold, ϕ; (b) an aggregate production function whose parameters include a technology or productivity "level", B, an infrastructure, M, a social space, N, and an elasticity of production, β.

If a society's population is below M, it cannot adopt the production technology in question for it cannot populate both the infrastructure and labor force. If it is close to or above N, the social space has been drastically reduced and the standard of living must fall below the family welfare threshold, implying that the population is infeasible. The system is feasible for populations between M and N. The dynamics of such a system can display all the simple and complex possibilities: convergent growth, cycles, erratic fluctuations, and collapse. If continuous (exponential) productivity improvement is incorporated, then growth or fluctuations around a rising trend are possible or, as before, growth, possibly expanding fluctuations around a rising trend followed by a collapse. All of these possibilities have been derived elsewhere.[5]

2.3 Expanding the Concept of a Macro Economy II

As population grows within an economy, if, eventually, the average standard of living begins to fall and if people eventually realize what is happening, growth might be restored by expanding the social space. Without any innovations in administrative technology, one way to accomplish this would be to split the economy.

(viii) Replication and Merging of Economies
By dividing the population, two similar economies can be created in place of one. This can only be done if the original economy is large enough to meet the infrastructural needs of both, that is, it must be larger than 2M and still have population left over to make up a labor force for each. Then growth can continue until, once again, the diseconomies begin to impinge on productivity and the standard of living begins to fall, then the same fission can occur again. The process can continue so long as the social space can be expanded in this way.

(ix) Environmental Space
In addition to the internal diseconomies implied by resource scarcity and social space, external diseconomies should be recognized that derive from the total population of *all the economies together*. These diseconomies are, for example, caused by the exhaustion of the environment's waste absorbing capacity. This capacity can-for a given technology-be stated in terms of the *environmental space* available which in turn depends on the total population density. In addition, as resources become scarce and the cost of extracting and refining them grows, diminishing absolute returns to the work force can eventually come to pass as the total world population gets large. The internal diseconomies can be overcome by replication, the external ones cannot. *Once the world is full in the sense that external diseconomies become important, the replication of economies with the same basic structures must come to an end.* If, when this state is attained, a collapse occurs due to a very powerful drop in productivity, the population may reorganize itself by fusing some of the previous groups into a smaller number of economies with the same technology as before. Then the stage is set for a new growth process through internal growth

---

[5] An exhaustive dynamic analysis is given in Day and Min (1996).

of the individual economies and through a resumption of replication. In this
way, fluctuations in the *number* of economies, as well as in total population,
could ensue, perhaps in a highly irregular way for a very long time.

2.4 Expanding the Concept of a Macro Economy III

In addition to the process of replication, social space might also be expanded
if there exist the following.

(x) Alternative Socioeconomic Systems
Suppose there are several different types of socioeconomic systems, each characterized by the ingredients just described but each with distinct parameters.
These alternatives represent different "family values", "ways of life", "development blocks", each with qualitatively distinct administrative/production
technologies. Let us assume that the technologies have a natural order so that
each successive system in the order so that each successive system in the order requires a greater overhead of human capital but produces a greater social
space that would permit higher attainable production and population levels
than its predecessors. Each such system also "creates" a characteristic environmental space which may expand-or constrict-from system to system.

(xi) Integration and Disintegration of Economies
Given these alternatives, a society may be able to reorganize itself by integrating separate economies and adopting a new system if its current population
is sufficient to populate the new, more demanding infrastructure. If this new
system expands the social space, then further growth in the total population is
possible. If so, then growth within the new more advance type of economy can
continue until the diseconomies of declining social space begin to impinge on
it, in which case, replication of economies could in principle take place by the
same fission process as before, or a further integration of existing economies
to form a still more advanced type of socioeconomic system, if one exists, with
attainable infrastructural requirements. Thus, replication and integration can
both play a role in economic population growth and economic evolution.
If in this process productivity declines enough to cause a drop in population
and a switch to a new more productive system fails to occur, the now unpro-
ductive economies can disintegrate and revert to a less advanced system that
requires a smaller infrastructure.

(xii) Learning by Doing
Still another mechanism to be considered that enhances the potential for continuing growth is the continuous productivity increase already mentioned in
the discussion above. In the expanded theory this phenomenon is incorporated in a way suited to the existence of alternative technological regimes.
Continuing productivity advance based on experience or learning by doing
can only occur within an "active" system, that is, the one with the currently

adopted basic technology. As experience within a given regime accumulates, output per unit of labor increases. But each distinct technology is assumed to have a maximum potential productivity, B, and that difference between B and the current level of technology B represents the potential improvement through learning by doing. The rate at which learning enhances productivity is assumed to be proportional to the potential improvement. In this way, the level of productivity of a given technology can increase when it is being used. I also assume that this process does not modify the social and environmental spaces.

3 The Multiple Phase Dynamics

3.1 The Organizational Options

Let us suppose there exists a menu of alternative socieconomic systems, each with distinct parameters of household, production, infrastructure, and social and environmental space. A given economy that belongs to one of them has several options in any generation: (i) it can continue to grow within the same system; (ii) it can divide so as to form two similar, more or less independent economies, each with the same system; (iii) it can merge with another similar economy to form a new economic unit with the same basic system as before; (iv) it can integrate with one or more economies to form a new, much larger economy with more advanced infrastructural requirements and a much larger social space, and possibly a much larger environmental space than before; (v) it can disintegrate into several smaller economies, each with a simpler system and each with smaller infrastructural requirements than before.

3.2 The Optimization Criteria

The "choice" among these options is guided in the present theory by the sole criterion of the average standard of living or welfare in terms of output per family for the current generation. This is in contrast to the optimal population growth theory of Dasgupta or Lane which characterizes an economy using an intertemporal optimization that takes into account (and determines) the standard of living and demoeconomic behavior of all future generations, forever. Whatever one may think of the desirability of an infinite horizon, I take it as obvious that doing the best for the present generation, given its current population, is already a considerable intellectual and organizational challenge and, no doubt, in itself an exaggeration of actual capabilities. Moreover, in the present theory a one period look ahead on a generational time scale implies a 25 year time horizon. With the discount factors used by contemporary growth theorists, this implies a minuscule weight on the benefits accruing to future generations. If an extreme assumption must be made-as indeed it must-it is far more plausible to assume that the choice of family size is based entirely on the preferences of the current generation, and that is what the present theory does.

3.3 Phase Switching

Given the alternatives listed above and the constraints built into the technology in terms of infrastructural requirements and the limits implied by social and environmental spaces, growth cannot continue forever within any given economy but can continue as long as the replication of economies within a given system and/or integration and switching to more advanced systems is possible. Every such switch changes the structure of the system and occurs endogenously on the basis of the generational standard of living criterion.
Growth, however, is not the inevitable outcome of the dynamic process implied by the theory. Instead, the other options involving merging or disintegrating can occur so that very complex demoeconomic histories are potentials that depend on all the parameter values.

3.4 Scenarios

A given sequence of phase switchings among the technological systems and numbers of economies within them is a *scenario*. The following indicate characteristics the various kinds of scenarios that can occur within the framework of this theory.

(i) Growth within a given economy is bounded.
(ii) If the social space is small relative to the environmental space, then growth can continue by means of replication.
(iii) If there are no more advanced regimes, then growth can terminate in fluctuations both in population and in the number of economies. Demise may also occur.
(iv) As long as more advanced regimes are available, then growth can continue by means of integration and switching to one of them.
(v) If there are a finite number of systems, then, depending on the parameter values, the model's histories could converge-possibly after many periods of local chaos to a classical equilibrium-or exhibit endless fluctuations, eventually sticking with a given regime or cycling in a nonperiod fashion through an endless sequence of regimes with replication, merging, integration, and disintegration with jumping and reverting among systems. Or histories may eventually lead to a collapse and demise.
(vi) When learning by doing is allowed and if the productivity potential of each technology is finite, then convergence to a classical economic equilibrium cannot occur. Instead, continued growth, including replication and integration, is accelerated. If in addition there is a finite number of technologies, fluctuations occur almost surely with an ever increasing chance of complete collapse.

(vii) Unstable fluctuation and collapse can be postponed indefinitely with the addition of successively more advanced technologies and infrastructures-*if they expand the environmental space.*

A comprehensive theoretical analysis of these possibilities and the parametric conditions under which each can occur is carried out elsewhere.[6]

4 Mimicking Economic Development in the Very Long Run: Evaluating the Theory

4.1 The Cultures

Historians of the nineteenth century noticed that prior to the industrial takeoff economies had passed through distinct stages of development characterized by differences in production technology and in the organization of exchange and governance. Archaeologists, aided by modern methods of dating materials, began extending this picture backwards in time. By now they have constructed an approximate but coherent chronology of major developments on a worldwide basis that stretches back to the earliest traces of a human presence.
Briefly, the great variety of human societies can be roughly grouped into a relatively small number of stages based on production technology and social infrastructure. To describe the major developments throughout the entire span of Homo sapiens and to take advantage of the known archaeological information, a reasonable minimal specification would be:

(i) Hunting and Gathering
(ii) Settled (Village) Agriculture
(iii) Complex Societies and City State Civilizations
(iv) Trading Empires
(v) Industrial States
(vi) The Global Information Economies

These names are, of course, only suggestive. It is not implied, for instance, that hunter-gatherers only hunt and forage or that agrarians never hunt nor gather wild foods. Nor do we wish to imply by the term "city state" that citizens never engaged in hunting or that hunters-gatherers were entirely absent in later stages. The division merely reflects the roughly dominant forms of social organization and economic activity. The technology regimes incorporated

---

[6] Day, Chapters 21-23 (1999). Of course, capital required for the infrastructure and for production and capital accumulation should be incorporated in the theory, but I will not go into that aspect of the story here. For discussion of capital accumulation with multiple phases, see Day and Zou (1994).

in the theory are idealizations of these rough stages. The mechanisms of replication/merging and of integration/disintegration are also idealized reflections of historical fact.

It shall be supposed here that at any one time the world population is dominated by a single socioeconomic system so that all of its economies are based on the same family function and the same socioeconomic technologies. Let us refer to the collection of such economies at a given time as a *culture*. The essential characteristics of these systems can be summarized as follows.

1. The several systems form an advancing sequence of increasing infrastructures and social spaces.
2. Demoeconomic conditions are a part of the prerequisites for the advance from one system to another. Thus, for example, hunting and food collecting people did not adopt agriculture until the declining productivity of their own culture made a switch desirable. They integrated to form more or less settled tribal societies when the economic conditions became relatively favorable for agriculture.
3. Disintegrations followed by eventual reintegrations have occurred from the second through the fourth and through the fifth stages.
4. There have been more or less continuous improvements of productivity within each epoch, and the rates of improvement seem to have increased successively.
5. Although population fluctuation is an important aspect of the story, the long run trend is strongly positive, and, viewed over a hundred thousand years of modern human evolution, appears to be explosive.
6. The bounds within which the entire human population could live as hunting and food collecting peoples have been exceeded many fold. Likewise, the number of people existing today could not have lived in any epoch prior to the industrial revolution. A reversion to an earlier system could only occur if it were accompanied by a drastic fall in population.

Of course, historical development through these stages has taken place in fits and starts, and at different times at different places. This is partly because the world is very heterogeneous in terms of topography and resource endowment, which means that similar technologies can have different productivities, and partly because many societies were more or less isolated from one another, which, in combination with even tiny perturbations in technology and/or social parameters, can make huge differences in the sequencing and timing of the major transitions.

4.2 A Model Generated History

The history generated by a given model based on the theory is, in effect, a scenario described by the episodes that make it up. An episode is a period of time during which the number of economies and the system governing them does not change. The following variables describe a given model history:

- the time of entry into each episode
- the duration of each episode
- the governing system in each episode
- the governing number of economies using the governing system
- number of households (from which population can be estimated)
- aggregate production
- average welfare per family
- number of children who survive to adulthood
- average family size
- the vector of technology levels (one level for each system)
- the size of the aggregate infrastructure
- the size of the total labor force
- the social slack
- the environmental slack

The specific mathematical forms and parameter values for the family and production functions are given in the references cited. Using them, a simulation was begun with an initial population of 100 families ($X_Q = 100$) and was continued for 4,185 periods or generations, a span of a little over 100,000 years. The graph of population for this run, as shown in figure 1, is virtually a vertical line over the present, caused by explosive growth after a takeoff a few centuries ago. Very close to the present, fluctuations can be observed, but, in terms of sheer numbers, human population-relative to the present-appears utterly insignificant until the most recent centuries.

This picture, however, is quite misleading, as can be seen by blowing up the time scale and plotting the data for shorter time spans. This is done in figure 2. Panel (a) plots population for system 1 in millions of families. We see that rapid growth appeared only after some 25 millennia. Then irregular fluctuations of increasing magnitude appear. Panel (b) plots population for systems 2, 3, and 4, also in millions of families for some 300 generations. Prominent fluctuations are featured, no doubt an exaggeration of reality. Panel (c) plots population in billions of families for systems 4, 5, and 6 and brings the story up to the end of the twentieth century.

Turning to the underlying economic forces, we find much more going on in terms of structural evolution. This can be seen in figure 3, which displays the dominant system index at each time. The initial population in our simulation adopted the first system and remained with it for well over 3,000 generations. Growth during this long epoch thus occurred by means of the fission process. A more detailed presentation of this epochal evolution is presented in figure 4. Panel (a) gives the system indexes from late in the system 1 epoch through to the "permanent" switch to system 4. Early in this evolution, temporary jump to system 2 occurs. It involves the integration of the very large number of hunting bands into a considerably smaller number of agricultural economies. They disintegrate, however, within a generation back into the original number of system 1 groups. Then structural fluctuation occurs, involving successive

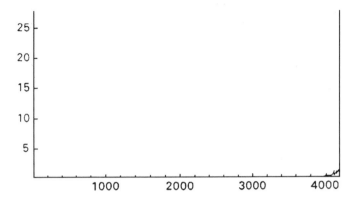

Fig. 1. A Simulated Population History. Time is measured in "generations" of 25 years; population in billions of families.

integrations and disintegrations, until the society locks into system 2 in period 3,784 or about 8050 B.C. Growth then continues within this village agriculture system by replication for 182 generations or 4,550 years. A similar sequence of structural fluctuations occurs between systems 2 and 3 and systems 3 and 4, with corresponding fluctuations in the number of economies as integrations and disintegrations bring about system jumps and reversions.

In panel (b) the story is continued. The switch to system 4 shown in panel (a) is indeed not permanent. A reversion occurs in system 3, followed by reintegration; also integration and disintegration between 4 and 5. The run terminates with a jump to system 6 (the global information economy), which takes place through an integration of industrial economies, then a reversion followed by another jump. Note that the time scales used in diagrams (a) and (b) are different and obscure the fact that the great instabilities in a structural sense are compressed into the 10,000 years since the advent of agriculture.

4.3 The Archaeological and Historical Record

In reality, various geographical areas traversed these stages at very different times. Certainly, however, we know that the advance through them did not increase uniformly from a lower to a higher index. Rather, progress from one to another, especially in earlier times, was interrupted by reversions to lower level stages. Moreover, fluctuations in income, population, and capital have been typical.

The overall picture is one of growth at fluctuating rates with sometimes smooth, sometimes turbulent transitions when jumps and reversions occurred until a "higher" stage became firmly established. But all of this is what our theory would "predict", and what the example shown actual does.

Now let us consider behavior within epochs and in the transitions between

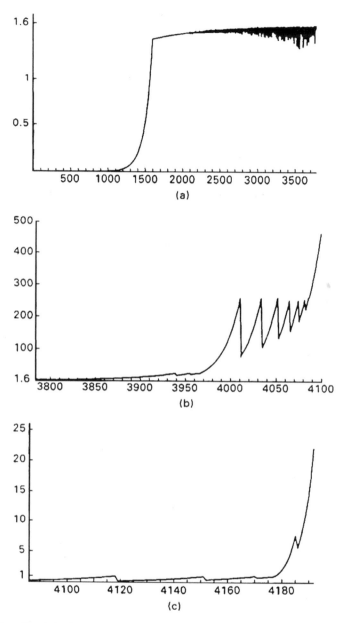

Fig. 2. Details of the Population Dynamics, (a) System 1, population in millions of families, (b) Systems 2, 3, and 4, population in millions of families, (c) Systems 4, 5, and 6, population in billions of families. Note the changing time scale from (a) to (c).

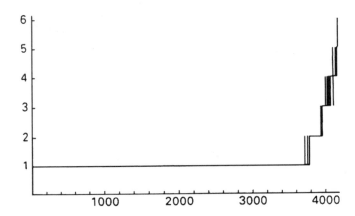

Fig. 3. Simulated History of Structural Change in Terms of the Dominant Systems Index.

them, beginning with hunting and food collecting. It is well known that the diffusion of hunting and food collecting cultures throughout the world occurred through a process of fission and migration with relatively little elaboration of infrastructure but with advances of technology that involved a gradual improvement in utensils, weapons, and other material artifacts. Our theory both reflects and explains this fact.

The reason for the cessation of this expansion and the subsequent settlement of people into more or less fixed agricultural villages is less obvious and still debated. If Binford, Cohen, Boserup, and others are right, then the regime switch was not due to the discovery of agriculture, which must have occurred long before the switch. Rather, it was due to the necessary decline in the productivity of the earlier way of life when the world became "full" which made farming relatively more efficient, given the levels of population that had been reached.

Our theory explains the early growth in terms of replication through fission, a well established fact, and the switch to agriculture in terms of the reorganization of production due to the relatively greater productivity of labor in the new regime, given the larger population and its greater social and environmental spaces. Thus, more people can live cohesively in a village than in a hunting band, and far more people can live on earth under agriculture.

The process of expanding agrarian settlement from 9000-3000 B.C. and the subsequent emergence of city states in the Ancient Near East has been described in meticulous terms by Nissen. Of special interest is his explanation of the internal conflicts that led to a reversion back to individual village organizations and the continuing fluctuation between these forms for an extended period. Saggs, who gives a survey of civilization before the classic period, explained why, because of the unusually favorable conditions for wild animals and plants along the Nile, people in Egypt settled down later than elsewhere.

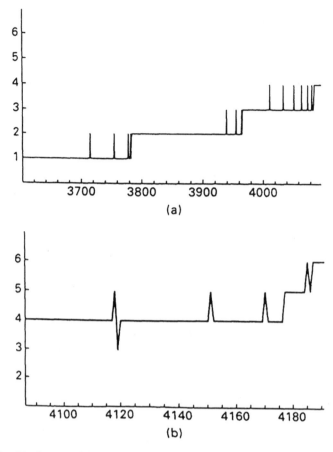

Fig. 4. The Evolution of Socioeconomic Systems, (a) Systems 1, 2, 3, and 4. (b) Systems 4, 5, and 6. Note that structural fluctuations occur between 1 and 2, 2 and 3, and 3, and 4 and 5.

He also describes how, as population grew, towns began to form from 5000 B.C. onward and then integrated to form a unified state, combining upper and lower Egypt about 3000 B.C. Scarre observes how a similar transition occurred in Greece about 1800 B.C. when the cluster of villages making up Attica unified politically to form the city state of Athens.

Much is known about the vast extension in administrative infrastructure associated with the regime switches in Mesopotamia, Egypt, and Greece, developments only possible with sufficiently large and productive populations divided between production per se and administrative functions.

Of special interest to the present theory is the process of the repeated integration of villages to form the complex societies of Burundi and Polynesia and their disintegration back to collections of independent villages. This history, described by Sagan, involves a switching and reswitching between levels of socioeconomic organization that is predicted by our model for well denned conditions of infrastructural requirements and productivity.

Another possibility that occurs generically in our theory is that of collapse and demise, a developmental outcome known to have occurred at various times and places in the archaeological and historical records. Iseminger summarizes an example discovered relatively recently in the broad plain east of St. Louis. During the period 9500-600 B.C., hunter-gatherers set up seasonal villages and later, permanent settlements. By 1200 A.D. a substantial city that archaeologists call Cahokia came to dominate the surrounding territory. Two centuries later it was abandoned and no "ties have been established between the great city an any historical tribe".

A couple of years ago, Katie Pollard, a young mathematics major at Claremont, simulated my model using data describing the reconstructed history of the Anasazi Indians in Chaco Canyon described by Lightfoot. Her model traces these people through their initial "hunting and gardening," village agriculture and centralized (city state like) systems, the fluctuation between these regimes, and the ultimate collapse and disappearance.

The replication mechanism that played such an important role in the diffusion of the hunting and food collecting culture is also evident in the diffusion of the city state. The classic description of the process is Herodatus' story of the division of Lydia's population and the subsequent colonization of North Africa and Italy. He also relates the belief of people in a city near the Bosporus whose citizens claimed that they were founded by a colonial expedition from Egypt.

Throughout the world, trading empires eventually arose through the widespread political and economic domination of surrounding territories by larger, more powerfully organized, and more effectively coordinated agglomeration of people. We might include the feudal era through the Renaissance in this epoch which is distinguished by repeated integrations and disintegrations of smaller city states and principalities as empires rose and fell. All this can be explained in terms of the theory at hand and mimicked by computational simulations. One thinks of Egypt, Persia, Greece under Philip and Alexander, Rome, China, and India.

Obviously, a great variety of geographical, social, and even psychological factors were involved in these examples and none were alike in detail. Yet, all the historical details had to work themselves out within a framework of interacting technological and demoeconomic forces roughly modelled by the present theory.

With the Industrial Revolution a vast expansion in the resources devoted to infrastructure took place. Elaborate education and scientific establishments, multiple levels of representative government, bureaus for monitoring economic activities of many kinds (banking, trade, production, etc.), elaborate systems for adjudicating economic and social conflict, public goods for recreation, communication, transportation, etc. And integration and disintegration continued, which brings us to current developments on the world scene.

5 The Lessons for the Present and Future

Associated with the rise of the nation state is an explosive increase in population and a considerable instability in the composition of the individual economic units. From the point of view of the present theory, it is not mere fluctuations in business that characterizes this institutional instability *but rather the integration and disintegration of political economic units* throughout the nineteenth and twentieth centuries. Also noteworthy has been the elaboration of infrastructure on a global basis: earth satellite systems, international courts and assemblies, trade agreements, and the vast complex of research organizations that feed technical advances. With the spread of jet aircraft, airport facilities, satellite communications, and the worldwide web we have entered the global information economy.

Our grossly aggregative theory would seem to provide too course a sieve to filter out the salient features of modern history which involve such intricately elaborated and inter-connected institutions among so many levels of organization as now exist. Yet, if the facts have been interpreted correctly, then our theory contributes a lot to an understanding the evolution of humanity through its various cultural forms-not in detail, of course, but in some of its salient aspects. If that is so, then we are entitled to draw implications for understanding events in our own time and for considering policies that will shape events in the future. Let us summarize some of its most important implications.

5.1 Infrastructure and Productivity

The theory incorporates a crucial link between infrastructure and productivity. The productivity of a society by any measure (its wealth, political power, size, and welfare distribution) depends on an effective work force whose productivity depends in turn on the existence of an appropriately developed infrastructure with sufficient resources to sustain the population as a whole. As population grows, infrastructure must also. It is not just the size of the infrastructure but its functions and organization that must change. When population begins to become excessive relative to its infrastructure, productivity must fall. To avoid fluctuations or even collapse, *population must be stabilized or the infrastructure transformed.*

5.2 The Disintegration of an Industrial Economy: The Soviet Bloc

Consider the former Soviet Bloc. Here we see something like the kind of reversion our theory predicts: a large complexly organized economy disintegrating into a number of smaller ones. In terms of the theory spelled out here, the causes are clear: the system outgrew the infrastructure required to continue growing in an effective manner. A population of such great size cannot persist within *that kind* of regime. A new one is required and that is what the transition is about. The presumption, both inside the former Soviet economies and outside, is that the new regime should be based on markets and private property, that is, on a different administrative technology.

Private property and the market economy depend on the state-*the right kind of state*-one that has created the right kind of public infrastructure within which private initiative can thrive *in a way that enhances the system as a whole.* This means an accumulation of laws defining the rights, obligations, opportunities, and limitations of public and private actions; a system of courts for interpreting the law and adjudicating disputes about its application; an effective system of representative government to adjust the law in response to changing conditions so as to engage the willing participation of most of the people most of the time; a large scientific and educational establishment to provide competent participants in private and public institutions; a system of monitoring to ensure standards of quality on the basis of which specialized production and trade can flourish. Most of all, it needs institutions that create a sense of common purpose and commitment so that the population forms a cohesive body that spends most of its energies on symbiotic activity rather than on destructive social conflict.

We know of the great cultures that have accomplished enough of these things to have played a powerful role in shaping the world as we know it. We also know that all of them have eventually failed in providing some of these crucial ingredients. In the midst of the transition from a culture that has failed to another regime, it is difficult, indeed, to anticipate the outcome. Certainly, the situation in Eastern Europe reflects this problematic aspect of the transition process. Will it go through a sequence of integration and disintegration as chaotically as has occurred at various places and times in the past?

5.3 Infrastructure and America in Transition

In the midst of our own spectacular American transition into the global information economy, we recognize the decline in the aspects of welfare by which the ascendant quality of American life in the first half of the twentieth century was measured: infant mortality, literacy, educational attainment, material well being, public safety, longevity, and the sense of unlimited individual opportunity. The fact is, *our situation has substantially worsened in these terms both absolutely and relative to many other countries in the last quarter century or more.* No doubt, there are many causes that have contributed. The theory developed here suggests that we look at infrastructure and population as key elements in an explanation. Let us take one prominent example: the modern city.

Many cities in the world now exceed in size the population of entire nation states of present and former times. Consider one case in point: Los Angeles. Los Angeles has a population roughly the same magnitude as Denmark. Yet it has a single mayor, a single police chief, a single superintendent of schools. In short, a single layer of government. Denmark, by way of contrast, has several layers of government, many mayors, many police chiefs. In this sense, it has far more infrastructure than Los Angeles has. Or, consider this: when the first census of the United States of America was taken in 1780, the population of the country was about 4 million, roughly that of Los Angeles now. But the U.S. population was divided into 13 states with 13 governors, 13 legislatures, and 13 state supreme courts, not to mention county and city governmental institutions. All this in addition to the institutions of the Federal Government. Can it be that the U.S. has outgrown its governmental infrastructure and outgrown it by far? Is this the reason representative government is seen to be unrepresentative by a growing body of alienated citizens? Can the basic problem facing this country be one of *too little government* and not one of too much?

Suppose the answer is, yes. Then our theory suggests two possibilities. First, our most populous states could split in two or three, as some have already suggested. Second, in order to restore participatory government at the local level, counties, cities, and towns could be created within the new, smaller state borders with, say, a constitutional provision for towns to be re-zoned so as to maintain a maximum limit of somewhere between 10,000 and 100,000 people within the smallest political unit. Local police, local fire departments, local schools, and all the local public services would be re-established. The police functions of the new state government would be limited to those of existing state governments. Many other functions would be reallocated from what is now the city to the new smaller city and town units.

5.4 Can Environmental Space be Expanded?

Finally, we should ask if new administrative and production technologies can continue to be designed so as to enable population growth to continue? Many scientists argue that there is some kind of bound, perhaps one much bigger than the present world population-but perhaps also smaller.[7] If so, continued growth could eventually lead to drastically overburdened infrastructure and drastically reduced social and environmental slack with all the attending instabilities and possibilities for collapse derived from our theory.

To prevent this squashing against the limits of growth, the theory above identifies three key aspects of it for attention:

---

[7] Such an ultimate bound was suggested by a National Academy of Sciences panel convened as long ago as 1968 as lying somewhere between 6 and 25 billion people. See Cohen for a discussion of the issue and for much smaller estimates.

(i) the externality generating effects of aggregate population;
(ii) the propensity for a greater than ZPG rate of reproduction;
(iii) the vast infrastructural complexities of advanced stages of development.

There would seem to be three corresponding policy objectives:

(i) enhance pollution abatement, encourage resource conservation, and expand research on new technologies, new behavioral rules, and new modes of organization that can arrest the debilitating aspects of growth;
(ii) lower or eliminate population growth;
(iii) elaborate and augment infrastructure with the objective in particular of restoring public services at the local level that are essential for participatory democracy and private enterprise.

Without success in the pursuit of all these objectives, the likelihood of a collapse would seem to be very high. Because the current velocity of the process is so great, the urgency for action along these lines seems to be rising.

5.5 The Time Scale of Collapse

Although our theory explains economic evolution in the long run, its mechanisms of replication and merging, integration and disintegration, and regime switching take place within a generational time scale. When economies have disintegrated in the past, they have often done so within a fraction of a biblical life. Certainly, within our time the Soviet Bloc's disintegration was not wholly unanticipated, but the speed with which it occurred came as a complete surprise. Other economies, including our own, show many symptoms of overdevelopment, declining productivity, diminishing well being, and inadequate administrative infrastructure. The multiple phase theory of macroeconomic evolution would seem, indeed, to hold lessons for us now.

References

Boserup, E.: 1996, Development theory: An analytical framework and selected application, *Population and Development Review* **22**, 505–515.

Day, R. and J.-L., W.: 1989, *Economic Gowth in the Very Long Run: On the Multiple-Phase Interaction of Population, Technology, and Social Infrastructure*, Economic Complexity: Chaos, Sunspots, Bubbles and Nonlinearity, barnett, w., and geweke, j.k. edn, Cambridge University Press, Cambridge, chapter 11.

Day, R. and Min, Z.: 1996, Classical economic growth theory: A global bifurcation analysis, *Chaos, Solitions and Fractals* **7**(12), 1969–1988.

Day, R. and Zou, G.: 1994, Infrastructure, restricted factor substitution and economic growth, *Journal of Economic Behavior and Organization* **23**, 149–166.

Easterlin, R.: 1978, *The Economics and Sociology of Fertility: A Synthesis*, Historical Studies of Changing Fertility, tilly, c. edn, Princeton University Press, Princeton, chapter 2.

North, D.: 1981, *Structure and Change in Economic History*, W.W. Norton and Co., New York.

Why Economics Must Abandon its Theory of the Firm

D 21

S. Keen*

1 In with the new, out with the old?

The raison d'etre of this book is the belief that significant new currents are developing in and on the fringes of economics. A moot point is whether these new interdisciplinary currents from complex systems and econophysics will simply embellish what is known, or whether they may in time transform economics itself.

In part the answer to this question depends on the soundness of existing economics. In this chapter, I show that, at least in the area known as the theory of the firm, the new must completely abandon the old, because the latter is based on mathematical fallacies.

2 The neoclassical theory of markets & profit maximization

By the old theory, I mean the models of perfect competition and monopoly that are the staple of undergraduate and postgraduate education, and the basis of the belief that in competitive markets, price is equal to marginal cost.

---

* The author would like to thank John Legge, (La Trobe University), Geoff Fishburn (University of New South Wales), Russell Standish (University of New South Wales), Mike Honeychurch (University of Melbourne), Robert Vienneau (ITT Industries Advanced Engineering Division), Trond Andresen (Norwegian Institute of Technology), Joanna Goard (University of Wollongong), Michael Kelly (Illinois Institute of Technology), Karol Gellert (University of Western Sydney), Raja Junankar (University of Western Sydney), Greg Ransom (UCLA Riverside) and members of the HAYEK-L internet discussion list for useful insights and comments on earlier drafts.

A core proposition of this theory, that the demand curve facing the individual firm is horizontal, is mathematically false and has been known to be so since 1957.

The false but still widely believed proposition[1] is that, because it is so small, the individual competitive firm is a "price taker" that has no influence on the market price. Thus while the market demand curve $P(Q)$ is negatively sloped $\left(\frac{dP}{dQ} < 0\right)$, the demand curve facing the individual competitive firm producing output q_i (where $Q = \sum_{i=1}^{n} q_i$) is horizontal at the price set by the market $\left(\frac{dP}{dq} = 0\right)$.

Since a monopolist experiences the industry demand curve, the profit maximization output level for the monopolist is where marginal revenue, which is less than price, equals marginal cost:

$$MR_M = \frac{d}{dQ}(P \cdot Q) = P \cdot \frac{dQ}{dQ} + Q \cdot \frac{dP}{dQ} = P + Q \cdot \frac{dP}{dQ} < P \qquad (1)$$

A competitive firm also maximizes profit by equating its marginal revenue and marginal cost, but in its case, marginal revenue equals the market price:

$$MR_{PC} = \frac{d}{dq}(P \cdot q) = P \cdot \frac{dq}{dq} + q \cdot \frac{dP}{dq} = P + q \cdot \frac{dP}{dq} = P + q \cdot 0 = P \qquad (2)$$

In the aggregate, these identical profit maximization behaviors but different market conditions lead to monopolies charging a higher price and producing a lesser quantity (at which marginal revenue equals marginal cost) than competitive industries (who produce where price equals marginal cost). The propositions that $\left(\frac{dP}{dQ} < 0\right)$ while $\left(\frac{dP}{dq} = 0\right)$ thus play a pivotal role in neoclassical theory. However they are mathematically incompatible, as Stigler first showed in 1957 with this simple application of the chain rule:

$$\frac{dP}{dq_i} = \frac{dP}{dQ}\frac{dQ}{dq_i} = \frac{dP}{dQ} \qquad (3)$$

The implicit proposition that $\frac{dQ}{dq_i} = 1$ is simply a statement that firms are independently managed, so that a change in one firm's output does not instantaneously cause a change in any others (though of course competitive feedback in the market place may cause changes over time). The expansion in (4) details this proposition. Consider an industry with n firms and an aggregate output of Q units. Then:

---

[1] A minority of economists are aware that it is false, but adhere to a more sophisticated argument about convergence of marginal revenue to price as the number of firms increases. This argument is considered below.

$$\frac{dP}{dq_i} = \frac{dP}{dQ} \cdot \frac{dQ}{dq_i} \tag{4}$$

$$= \frac{dP}{dQ} \cdot \frac{d}{dq_i} \sum_{j=1}^{n} q_j$$

$$= \frac{dP}{dQ} \cdot \frac{d}{dq_i} (q_1 + q_2 + \dots + q_i + \dots + q_n)$$

$$= \frac{dP}{dQ} \cdot \left(\frac{d}{dq_i} q_1 + \frac{d}{dq_i} q_2 + \dots + \frac{d}{dq_i} q_i + \dots + \frac{d}{dq_i} q_n \right)$$

$$= \frac{dP}{dQ} \cdot (0 + 0 + \dots + 1 + \dots + 0)$$

$$= \frac{dP}{dQ}$$

I have personally experienced neoclassical economists reacting dismissively to this simple piece of mathematics, often with the argument that the proposition that $\frac{dP}{dq} = 0$ is "just an assumption" that competitive firms are "price takers",[2] and it is therefore not amenable to mathematical deconstruction. Such an argument is nonsense, since when this "assumption" is paired with the core belief that the market demand curve is negatively sloped $\left(\frac{dP}{dQ} < 0 \right)$, it leads to mathematical contradictions. Since competitive firms are independent, the amount that the ith firm expects the rest of the industry Q_R to vary its output in direct response to a change in its output q_i is zero: $\frac{d}{dq_i} Q_R = 0$.[3] The assumption that marginal revenue equals price for the ith firm means that $\frac{d}{dq_i} (P \cdot q_i) = P$. Now introduce $\frac{d}{dq_i} Q_R$ and $\frac{dP}{dq_i} = \frac{dP}{dQ} \cdot \frac{dQ}{dq_i}$ into $\frac{d}{dq_i} (P \cdot q_i) = P$ and expand:

---

[2] This term itself raises another unanswered question, that if all firms are "price takers", who "makes" the price? If the answer is "the market", the question remains how since every firm in this market is supposed to have no role in setting price.

[3] This doesn't mean that the amount other firms vary their output by is always zero, or that the other firms will not in time respond to the impact that the change in the ith firm's behavior has on the overall market; only that the amount of variation in direct and immediate response to a change in output by the ith firm is zero.

$$\frac{d}{dq_i}(P \cdot q_i) = P \cdot \frac{d}{dq_i}q_i + q_i \cdot \frac{d}{dq_i}P \tag{5}$$

$$= P + q_i \cdot \left(\frac{d}{dQ}P \cdot \frac{d}{dq_i}Q\right)$$

$$= P + q_i \cdot \left(\frac{d}{dQ}P \cdot \frac{d}{dq_i}(q_i + Q_R)\right)$$

$$= P + q_i \cdot \left(\frac{d}{dQ}P \cdot \left(\frac{d}{dq_i}q_i + \frac{d}{dq_i}Q_R\right)\right)$$

$$= P + q_i \cdot \left(\frac{d}{dQ}P \cdot \left(1 + \frac{d}{dq_i}Q_R\right)\right)$$

Thus the "assumption" that $\frac{d}{dq_i}(P \cdot q_i) = P$ is only compatible with $\frac{dP}{dQ} < 0$ if $\frac{d}{dq_i}Q_R = -1$, which contradicts the concept of firm independence. This is proof by contradiction that the slope of the demand curve for the ith firm must equal the slope of the market demand curve.

This argument will not perturb sophisticated neoclassical economists, since they believe that Stigler showed that while $\frac{dP}{dq_i} = \frac{dP}{dQ}$, perfect competition is a limiting case of actual competitive behavior as the number of firms in an industry rises. Assuming n identical firms each producing q units, Stigler introduced n and Q into the expression for the ith firm's marginal revenue:

$$\frac{d}{dq_i}(P \cdot q_i) = P + q\frac{dP}{dQ} \tag{6}$$

$$= P + \frac{Q}{n}\frac{P}{P}\frac{dP}{dQ}$$

$$= P + \frac{P}{n \cdot E}$$

Stigler correctly argued that "this last term goes to zero as the number of sellers increases indefinitely" (Stigler 1957: 8), so that marginal revenue for the ith firm converges to market price as the number of firms rises. Though true, this is irrelevant, since the price that the marginal revenues of *profit maximizing* firms converge to is not the "competitive, price equals marginal cost" market price, but the "monopoly, aggregate marginal revenue equals marginal cost" market price. Economists have not realized this because they believe that the aggregate profit maximization position (marginal revenue equals marginal cost) is consistent with all individual firms equating their marginal revenues and marginal costs. This belief is mathematically false.

3 Profit maximization formulae

Economists believe that firms maximize profits by producing the quantity at which their marginal revenue and marginal cost are equal:[4]

$$mr_i(q) - mc_i(q) = 0 \tag{7}$$

This false belief emanates from an aggregation fallacy. Marginal revenue is defined as the change in the firm's revenue given a change in its output; but in a multi-firm industry, changes in a firm's revenue can occur because of the independent actions of other firms. Defining tr_i as the total revenue function of the ith firm, we have:

$$tr_i = tr_i\left(\sum_{j\neq i}^{n} q_j, q_i\right) \tag{8}$$

Defining Q_R as the output of the rest of the industry $\left(Q_R = \sum_{j\neq i}^{n} q_j\right)$, a change in revenue for the ith firm is properly defined as:

$$dtr_i(Q_R, q_i) = \left(\frac{\partial}{\partial Q_R} P(Q) \cdot q_i\right) dQ_R + \left(\frac{\partial}{\partial q_i} P(Q) \cdot q_i\right) dq_i \tag{9}$$

The standard "profit maximization" formula for the individual firm ignores the effect of the first term on the firm's profit.[5] In what follows, I refer to $\frac{\partial}{\partial q_i} P(Q) \cdot q_i$ as *own-output marginal revenue*.

It is therefore obvious that if all firms set own-output marginal revenue equal to marginal cost, the individual and aggregate quantities produced will *not* be profit-maximizing. However we can use the aggregate impact of firms following the incorrect formula to both quantify how erroneous the formula is as a guide to true profit maximization, and then work out the correct formula. In the following derivation I use the simple rule for the aggregation of marginal costs that $mc_i(q_i) = MC(Q)$.[6]

---

[4] This implicitly contradicts game theory, where equating marginal cost and marginal revenue is acknowledged to not be profit-maximizing. But many economists do not seem to be aware of this contradiction.

[5] This is not changes in the output of the rest of the industry in direct response to a change in output by the ith firm, which is zero as discussed above $\left(\frac{d}{dq_i} Q_R = 0\right)$, but simply changes that all other firms are making to output $\left(\frac{d}{dq_i} Q_R = 0\right)$ as they independently search for a profit-maximizing level of output

[6] This aggregation rule is accurate regardless of the structure of the industry. However issues do arise when one wants to compare the welfare effects of different industry structures, as I discuss below.

$$\sum_{i=1}^{n}\left(\frac{d}{dq_i}\left(P\left(Q\right)\cdot q_i - TC_i\left(q_i\right)\right)\right) \tag{10}$$

$$= \sum_{i=1}^{n}\left(P\left(Q\right) + q_i\frac{d}{dq_i}P\left(Q\right)\right) - \sum_{i=1}^{n}\left(\frac{d}{dq_i}TC_i\left(q_i\right)\right)$$

$$= n\cdot P\left(Q\right) + \sum_{i=1}^{n}\left(q_i\cdot\frac{d}{dQ}P\left(Q\right)\right) - \sum_{i=1}^{n}mc\left(q\right)$$

$$= n\cdot P\left(Q\right) + \frac{d}{dQ}P\left(Q\right)\cdot\sum_{i=1}^{n}q_i - \sum_{i=1}^{n}MC\left(Q\right)$$

$$= n\cdot P\left(Q\right) + Q\cdot\frac{d}{dQ}P\left(Q\right) - n\cdot MC\left(Q\right)$$

$$= \left(n-1\right)\cdot P\left(Q\right) + \left(P\left(Q\right) + Q\cdot\frac{d}{dQ}P\right) - n\cdot MC\left(Q\right)$$

$$= \left(n-1\right)\cdot P\left(Q\right) + MR\left(Q\right) - n\cdot MC\left(Q\right)$$

$$= 0$$

Equation (10) can be rearranged to yield:

$$MR\left(Q\right) - MC\left(Q\right) = -\left(n-1\right)\cdot\left(P\left(Q\right) - MC\left(Q\right)\right) \tag{11}$$

Since $(n-1)$ exceeds 1 in all industry structures except monopoly, and price exceeds marginal cost,[7] the RHS of (11) is negative except in the case of a monopoly. Thus industry marginal cost *exceeds* marginal revenue in a multi-firm industry if each firm equates its own-output marginal revenue to marginal cost, so that part of industry output is produced at a loss. These losses at the aggregate model must be born by firms within the industry, so that firms that equate their own-output marginal revenue to marginal cost are producing part of their output at a loss. They therefore cannot be profit-maximizers.

Equation (10) can be used to derive the actual profit-maximizing quantity for the industry and the firm by putting $MR\left(Q\right) - MC\left(Q\right)$ on the RHS and taking $(n-1)\left(P\left(Q\right) - MC\left(Q\right)\right)$ inside the summation:

---

[7] As Stigler argued, if all firms are profit maximizers that equate their own-output marginal revenues and marginal costs, then the limit of (P(Q)-MC(Q)) is zero as the number of firms rises indefinitely, and this limit is approached from above so that (P(Q)-MC(Q)) is always non-negative.

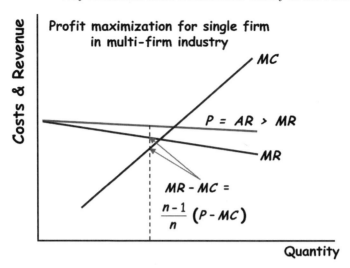

Fig. 1. The general profit-maximizing rule in a multi-firm industry

$$\sum_{i=1}^{n} \left\{ mr_i\left(q_i\right) - mc\left(q\right) - \frac{n-1}{n} \cdot \left(P\left(Q\right) - MC\right) \right\} = MR\left(Q\right) - MC \quad (12)$$

Setting the RHS of (12) to zero identifies the industry-level output Q_K and firm level output q_k that maximize profits, and reveals the true individual firm profit-maximizing strategy:

$$mr_i\left(q_k\right) - mc\left(q_k\right) = \frac{n-1}{n} \cdot \left(P\left(Q_K\right) - MC\left(Q_K\right)\right) \quad (13)$$

The two formulas (7) and (13) obviously correspond for a monopoly. However for a multi-firm industry, the correct formula (13) indicates that firms maximize profits, not by equating their own-output marginal revenue and marginal cost, but by producing where their own-output marginal revenue *exceeds* their marginal cost. The following graph illustrates the irony that, for an academic discipline that is obsessed with intersecting curves, the true profit-maximizing output level occurs where the curves do *not* intersect:

This correct profit-maximization formula has a number of consequences that contradict accepted economic belief and make the theory effectively meaningless.[8] In brief:

---

[8] There has been a recent trend in neoclassical economics to try to re-derive all the conventional results using game theory. My paper does not directly address

1. Given comparable cost functions, competitive markets produce the same quantity/price outcomes as monopolies;
2. What economists define as "welfare loss" is an inevitable outcome of profit-maximizing behavior, rather than due to monopoly behavior: profit-maximization is incompatible with welfare maximization; and
3. Given realistic non-comparable cost functions, monopolies will in general have lower marginal costs. Properly amended neoclassical theory therefore predicts that monopoly will result in *higher* output and lower prices than competition.

4 Perfect competition equals monopoly

Consider a linear demand curve $P(Q) = a - b \cdot Q$ and n firms facing the identical marginal cost function $mc(q) = c + d \cdot q$, where a, b, c, d & e are all positive constants.[9] Using $\frac{dP}{dq_i} = \frac{dP}{dQ}$, marginal revenue for the ith such firm is:

$$mr_i = P + q_i \cdot \frac{dP}{dQ} \qquad (14)$$
$$= a - b \cdot Q - b \cdot q_i$$

The false "profit maximizing" formula (7) predicts that the output for the single firm will be:

$$q = \frac{a - c}{(n+1) \cdot b + d} \qquad (15)$$

Aggregate output $Q = n \cdot \frac{a-c}{(n+1) \cdot b + d}$ converges to the perfect competition ideal $\frac{a-c}{b}$ as $n \to \infty$.

The correct profit maximizing formula (13) yields:

$$q = \frac{a - c}{2 \cdot n \cdot b + d} \qquad (16)$$

Aggregate output is therefore:

$$Q = n \cdot \frac{a - c}{2 \cdot n \cdot b + d} \qquad (17)$$

---

this recent fad; however my conclusions concerning cost curve aggregation are relevant to this literature, and I discuss the applicability of game theory to the concept of competitive markets briefly in my conclusion.

[9] I return to the issue of what cost functions can be if they are to be comparable for different scales of operation later.

If $n = 1$, this coincides with (7)'s prediction for a monopoly. But as $n \to \infty$, the limiting output is precisely half that predicted by (7) :

$$\lim_{n \to \infty} n \cdot \frac{a - c}{2 \cdot n \cdot b + d} = \frac{a - c}{2 \cdot b} \tag{18}$$

(13) results in a much larger profit for each individual firm in the industry than (7). Profit is total revenue minus total cost, where total cost is the integral of marginal cost. Using k for fixed costs, in general profit $\pi(q)$ is:

$$\pi(q) = P(Q) \cdot q - tc(q) \tag{19}$$

$$= (a - b \cdot n \cdot q) \cdot q - \left(k + c \cdot q + \frac{1}{2} \cdot d \cdot q^2 \right)$$

(7)'s quantity q_c yields a profit level for each firm of:

$$\pi(q_c) = \left(\frac{1}{2} \frac{(a - c)^2 \cdot (2 \cdot b + d)}{((n + 1) \cdot b + d)^2} \right) - k \tag{20}$$

(13) yields a profit level of:

$$\pi(q_k) = \left(\frac{1}{2} \frac{(a - c)^2}{2 \cdot b \cdot n + d} \right) - k \tag{21}$$

The two profit levels are equal for a monopoly (where $n = 1$) but for $n > 1$, (13)'s profit level necessarily exceeds (7)'s:

$$\pi(q_k) - \pi(q_c) = \frac{1}{2} \cdot b^2 \cdot \frac{(n - 1)^2 \cdot (a - c)^2}{(2 \cdot b \cdot n + d) \cdot ((n + 1) \cdot b + d)^2} \tag{22}$$

As noted above, all the parameters are positive. Equation (22) therefore necessarily exceeds zero for $n > 1$. The accepted "profit maximization" formula (7) therefore cannot be profit-maximizing.

A numerical example indicates just how substantially (7)'s level of output exceeds the profit-maximizing level for an individual firm. With the parameters $n = 100, a = 100, b = \frac{1}{1000000}, c = 20, d = \frac{1}{100000}, k = 10000$, (7) results in an output level of 720 thousand units and a profit of \$3.1 million per firm. The revised formula (13) results in an output level of 381 thousand units and a profit of \$15.2 million per firm. Figure 3 illustrates the difference in profits as a function of the number of firms.

Therefore profit-maximizing competitive firms will in the aggregate produce the same output as a monopoly, and sell it at the same price (given the same cost function, of which more later). The "welfare comparisons" of perfect competition and monopoly, which play such an important role in the

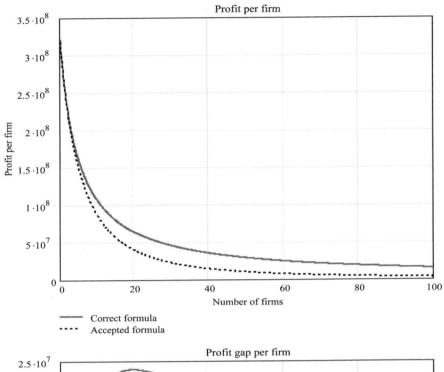

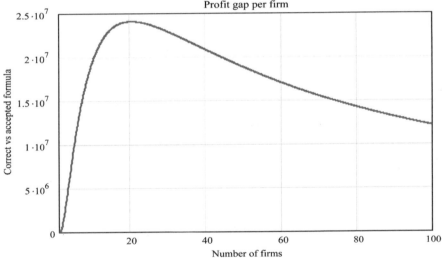

Fig. 2.

indoctrination of neoclassical economists,[10] and the peculiar radicalness of economists that leads them to criticize corporations for setting price above marginal cost, are thus mathematically false.

5 Profit maximization and welfare

This is why I previously described Stigler's relation $MR_i = P + \frac{P}{n \cdot E}$ as correct but irrelevant: while the ith firm's own-output marginal revenue will converge to the market price as the number of firms in the industry rises, the market price to which convergence occurs is the "monopoly" price. If we feed Stigler's Relation into the true profit maximization formula, we get:

$$P + \frac{P}{n \cdot E} - MC = \frac{n-1}{n} \cdot (P - MC) \qquad (23)$$
$$\left(1 + \frac{1}{E}\right) \cdot P = MC$$

The LHS of (22) is aggregate industry marginal revenue: $MR = \left(1 + \frac{1}{E}\right) \cdot P$. Price in a competitive industry with profit-maximizing firms therefore converges to the "monopoly" price, where aggregate marginal revenue equals aggregate marginal cost. The only way it could converge to the "competitive" price would be if firms were *not* profit-maximizers: profit-maximization and welfare-maximization (as defined by neoclassical economics) are thus incompatible.

6 Limitations on cost functions for output comparability

While the above analysis presumes that the same cost function can be used for (small) competitive firms as for (larger) monopolies, this presumption can only apply in three restrictive cases:

1. where the monopoly comes into being by taking over and operating all the firms of the competitive market;
2. where the monopoly and the competitive firms operate under conditions of constant identical marginal cost; or
3. where the monopoly and competitive firms have differing marginal costs that happen to result in equivalent aggregate marginal cost functions.

---

[10] Indoctrination may appear to be a strong word here, but since the standard tuition of economists involves the inculcation of a provably false proposition, I think indoctrination is a more suitable word than "education".

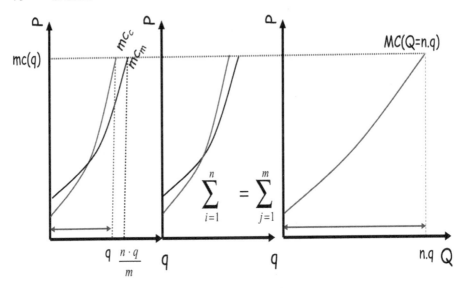

Fig. 3.

Consider an n-firm competitive industry and an m-plant monopoly. For the aggregate marginal cost curves to coincide, then the (horizontal) aggregation of the quantities produced at each level of marginal cost must sum to the same aggregate marginal cost function. This gives us the aggregation of output condition that $Q = n \cdot q_c = m \cdot q_m$, where q_c is the output of a competitive firm and q_m is the output of a monopoly plant at the same level of marginal cost. Consider two arbitrary marginal cost curves mc_c and mc_m. In general, the horizontal summation of arbitrary curves gives a diagram like Figure 5:

If $m = n$—if the monopoly simply takes over all the competitive firms—then the two curves mc_c and mc_m coincide, and any function will work. If however $m < n$ (the monopoly has less plants and operates on a larger scale than the competitive firms), then Figure 5 has to be amended in two ways: firstly, the curves can't intersect, since at the level of intersection q_x, $m \cdot q_x < n \cdot q_x$ whereas the aggregation condition is that $m \cdot q \equiv n \cdot q$. Secondly, and for the same reason, the y-intercept must be the same. This gives us Figure 6:

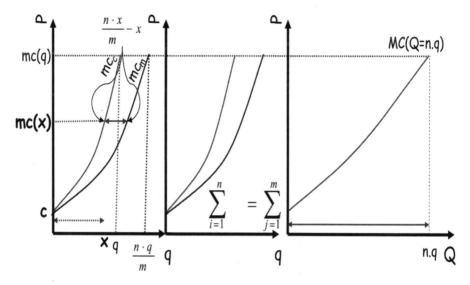

Fig. 4.

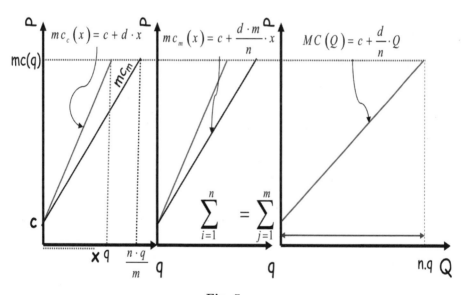

Fig. 5.

Again, the condition that $Q = m \cdot q \equiv n \cdot q$ shows that this figure must be amended. The maximal marginal cost level shown of $mc(q)$ results in each competitive firm producing q units of output and each monopoly plant producing $\frac{n}{m} \cdot q$ units (so that the aggregate output in both cases is $Q = n \cdot q$). The same condition applies at any intermediate level of marginal cost $mc(x)$, as shown in Figure 6: the monopoly's plants must produce $\frac{n}{m} \cdot x$ units of output at the same marginal cost that results from x units of output from each competitive firm so that in the aggregate $Q(x) = n \cdot x = m \cdot \frac{n}{m}x$. This is only possible if mc_c and mc_m are multiple functions, where the slope of mc_m is $\frac{m}{n}$ times the slope of mc_c.

With any more general nonlinear marginal cost function—even linear marginal cost functions where the slopes don't have this correspondence— the aggregate marginal cost curve for a competitive industry *must* differ from that for a monopoly. Therefore, *according to properly amended neoclassical theory*, whichever market structure has the lower marginal costs will produce the greater output. In general, monopolies—or rather the larger plants that tend to accompany more concentrated industry structures—will have lower marginal costs than competitive firms. Rosput (1993) gives the following illustration of how greater economies of scale can result in lower marginal costs, even with the same technology (in gas pipelines):

"Simply stated, the necessary first investment in infrastructure is the construction of the pipeline itself. Thereafter, additional units of throughput can be economically added through the use of horsepower to compress the gas up to a certain point where the losses associated with the compression make the installation of additional pipe more economical than the use of additional horsepower of compression. The loss of energy is, of course, a function of, among other things, the diameter of the pipe. Thus, at the outset, the selection of pipe diameter is a critical ingredient in determining the economics of future expansions of the installed pipe: *the larger the diameter, the more efficient are the future additions of capacity and hence the lower the marginal costs of future units of output.*" (Rosput 1993: 288; emphasis added)[11]

The general rule of Adam Smith's pin factory also comes into play: specialization lowers marginal costs. Walmart outcompetes the small corner shop in part because of the greater efficiency of its specialized employees and infrastructure.

---

[11] Economies of scale in research and technology will also favor larger-scale operations. While these are ruled out in the standard comparison with identical marginal cost curves, they cannot be ruled out in the general case of differing marginal cost curves.

7 The sum of the parts

When we collate all the above issues, the remaining theory is effectively devoid of content.

What is described as a profit-maximization rule does not maximize profits. This can be replaced with my correct formula, but when this is done the theory loses one of its major conclusions, the superiority of competition to monopoly. If cost functions are comparable, there is no difference in the behavior of competitive or monopolized industries—both will produce the same output at the same price, with the same deadweight loss of welfare. When the limitations on the strict comparability of cost functions are considered, it is obvious that in general monopolies will have lower marginal costs (and of course lower per unit fixed costs), so that monopolies will produce a greater quantity than (necessarily smaller scale) competitive firms, and sell it at a lower price. Far from supporting competitive behavior (which has been a hallmark of economic theory since its inception), properly amended neoclassical theory apparently supports monopolization.

With profit-maximizing firms producing off their marginal cost curves and aggregate output occurring where marginal revenue equals marginal cost, supply and demand analysis becomes impossible because a supply curve cannot be independently derived. General equilibrium analysis has normally presumed that profit-maximizing behavior and competitive markets ensure that price equals marginal cost in all markets. This presumption is invalid, so that much of "General Equilibrium" analysis is invalid. There is some limited "GE" work with non-competitive markets, but this is far less definitive than the falsely-grounded "competitive" analysis.

The conventional theory of the firm is thus an empty shell. Either economics must reverse long-held propositions concerning competition, or an alternative theory must be developed. The question is, what could replace the conventional theory? Many neoclassical economists would nominate game theory. Game theory is not dependent on the concept of profit maximization, and superficially it reaches the accepted conclusions about the superiority of competitive market structures over more concentrated ones. But there are substantial limits on its applicability.

8 Game theory to the rescue?

The "Prisoner's Dilemma" generates a reward table that favors the firm that produces the "Cournot" quantity (in my terms, that found by equating own-output marginal revenue to marginal cost) if the other firm follows the profit-maximizing formula $mr_i(q_k) - mc(q_k) = \frac{n-1}{n} \cdot (P(Q_K) - MC(Q_K))$. Using my algebraic example of two identical firms facing an identical rising linear marginal cost function, Figure (6) shows the quantities produced for the 4 feasible combinations where each firm applies either the conventional formula

80   S. Keen

or the correct formula, and Figure (??) shows the change in profit from the profit-maximizing level.

		Firm 2	Firm2
		MR = MC	MR - MC = 1 / 2 (P - MC)
Firm 1	MR =	$q1 \rightarrow -\dfrac{-a+c}{3b+d}$	$q1 \rightarrow -\dfrac{-2\,ab+2b\,c-a\,d+c\,d}{5b^2+5b\,d+d^2}$
	MC	$q2 \rightarrow -\dfrac{-a+c}{3b+d}$	$q2 \rightarrow -\dfrac{-ab+b\,c-a\,d+c\,d}{5b^2+5b\,d+d^2}$
Firm 1	MR - MC =	$q1 \rightarrow -\dfrac{-ab+b\,c-a\,d+c\,d}{5b^2+5b\,d+d^2}$	$q1 \rightarrow -\dfrac{-a+c}{4b+d}$
	1 / 2 (P - MC)	$q2 \rightarrow -\dfrac{-2\,ab+2b\,c-a\,d+c\,d}{5b^2+5b\,d+d^2}$	$q2 \rightarrow -\dfrac{-a+c}{4b+d}$

Fig. 6.

Clearly the firm that "defects" gains a greater profit, so that the "Nash equilibrium" is where both firms defect, resulting in the output level (and price) predicted by the conventional formula (which is of course not profit-maximizing).At first glance, this appears to restore the conventional outcome— though not as a profit-maximizing non-interactive result, but as one due to competitive behavior where each firm takes account of the behavior of all other firms. The output level that results is higher than the profit-maximizing level, while the price is lower, restoring the welfare lost by profit-maximizing behavior. However, there are many well-known problems with this argument, and one new one added by our research.

Commencing with the one aspect of the latter first, while this result appears to restore the neoclassical presumption in favor of competition over collusion, it does not restore the presumption against monopoly, because the analysis assumes identical marginal costs for the two competitive firms. While this is valid in the case of comparing two colluding to two competing firms, it is not valid when comparing two or more (competing or colluding) firms to one single firm. As indicated above, only in 3 restrictive cases will the cost functions of two or more firms coincide with that of a single firm (or other concentrated industry structure). In general, the marginal cost functions *will* differ, and the firm with the larger plants will have the lower costs. In this general case, algebra alone can't decide which results in the higher output and the lower prices for consumers. Instead, the cost functions of actual firms would have to be empirically researched to work out whether competition would results in a higher output than a more concentrated industry structure.

Secondly, it is well-known that while the one-off Prisoners' Dilemma has a "competitive" equilibrium outcome (price equals marginal cost), the repeated game converges to the "cooperative" outcome (marginal revenue equals marginal cost; Ellison 1994). It is rather hard to sustain a model of "perfect competition" in which firms only ever "do it" once.

Thirdly, the standard Prisoner's Dilemma outcome requires the players to have full knowledge, not only of their own situation, but also that of their opponent. This is quite acceptable in the situation where the game was first developed: two prisoners who did commit a crime both know that they did, and therefore know what each could do given the incentive of a lesser sentence for implicating the other. But it is unacceptable in the case of two supposedly independent firms: if they in fact know each other's cost functions, then are they independent or collusive? There is also the problem of "infinite regress": if you know what your opponent is likely to do, and he/she knows what you are likely to do, then it is best to do the opposite; but since you both know that, you'll do the opposite of the opposite; but because you both know that... (Strait 1994).

While neoclassical authors suggest solutions, the "real world" response to this dilemma is that in firms do not behave as game theorists expect, but simply follow "rules of thumb". This necessity for "rules of thumb" rather than optimizing behavior is reinforced by another obvious but generally unacknowledged problem with game theory, the "curse of dimensionality" (Rust 1997; Marks 2000). While a problem like the 2 person 2 state Prisoner's Dilemma has only 4 feasible outcomes, adding additional players (and time steps) can make the number of feasible outcome prohibitively large. Ten players results in 2^{10} or 1024 potential outcomes in a one-shot game and 2^{20} or over one million outcomes in a game with just a one period memory. The general formula is $Strategies^{Players \cdot (Memory+1)}$, where $Memory$ signifies the number of preceding rounds remembered by players.

Clearly it is impossible for real world firms to keep track of this many potential outcomes, and yet game theory was supposed to make economics more realistic by modelling interactive behavior. With so many possibilities available, then rather than exhaustively considering each one to find the Nash Equilibrium, as game theory implies, firms would instead behave like chess players faced with a similar bewildering range of possibilities and simply develop heuristic approaches rather than attempt to optimize.

An obvious heuristic (in this hypothetical world of a well behaved market demand curve and rising marginal cost) is to simply vary output in one direction, and continue in that direction if profit is increasing, but reverse direction if it should fall. Modelling by a colleague and me (Standish & Keen 2004) shows that this algorithm results in a market inhabited by rational profit maximizers converging to the profit-maximizing solution given by our formula.

This result, which appears contrary to standard game theory, occurs because while the end outcome of the "defect" strategy results in a higher profit for the defector, the interim steps from the profit-maximizing equilibrium result in a fall in profit for at least one of the firms in an environment where each firm is independently seeking its profit maximum.

Suppose that a particular combination of changes results in Firm 1's profit rising and Firm 2's falling—Firm 1 increases output by 1, Firm 2 reduces output by 1: signify this new location by (1,-1). Firm 1 will then continue to increase output in the next iteration; if Firm 2 did nothing, then the next iteration would be (2,-1) which involves a still higher profit for Firm 1 and still lower for Firm 2.

But Firm 2 will *not* do nothing: instead, it will go from decreasing production to increasing production (since its previous strategy reduced its profit). The next iteration will take the firms to (2,0) or (2,1), not (2,-1). At this point, both firms experience a fall in profit which will lead them to reduce output back to (0,0). These feedbacks will keep both firms within the orbit of the profit maximizing equilibrium.

Only if the feedback effects of one firm's change in behavior on the other is positive can a change in output in a particular direction be sustained. This does occur if both firms start at the position given by MC=MR: if both firms reduce their output, then both will increase their profit. The profit maximizing equilibrium is therefore locally stable, whereas the "Nash equilibrium" is locally unstable. The following figures show the outcome with the parameter values a=100, b=1/10000, c=.01, d=0.001 & k=100000. Figure (8) shows the output levels, and Figure (8) shows the change in profit with respect to the profit given by the profit-maximizing formula.

Outputs		Firm 2	Firm 2
		MR = MC	MR - MC = 1 / 2 (P - MC)
Firm 1	MR =	q1 → 76915.4	q1 → 77411.6
	MC	q2 → 76915.4	q2 → 70960.6
Firm 1	MR - MC =	q1 → 70960.6	q1 → 71421.4
	1 / 2 (P - MC)	q2 → 77411.6	q2 → 71421.4

Fig. 7.

The standard result applies that the "defect" strategy results in the highest profit level for the defector. However, when the local stability of the two strategies are compared, a very different picture emerges: if both firms start at the "Nash equilibrium" level, both will increase profit if both reduce their output. This process continues until both are producing at the levels given by our profit-maximizing formula. The "Nash equilibrium" is locally unstable (see Figure (8)).

On the other hand, if both firms start at the profit-maximizing level, then there is no pattern of output changes that will increase profit for both firms. As a result, their output levels orbit around the profit-maximizing level: this output combination is locally stable (See Figure (8)).

Profit Change		Firm 2	Firm 2
		MR = MC	MR - MC = 1/2 (P - MC)
Firm 1	MR =	-21128.487109044101	24820.365938755218
	MC	-21128.487109044101	-45925.108233982697
Firm 1	MR - MC =	-45925.108233982697	0.0
	1/2 (P - MC)	24820.365938755218	0.0

Fig. 8.

	-3	-2	-1	0	1	2	3
-3	23.0683 23.0683	15.3771 23.0716	7.68584 23.0737	-0.0054 23.0746	-7.69664 23.0743	-15.3879 23.0728	-23.0791 23.0701
-2	23.0716 15.3771	15.3803 15.3803	7.68894 15.3823	-0.0024 15.3831	-7.69374 15.3827	-15.3851 15.3811	-23.0764 15.3783
-1	23.0737 7.68584	15.3823 7.68894	7.69084 7.69084	-0.0006 7.69154	-7.69204 7.69104	-15.3835 7.68934	-23.0749 7.68644
0	23.0746 -0.0054	15.3831 -0.0024	7.69154 -0.0006	0. 0.	-7.69154 -0.000599999	-15.3831 -0.0024	-23.0746 -0.0054
1	23.0743 -7.69664	15.3827 -7.69374	7.69104 -7.69204	-0.000599999 -7.69154	-7.69224 -7.69224	-15.3839 -7.69414	-23.0755 -7.69724
2	23.0728 -15.3879	15.3811 -15.3851	7.68934 -15.3835	-0.0024 -15.3831	-7.69414 -15.3839	-15.3859 -15.3859	-23.0776 -15.3891
3	23.0701 -23.0791	15.3783 -23.0764	7.68644 -23.0749	-0.0054 -23.0746	-7.69724 -23.0755	-15.3891 -23.0776	-23.0809 -23.0809

Fig. 9.

The "cooperate-defect" output combination is also marginally unstable (see Figure (8)): if both firms reduce output by more than one unit, then they will both increase profit which will lead to a divergence away from this strategy towards the profit-maximizing strategy:

The standard game theory outcome of the single-shot Prisoner's Dilemma is therefore dependent upon both firms knowing with certainty the outcome of adopting the extreme strategies, and ignoring all intermediate steps. If, however, there is any uncertainty, and they simply have to alter output levels and see what happens to profit, then the topology of their interactions will lead them to the profit-maximizing equilibrium.

Game theory is therefore a particularly tenuous foundation on which to resurrect the neoclassical world view. Though it has some merits—whereas the conventional equilibrium theory of the firm has none—an attempt to use

	-3	-2	-1	0	1	2	3
-3	-0.0063 -0.0063	-7.14814 7.13914	-14.29 14.2834	-21.4318 21.4264	-28.5737 28.5683	-35.7155 35.7089	-42.8574 42.8484
-2	7.13914 -7.14814	-0.0028 -0.0028	-7.14474 7.14134	-14.2867 14.2843	-21.4286 21.426	-28.5706 28.5666	-35.7125 35.7059
-1	14.2834 -14.29	7.14134 -7.14474	-0.0007 -0.0007	-7.14274 7.14214	-14.2848 14.2838	-21.4268 21.4242	-28.5689 28.5635
0	21.4264 -21.4318	14.2843 -14.2867	7.14214 -7.14274	0. 0.	-7.14214 7.14154	-14.2843 14.2819	-21.4264 21.421
1	28.5683 -28.5737	21.426 -21.4286	14.2838 -14.2848	7.14154 -7.14214	-0.000700001 -0.000700001	-7.14294 7.13954	-14.2852 14.2786
2	35.7089 -35.7155	28.5666 -28.5706	21.4242 -21.4268	14.2819 -14.2843	7.13954 -7.14294	-0.0028 -0.0028	-7.14514 7.13614
3	42.8484 -42.8574	35.7059 -35.7125	28.5635 -28.5689	21.421 -21.4264	14.2786 -14.2852	7.13614 -7.14514	-0.0063 -0.0063

Fig. 10.

	-4	-3	-2	-1	0	1	2	3
-4	30.9534 -0.0112	23.2127 7.08946	15.4719 14.1889	7.73116 21.2872	-0.0096 28.3843	-7.75036 35.4801	-15.4911 42.5748	-23.2319 49.6683
-3	30.958 -7.10686	23.2172 -0.0063	15.4763 7.09306	7.73546 14.1912	-0.0054 21.2882	-7.74626 28.384	-15.4871 35.4785	-23.228 42.5719
-2	30.9614 -14.2025	23.2205 -7.10206	15.4795 -0.0028	7.73856 7.09526	-0.0024 14.1921	-7.74336 21.2878	-15.4843 28.3823	-23.2253 35.4755
-1	30.9636 -21.2982	23.2226 -14.1978	15.4815 -7.09866	7.74046 -0.0007	-0.0006 7.09606	-7.74166 14.1916	-15.4827 21.286	-23.2238 28.3792
0	30.9646 -28.3939	23.2235 -21.2936	15.4823 -14.1945	7.74116 -7.09666	0. 0.	-7.74116 7.09546	-15.4823 14.1897	-23.2235 21.2828
1	30.9644 -35.4895	23.2232 -28.3894	15.4819 -21.2904	7.74066 -14.1926	-0.000600001 -7.09606	-7.74186 -0.0007	-15.4831 7.09346	-23.2244 14.1864
2	30.963 -42.5852	23.2217 -35.4851	15.4803 -28.3863	7.73896 -21.2886	-0.0024 -14.1921	-7.74376 -7.09686	-15.4851 -0.0028	-23.2265 7.09006
3	30.9604 -49.6809	23.219 -42.5809	15.4775 -35.4821	7.73606 -28.3846	-0.0054 -21.2882	-7.74686 -14.193	-15.4883 -7.09906	-23.2298 -0.0063

Fig. 11.

it to preserve the conventional outcomes of "perfect competition" and "price equals marginal cost in competitive markets" does not give definitive results. We therefore need an alternative theory. What should it be?

9 An appeal for empiricism

The answer to that question is beyond the scope of this paper. What is within its scope is an appeal that any replacement theory be based upon empirical data on the actual behavior of firms. The existing literature on this topic (Eiteman 1947 et seq., Haines 1948, Means 1972, Blinder et al. 1998—see Lee 1998 and Downward & Lee 2001 for surveys) reveals that the vast majority of actual firms have production functions characterized by large average fixed costs and constant or falling marginal costs. This cost structure, which is described as "natural monopoly" in economic literature and portrayed as an exception to the rule of rising marginal cost, actually appears to be the empirical reality for 95 per cent or more of real firms and products. Once a breakeven sales level has been achieved, each new unit sold adds significantly to profit, and this continues out to the last unit sold—so that marginal revenue is always significantly above marginal cost (more so even than in the mathematical analysis above).

The prices that rule in real markets are not the market clearing prices of neoclassical theory, but what Means termed "administered prices", set largely by a markup on variable costs, with the size of the markup reflecting many factors (of which the degree of competition is one).[12] Firms compete not so much on price but on heterogeneity: Competitors' products differ qualitatively, and the main form of competition between firms is not price but product differentiation (by both marketing and R&D). Schumpeter is more relevant to this reality of competition than Samuelson; Sraffa's (1926) analysis of costs makes more sense than diminishing marginal productivity; and Kalecki's (1937) analysis of the financial constraints to expansion better characterizes the limits to production than the chimera of rising marginal cost. This implies that a dynamic/evolutionary/nonequilibrium approach to modelling and characterizing competitive behavior is more appropriate than the structural, "taxonomic" approach that has dominated economics to date.

Such an approach to modelling is well outside the comfort zone of economists who have been schooled in the neoclassical tradition. But it is well within the

---

[12] These include the need to cover fixed costs at a levels of output well within production capacity, the desire to finance investment and/or repay debt with retained earnings, the impact of the trade cycle, and the degree of competition (so that empirical research gives some grounds by which a more competitive industry can be preferred to a less competitive one)

tradition of those interlopers into economics from complex systems analysis and econophysics. I urge these newcomers to rise to the challenge of providing a theory of firms and markets to replace the non-theory that economists currently accept.

References

Arrow, K.: 1959, Towards a theory of price adjustments, *in* e. a. M. Abramovitz (ed.), *The Allocation of Economic Resources*, Stanford University Press.

Aslambeigui, N. and Naples, M.: 1997, Scissors or horizon: Neoclassical debates about returns to scale, costs, and long run supply, 1926-1942, *Southern Economic Journal* **64**, 517–530.

Aumann, R.: 1964, Markets with a continuum of traders, *Econometrica* **32**, 39–50.

Aumann, R.: 1966, Existence of competitive equilibria in markets with a continuum of traders, *Econometrica* **34**, 1–17.

Bishop, R.: 1948, Cost discontinuities, declining costs and marginal analysis, *American Economic Review* **38**, 1–17.

Blinder, A., Canetti, E., Lebow, D. and Rudd, J.: 1998, *Asking About Prices: a New Approach to Understanding Price Stickiness*, Russell Sage Foundation.

Boland, L.: 1981, On the futility of criticizing the neoclassical maximization hypothesis, *American Economic Review* **71**, 1031–1036.

Conkling, R.: 1999, Marginal cost pricing for utilities: a digest of the california experience, *Contemporary Economic Policy* **17**, 20–32.

Cournot, A.: 1988, Of the competition of producers, *in* A. Daughety (ed.), *Cournot Oligopoly*, Cambridge University Press.

Downward, P. and Lee, F.: 2001, Post keynesian pricing theory reconfirmed? a critical review of asking about prices, *Journal of Post Keynesian Economics* pp. 465–483.

Eichner, A.: 1976, *The Megacorp and Oligopoly: Micro Foundations of Macro Dynamics*, Cambridge University Press.

Eiteman, W.: 1947, Factors determining the location of the least cost point, *American Economic Review* **37**, 910–918.

Eiteman, W.: 1948, The least cost point, capacity and marginal analysis: a rejoinder, *American Economic Review* **38**, 899–904.

Ellison, G.: 1994, Cooperation in the prisoner's dilemma with anonymous random matching, *Review of Economic Studies* **61**, 567–588.

Friedman, J.: 1983, *Oligopoly Theory*, Cambridge University Press.

Friedman, M.: 1953, The methodology of positive economics, *Essays in Positive Economics*, University ofChicago Press.

Groenewegen, P.: 1995, *A Soaring Eagle: Alfred Marshall 1842-1924*, Edward Elgar.

Haines, W.: 1948, Capacity production and the least cost point, *American Economic Review* **38**, 617–624.

Harrod, R.: 1934, Doctrines of imperfect competition, *The Quarterly Journal of Economics* **48**, 442–470.

Keen, S.: 2001, *Debunking Economics*, Sydney & London: Pluto Press & Zed Books.

Keen, S.: 2003, Standing on the toes of pygmies: Why econophysics must be careful of the economic foundations on which it builds, *Physica A* **324**, 108–116.

Kuenne, R.: 1998, *Price and Nonprice Rivalry in Oligopoly*, Macmillan.

Langlois, C.: 1989, Markup pricing versus marginalism: a controversy revisited, *Journal of Post Keynesian Economics* **12**, 127–151.

Lee, F.: 1996, Pricing and the business enterprise, *in* C. Whalen (ed.), *Political Economy for the 21st century*, ME Sharpe.

Lee, F.: 1998, *Post Keynesian Price Theory*, Cambridge University Press.

Makowski, L.: 1987, Are 'rational conjectures' rational?, *The Journal of Industrial Economics* **36**, 35–47.

Marks, R.: 2000, Evolved perception and the validation of simulation models, *in* C. C. K. S. M. R. S. H. Barnett, W. (ed.), *Commerce, Complexity and Evolution*, Cambridge University Press.

Marshall, A.: 1907, *Principles of Economics*, Macmillan.

Marshall, A.: 1925, Correspondence with professor a. l. bowley, *Memorials of Alfred Marshall*, Macmillan Publishing Company.

Martin, S.: 2001, *Advanced Industrial Economics*, Blackwell.

Mas-Colell, A.: 1983, Walrasian equilibria as limits of noncooperative equilibria. part i: Mixed strategies, *Journal of Economic Theory* **30**, 153–170.

Means, G.: 1972, The administered-price thesis reconsidered, *American Economic Review* **62**, 292–306.

Moss, S.: 1984, The history of the theory of the firm from marshall to robinson to chamberlin: the source of positivism in economics, *Economica* **51**, 307–318.

Nichol, A.: 1934, A re-appraisal of cournot's theory of duopoly price, *The Journal of Political Economy* **42**, 80–105.

Novshek, W.: 1980, Cournot equilibrium with free entry, *Review of Economic Studies* **47**, 473–486.

Novshek, W.: 1985, Perfectly competitive markets as the limits of cournot markets, *Journal of Economic Theory* **35**, 72–82.

Novshek, W. and Sonnenschein, H.: 1983, Walrasian equilibria as limits of noncooperative equilibria. part ii: Pure strategies, *Journal of Economic Theory* **30**, 171–187.

Pigou, A.: 1922, Empty economic boxes - a reply, *Economic Journal* **36**, 459–465.

Pigou, A.: 1927, The law of diminishing and increasing cost, *Economic Journal* **41**, 188–197.

Pigou, A.: 1928, An analysis of supply, *Economic Journal* **42**, 238–257.

Robbins, L.: 1928, The representative firm, *Economic Journal* **42**, 387–404.

Robertson, D.: 1924, Those empty boxes, *Economic Journal* **34**, 16–31.

Robertson, D.: 1930, The trees of the forest, *Economic Journal* **44**, 80–89.

Rosput, P.: 1993, *The Limits to Deregulation of Entry and Expansion of the US Gas Pipeline Industry*, Utilities Policy.

Rotwein, E.: 1959, On 'the methodology of positive economics', *The Quarterly Journal of Economics* **73**, 554–575.

Rust, J.: 1997, Using randomization to break the curse of dimensionality, *Econometrica* **65**, 487–516.

Sato, K.: 1979, A note on capital and output aggregation in a general equilibrium model of production, *Econometrica* **47**, 1559–1568.

Schmalensee, R.: 1988, Industrial economics: an overview, *Economic Journal* **98**, 643–681.

Schumpeter, J.: 1936, *The Theory of Economic Development*, Harvard University Press.

Shepherd, W.: 1984, 'contestability' vs. competition, *American Economic Review* **74**, 572–587.

Shove, G.: 1930, The representative firm and increasing returns, *Economic Journal* **44**, 93–116.

Simon, J., Puig, C. and Aschoff, J.: 1973, A duopoly simulation and richer theory: an end to cournot, *Review of Economic Studies* **40**, 353–366.

Sraffa, P.: 1926, The law of returns under competitive conditions, *Economic Journal* **40**, 538–550.

Sraffa, P.: 1930, The trees of the forest—a criticism, *Economic Journal* **44**, 89–92.

Standish, R. and Keen, S.: 2004, Emergent effective collusion in an economy of perfectly rational competitors, *Complexity International (submitted)* .

Stigler, G.: 1957, Perfect competition, historically considered, *Journal of Political Economy* **65**, 1–17.

Strait, R.: 1994, Decision analysis approach to competitive situations with a pure infinite regress, *Decision Sciences* **25**, 853–862.

Part II

Tools and Techniques

Use of Recurrence Quantification Analysis in Economic Time Series

J.P. Zbilut

C22

G10

1 Introduction

Considerable efforts have been expended to determine if economic time series can be modeled as nonlinear chaotic dynamics. A motivation has been the recognition that often, economic observables appear chaotic, although they are clearly generated by some form of determinism (Creedy and Martin 1994, Gandolfo 1996, Ormerod 1998). Unfortunately, these attempts have not been distinguished by unequivocal results. This follows the results of other sciences such as biology (Webber and Zbilut 1994). Whereas the physical sciences can generate reasonably long stationary data, economic sciences perforce depend upon imperfectly collected sources. Additionally, greater amounts of noise often attend such data. Some of the difficulties have been attributed to the algorithms used to quantify chaotic invariants, such as dimensions, entropies, and Liapunov exponents. Other, more traditional methods, such as FFTs have also exhibited well-known difficulties. As a result, much energy has been devoted to analyzing various methods of calculation and conditioning to real life data (Schreiber 1998).

In the case of economic data, a fundamental problem has not been addressed; namely, the correspondence of economic data to the fundamental assumptions of chaos and other fully determined models. Specifically, it is noted that chaotic dynamics are continuous, deterministic systems. Although the time series of such systems are random looking, processes which generate them are not: their behavior is, by definition, rigid (Zbilut et al. 1996). Economic systems, on the other had are subject to the vagaries of human agency. Although these facts are obvious, the consequences are seldom appreciated. To suggest that economic data is chaotic, would assume that such systems are ultimately very unstable. This comes as a result from the recognition that the way to change a chaotic system is to change its control variable or by creating specific perturbations, but, as is known, very small changes can produce significantly different behavior. As a result much energy has been devoted to analyzing various methods of calculation. Furthermore, the character of economic data places significant demands upon data analysis tools given that many such series cannot provide long data sets, and are not stationary. As an alternative to traditional model-based analysis, a very simple and straightforward method of analysis is proposed; namely recurrence quantification (RQA).

2 Recurrence Quantification Analysis

The notion of a recurrence is simple: for any ordered series (time or spatial), a recurrence is simply a point which repeats itself. In this respect, the statistical literature points out that recurrences are the most basic of relations (Feller 1968) and it is important to reiterate the fact that calculation of recurrences, unlike other methods such as Fourier, Wigner-Ville or wavelets, requires no transformation of the data, and can be used for both linear and nonlinear systems (Zbilut and Webber 1992, Zbilut et al. 1992). Because recurrences are simply tallies, they make no mathematical assumptions. Given a reference point, X_0, and a ball of radius r, a point is said to recur if

$$B_r(X_0) = \{X : ||X - X_0|| \leq r\}. \tag{1}$$

A trajectory of size N falling within $B_r(X_0)$ is denoted as

$$S_1 = \{X_{t,1}, X_{t,2}, ..., X_{t,i},\} \tag{2}$$

with the recurrence times defined as

$$T_1(i) = t_{i+1} - t_i; \ i = 1, 2, ..., N \tag{3}$$

3 Recurrence Plots

Given a scalar time series $\{x(i) = 1, 2, 3, ...\}$ an embedding procedure will form a vector, $X_i = (x(i), x(i + L), ..., x(i + (m - 1)L))$ with m the embedding dimension and L the lag. $\{X_i = 1, 2, 3, ..., N\}$ then represents the multi dimensional process of the time series as a trajectory in m-dimensional space. Recurrence plots are symmetrical $N \times N$ arrays in which a point is placed at (i, j) whenever a point X_i on the trajectory is close to another point X_j. The closeness between X_i and X_j is expressed by calculating the Euclidian distance between these two normed vectors, i.e., by subtracting one from the other: $||X_i - X_j|| \leq r$, where r is a fixed radius. If the distance falls within this radius, the two vectors are considered to be recurrent, and graphically this can be indicated by a dot.

An important feature of such matrixes is the existence of short line segments parallel to the main diagonal, which correspond to sequences $(i, j), (i + 1, j + 1), , (i + k, j + k)$ such that the piece of $X_j, X_{i+1}, ..., X_{i+k}$ is close to

$X_i, X_{i+1}, ..., X_{i+k}$ in series which are deterministic. The absence of such patterns suggests randomness (Eckmann, et al., 1987).

Thus recurrence plots simply correspond to the distance matrix between the different epochs (rows of the embedding matrix) filtered, by the action of the radius, to a binary 0/1 matrix having a 1 (dot) for distances falling below the radius and a 0 for distances greater than radius. Distance matrices are demonstrated to convey all the relevant information necessary for the global reconstruction of a given system, and thus represent an exhaustive representation of the studied phenomenon (Rao and Suryawanshi 1996) (see Fig. 1).

4 Recurrence Quantification

Because graphical representation may be difficult to evaluate, RQA was developed to provide quantification of important aspects revealed by the plot. Recurrent points which form diagonal line segments are considered to be deterministic (as distinguished from random points which form no patterns). Unfortunately, beyond general impressions of drift and determinism, the plots of themselves provide no quantification. As a result, Zbilut et al. (1992), and (Zbilut and Webber 1992) developed several strategies to quantify features of such plots originally pointed out by Eckmann, et al. (1987). Hence, the quantification of recurrences leads to the generation of five variables including: %REC (percent of plot filled with recurrent points), %DET (percent of recurrent points forming diagonal lines, with a minimum of two adjacent points), ENT (Shannon information entropy of the line length distribution), MAXLINE, length of longest line segment (the reciprocal of which is an approximation of the largest positive Liapunov exponent and is a measure of system divergence, (Trulla et al. 1996); and TREND (measure of the paling of recurrent points away from the central diagonal). These five recurrence variables quantify the deterministic structure and complexity of the plot. The application of these simple statistical indexes to the recurrence plots gives rise to a five dimensional representation of the studied series.

A) Time Series

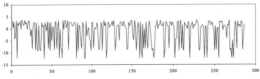

B) Vector   Embedding Matrix (EM)

3.4		0.6	3.1	-4.1	-3
0.6	0.6	3.1	-4.1	-3	3.7
3.1	3.1	-4.1	-3	3.7	-12.3
-4.1	-4.1	-3	3.7	-12.3	2.6
-3	-3	3.7	-12.3	2.6	1.6
3.7	3.7	-12.3	2.6	1.6	2.8
-12.3	-12.3	2.6	1.6	2.8	3.1
2.6					
1.6					
2.8					
3.1					
....					

The embedding procedure consists of building an *n* columns matrix (in this case *n* = 5) out of the original vector, by shifting the series by a fixed lag. (= 1, due to the discrete character of financial sequences). The rows of the embedding matrix (EM) correspond to subsequent windows of length (here = 5) (embedding dimension) along the sequence. The choice of the embedding dimension is a result of the need for having a space large enough to contain the changing dynamic. N.B. *n* points, in fact, are eliminated from the analysis as a consequence of shifting.

C) Distance Matrix (Euclidean norm between rows of the EM)

D) Recurrence Plots (RP) and their quantitative descriptors.

A **Recurrence Plot** results from a Distance Matrix by darkening the pixels located at specific (i,j) coordinates, corresponding to distance values between ith and jth rows lower than a predefined threshold (= radius).

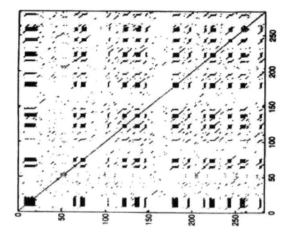

% Recurrence: this measure quantifies the fraction of the plot filled by recurrent points. It corresponds to the fraction of recurrent pairs over all the possible pairs of epochs or, equivalently, to the fraction of pairwise distances below the chosen radius.
% Determinism: percentage of sequential recurrent points forming diagonal line structures in the distance matrix. It corresponds to the amount of patches of similar characteristics along the sequence.
MAXLINE: length (in terms of consecutive points) of the longest recurrent line in the plot. (Inversely related to largest Liapunov exponent.)
ENTROPY: is defined in terms of the Shannon-Weaver formula for information entropy computed over the distribution of length of the lines of recurrent points and measures the richness of deterministic structuring of the series.
TREND :   indicates the degree of stationary of the relative frequency of recurrent points. (A rough derivative.)

Fig. 1. Techniques of RQA

This five dimensional representation gives a summary of the autocorrelation structure of the series and was also demonstrated, by means of a psychometric approach (Giuliani et al. 2000) to correlate with the visual impression a set of unbiased observers derive from the inspection of a set of recurrence plots.

When one needs to appreciate eventual changes in the autocorrelation structure at the level of single element of the series, it is not possible to rely solely on the "holistic" summaries given by the direct application of RQA to the global sequence, in these case use is made of a "windowed" version of RQA can be performed, such that for a time series $(s_1, s_2, ..., s_n)$, where $(s_j = j\tau_s)$ and $\tau_s =$ sampling time. For an N point long series

$$E_1 = (s_1, s_2, ..., s_n)$$
$$E_2 = (s_{1+w}, s_{2+w}, ..., s_{n+w})$$
$$E_3 = (s_{1+2w}, s_{2+2w}, ..., s_{n+2w})$$
$$...$$
$$...$$
$$...$$
$$E_p = (s_{1(p-1)w}, s_{2+(p-1)w}, ..., s_{n+(p-1)w})$$

(4)

with $w =$ the offset, and the number of epochs (windows), E_p, satisfies the relation, $N + (p-1) \leq n$.

The data obtained can also be used to obtain estimations of local Liapunov exponents, information entropy, or simply plotted as $N_{recurrences}$ vs. period (in the case of a time series); i.e., a histogram of recurrence times. In the case of histograms, strictly periodic points demonstrate instrumentally sharp peaks; whereas chaotic or nonlinear systems reveal more or less wider peaks depending upon the radius chosen and noise effects. The histogram of the distribution of recurrence times gives a sort of "nonlinear" analogue of a Fourier power spectrum and can be profitably used to derive scaling profiles of the studied systems. RQA can also be combined with other statistical techniques, including a "cross recurrence" version (Zbilut et al. 1998a,b, Gao 1999, Zbilut et al. 2000).

5 Determining Parameters for Nonstationary Series

As has been emphasized, RQA is useful for understanding nonstationary time series. Yet, since a given system may be changing state; i.e., the relevant degrees of freedom may change, the choice of m, L and r can become confounding. Unfortunately, most algorithms for such choices are based upon computer simulations of well-known, stationary examples. Typically, however, human systems are rarely stationary, and often exhibit rather sudden changes of state. Nonetheless, some guidelines can be established, based upon available research, and a careful consideration of the import of nonstationarity.

6 Choice of Embedding

In the context of nonstationarity, the notion of a "correct" embedding or delay is inappropriate as has been pointed out by Grassberger et al. (1991).

Instead it becomes important to remember that a sufficiently large embedding be chosen which will "contain" the relevant dynamics (as it may change from one dimensionality to another) as well as account for the effects of noise, which tend to inflate dimension. There are no clear guidelines relative to this question, except from what can be inferred from studies of noise. In this respect Ding et al. (1993) have indicated that noise will tend to require higher dimensions, even in the case of stationary dynamics.

Gao and Cai (2000) have studied this question in the context of a noisy Lorenz attractor, and concluded that an embedding of 6 is required to provide reasonable clarification of the dynamics. Because of the high complexity of human systems, we have empirically embedded in 10. Care, however, must be made to make sure that the system is not excessively noisy, since embedding will amplify such noise to the detriment of the real dynamics.

7 Choice of Lag

Choice of lag is governed by similar considerations. As a system changes from one dimension to another the effects of the lag are perforce changed. Thus, a so-called "optimal" lag in one embedding, becomes less so as the relevant dimension changes (Grassberger et al. 1991). Although there have been numerous proposals for choice of lag, chief among them the first local minimum of the autocorrelation or mutual information, they all are presented with the assumption of stationarity (Fraser and Swinney 1986, Holzfuss and Mayer-Kress 1986). What would appear to be more important is an understanding of how the data is acquired, as well as the system studied. Given that much financial data is discrete, a lag of one is usually sufficient.

8 Choice of Radius

The object of RQA is to view the recurrences in a locally defined (linear) region of phase space. Practically speaking, however, because of intrinsic and extrinsic noise, too small a value of r results in quantification of the noise only; whereas too large a value captures values which can no longer be considered recurrent. To get to the dynamics proper, a strategy is to calculate %REC for several increasing values of r and to plot the results on a log-log plot to determine a "scaling" region; i.e., where the dynamics are found. Figure 2 demonstrates such a strategy. If the data are extremely nonstationary, a scaling region may not be found. The guide then is the percent recurrence. A critical factor is that there be sufficient numbers of recurrences so as to make sense for computation of the other variables. A value of 1% recurrence tends to fulfill this criterion. Further verification can be obtained from an inspection of the recurrence plot: too sparse a matrix suggests a modest increase. Windowed RQA is especially informative. If a given window fails to achieve 1% recurrence, the radius should be increased, or the window enlarged.

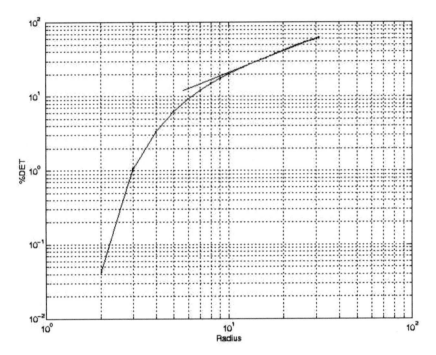

Fig. 2. Demonstration of finding an appropriate radius. %DET is calculated for several values of radius and plotted on a log-log plot. Where the line becomes scaling (here at approximately 10) is a good choice.

9 Example of Stock Market

RQA of a data series can begin in a number of ways, but one useful approach is to view the global recurrence plot. Frequently, this can identify some basic dynamics relative to multiplicative (intercorrelated vs. independent) processes. We have taken the stock index of the New York S&P 500 from January 6, 1986 until December 31, 1997, and performed such an analysis (Fransen and van Dijk 2000).

If one looks at the recurrence plot, two things are apparent (Fig. 3): 1) the data are not stationary, given the paling of the recurrences; and 2) within the nonstationary processes, there are several embedded stationary processes characterized by square structures, while the over-all funnel shape is typical of a transient. What is more interesting is the numerous box-like structures typical of local autocorrelated data. Furthermore many of these structures have additional "boxes" within them. These typically terminate abruptly, only to have another begin (Fig. 3, arrow). Thus one can conclude that multiplicative (intercorrelated) processes are present. If we take a histogram of recurrences (in lagged order), this impression is correct (Fig. 4). A scaling region can easily be identified. Scaling suggests a multiplicative process, while the hori-

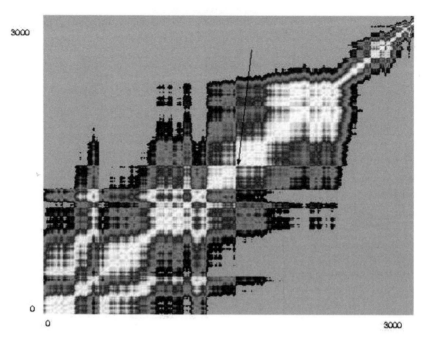

Fig. 3. Recurrence plot of stock market index (see text for details).

zontal regions suggest independent "noise-like" processes. The scaling region, however, is bounded by two non-scaling regions: the first is relatively horizontal, and the second has several peaks. Being quite fast, and of relatively equal probability, this first non-scaling region suggests noise of some type. The second region has several peaks. The end of the scaling region ends at 95 days and may suggest some quarterly process since the peak immediately to the right is about 125 days. Similarly, the next cluster is centered around 350 days and may be part of yearly cycles. However an area immediately adjacent near 500 is not clear as to its source. To obtain more information, a windowed RQA was done (Fig. 5). Using a 90 day window, it becomes clear that there is considerable variation in the series, but the RQA variables provide some hint as to their significance. Although there is considerable change in relative magnitude of the index, the %DET and the Liapunov approximation provide the degree of importance (see Fig. 5).

Several regions are numbered in the time series of the Index. A noticeable precipitous fall (1) is presaged by a minor decrease in DET (2a) and an increase in the Liapunov exponent. What is more noticeable is the area (2). Although the time series appears rather unremarkable except for its gradual trend upward, the DET (2a) and Liapunov (2b) are considerably unstable, which is immediately followed by a series increasing in its slope upward (3). (Instabil-

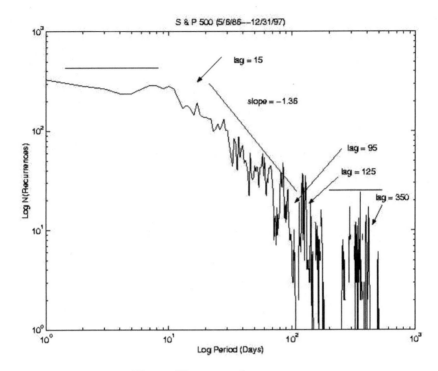

Fig. 4. Histogram of recurrences.

ity was determined by calculating a 30-day sliding window of 95% confidence limits. Variables falling outside the limits were considered unstable.) Note, however, that the DET (3a) and Liapunov (3b) are relatively stable, while the TREND clearly tracks variability. Thus, although this region is changing-it is a "stable" change, given that the DET and Liapunov remain relatively constant, suggesting an underlying stationary process. It appears obvious that a typical stock exchange index is quite complex, and although it may have features typical of stochastic processes, it also has areas of relatively significant determinism. To try and make sense of the process, we suggest that financial markets are characterized by singularities of the discrete data.

10 Lipschitz Conditions ("Terminal Dynamics")

A fundamental problem in the application of nonlinear dynamics to human systems is that fact that they are still classical: they require Lipschitz conditions to guarantee the uniqueness of solutions subject to prescribed initial conditions (Zak et al. 1997). For a dynamical system all the derivatives are bounded. This condition allows for the description of classical Newtonian dynamics within the traditional theory of differential equations, such that

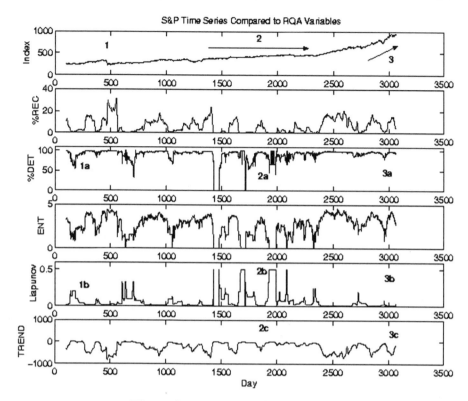

Fig. 5. Sliding window RQA analysis.

reversibility and predictability are guaranteed (recall that chaotic dynamics can be predicted if it were possible to know the initial conditions with infinite precision and devoid of noise) (Zbilut et al. 1996). This results in an infinite time of approaching an attractor. Clearly, however, such observations are not typical in real systems. One way to overcome these problems is to violate the requirement of Lipschitz conditions (Zak et al. 1997). By doing so, at "singularities" of the phase space, the dynamics forgets its past as soon as it approaches these singularities. Additionally, the architecture of such systems is able to be activated not only by external inputs and infinitesimal noise of any kind, but also by internal perturbations (Fig. 6). Such critical points can be placed in a network with others, which are weakly coupled. Consider, for example, a simple equation without uniqueness:

$$dx/dt = x^{1/3} \cos \omega t. \qquad (5)$$

At the singular solution, $x = 0$ (which is unstable, for instance at $t = 0$), a small noise drives the motion to the regular solutions, $x = (2/3\omega \sin \omega t)^{3/2}$ with equal probabilities. Indeed, any prescribed distribution can be implemented by using non-Lipschitz dynamics. It is important to emphasize, how-

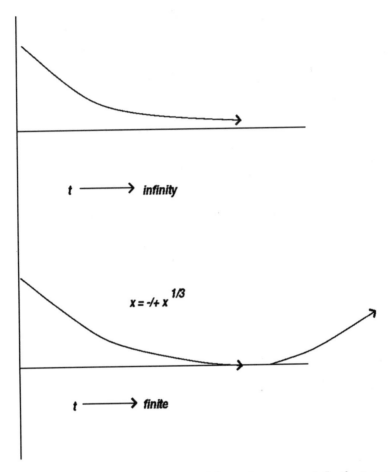

Fig. 6. Traditional dynamics and terminal dynamics compared. In the top panel, the dynamics never do reach the singular point, whereas, in terminal dynamics, the point is reached in a finite time and is able to be perturbed to continue on again.

ever, the fundamental difference between the probabilistic properties of these non-Lipschitz dynamics (N.B., we term these dynamics also "terminal dynamics", and "nondeterministic" dynamics) and those of traditional stochastic or differential equations: the randomness of stochastic differential equations is caused by random initial conditions, random force or random coefficients; in chaotic equations small (but finite) random changes of initial conditions are amplified by a mechanism of instability. But in both cases the differential operator itself remains deterministic. Thus, there develop a set of "alternating," "deterministic" trajectories at stochastic singular points. This is the import of the "square" regions of the recurrence plot": they are the "trajectories" which alternate with singular points on the identity line.

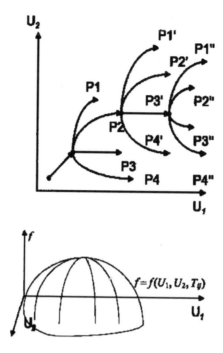

Fig. 7. Connected terminal dynamics can demonstrate multi-choice probability distributions sensitive to type and kind of perturbation (noise) at each singular point (top). Thus one can speak of a "stochastic attractor" (bottom).

One additional note: although there are many models which add stochastic terms, these terms are added to the entire dynamic. The model here proposed would suggest that the stochastic aspects appear only at the singular points, and thus do not distort the general dynamic of the trajectory. The difficulty, of course, is to determine the proper form of the deterministic "trajectories" and their related probability distribution functions. At each singular point, a variety of connecting possibilities are admitted-each with their own likelihood of being realized. Furthermore, the strength and type of excitation conditions these possibilities (Fig.7). Thus, the final problem is cast in the form of a combinatorial problem, resulting in a "stochastic attractor".

References

Creedy, J. and Martin, V.: 1994, *Chaos and Non-Linear Models in Economics*, Edward Elgar Publishing Limited.

Ding, M., Grebogi, C., Ott, E., Sauer, T. and Yorke, J.: 1993, Estimating correlation dimension from a chaotic time series: When does plateau onset occur?, *Physica D* **69**, 404–424.

Feller, W.: 1968, *An Introduction to Probability Theory and its Applications. Vol. 1*, Wiley.

Fransen, P. and van Dijk, D.: 2000, *Nonlinear Time Series Models in Empirical Finance*, Cambridge University Press.

Fraser, A. and Swinney, H.: 1986, Independent coordinates for strange attractors from mutual information, *Physical Review A* **33**, 1134–1140.

Gandolfo, G.: 1996, *Economic Dynamics*, Springer-Verlag.

Gao, J.: 1999, Recurrence time statistics for chaotic systems and their applications, *Physical Review Letters* **83**, 3178–3181.

Gao, J. and Cai, H.: 2000, On the structures and quantification of recurrence plots, *Physics Letters A* **270**, 75–87.

Giuliani, A., Sirabella, P., Benigni, R. and Colosimo, A.: 2000, Mapping protein sequence spaces by recurrence quantification analysis: a case study on chimeric sequences, *Protein Engineering* **13**, 671–678.

Grassberger, P., Schreiber, T. and Schaffrath, C.: 1991, Non-linear time sequence analysis, *International Journal of Bifurcation and Chaos* **1**, 521–547.

Holzfuss, J. and Mayer-Kress, G.: 1986, An approach to error estimation in the application of dimension algorithms, *in* M.-K. G. (ed.), *Dimensions and Entropies in Chaotic Systems*, Springer-Verlag.

Ormerod, P.: 1998, *Butterfly Economics*, Pantheon Books.

Rao, C. and Suryawanshi, S.: 1996, Statistical analysis of shape of objects based on landmark data, *Proceedings of the National Academy of Sciences USA* **93**, 12132–12136.

Schreiber, T.: 1998, *Interdisciplinary Application of Nonlinear Time Series Methods*, Physics Reports 2.

Trulla, L., Giuliani, A., Zbilut, J. and Webber, J.: 1996, Recurrence quantification analysis of the logistic equation with transients, *Physics Letters A* **223**, 225–260.

Webber, J. C. and Zbilut, J.: 1994, Dynamical assessment of physiological systems and states using recurrence plot strategies, *Journal of Applied Physiology* **76**, 965–973.

Zak, M., Zbilut, J. and Meyers, R.: 1997, *From Instability to Intelligence: Complexity and Predictability in Nonlinear Dynamics*, Springer-Verlag.

Zbilut, J., Giuliani, A. and Webber, J.: 1998a, Recurrence quantification analysis and principal components in the detection of short complex signals, *Physics Letters A* **237**, 131–135.

Zbilut, J., Giuliani, A. and Webber, J.: 1998b, Detecting deterministic signals in exceptionally noisy enviroments using cross recurrence quantification, *Physics Letters A* **246**, 122–128.

Zbilut, J., Giuliani, A. and Webber, J.: 2000, Recurrence quantification analysis as an empirical test to distinguish relatively short deterministic versus random number series, *Physics Letters A* **267**, 174–178.

Zbilut, J., Hubler, A. and Webber, J.: 1996, Physiological singularities modeled by nondeterministic equations of motion and the effect of noise, *in* M. Millonais (ed.), *Fluctuations and Order: The New Synthesis*, Springer-Verlag, pp. 397–417.

Zbilut, J., Koebbe, M. and Mayer-Kress, G.: 1992, Use of recurrence plots in the analysis of heart beat intervals, *Proceedings Computers in Cardiology IEEE Computer Society* pp. 263–266.

Zbilut, J. and Webber, J. C.: 1992, Embeddings and delays as derived from quantification of recurrence plots, *Physics Letters A* **171**, 199–203.

Quasilinear Aggregation Operators and Preference Functionals

L. D'Apuzzo

Do1

1 Introduction

The evaluation of the alternatives is a crucial point in a decision process. Usually, for every alternative the Decision Maker has at its disposal n estimates that can be either degrees of satisfaction of the alternative to n criteria, or judgements of the n experts, or evaluations of n possible consequences of the alternative. In any case, before making a choice, the Decision Maker has to translate the n local estimates in a real number representing the global evaluation of the alternative; so he need an aggregation operator. The questions is: what operator? In order to give an answer we first have to inquire about the properties that an aggregation operator should satisfy and, consequently, about the general form of an aggregation operator verifying suitable conditions. The papers of Aczél and Saaty (1983), D'Apuzzo et al. (19,Aczél6690), Skala (1991), Basile and D'Apuzzo (1996), D'Apuzzo and Squillante (2002), suggest answers to our questions. From above mentioned papers we get that an answer to the question concerning the choice of the operator is given by the class of quasi linear means, $\phi \wedge -1(\sum_i p_i \phi(u_i))$, each one generated by a strictly monotone, continuous function defined over a real interval. Analitycal properties of quasi-linear means have been widely investigated by deFinetti (1931), Hardy et al. (1952), Aczél (1966) these operators were characterized as associative operators by de Finetti. Following Basile and D'Apuzzo (1996), D'Apuzzo and Squillante (2002) we introduce in section 1 the *quasilinear aggregation operators*

$$F(a_1, ..., a_n; p_1, ..., p_n) = \phi \wedge -1 \left(\sum_i p_i \phi(a_i) \right) \qquad (1)$$

as constituents the class of weighted averaging aggregation operators; moreover, following Basile and D'Apuzzo (1996), we show that a comparison among these operators can be modelled in terms of preoder stated in the set of the generating functions ϕ. In section 2 we report the results of D'Apuzzo and

Squillante (2002) in which the above operators are applied in the context of the Decision Making under Uncertainty to give a decision model generalizing the Expected Utility model. In the proposed model the functional evaluating lotteries is chosen from time to time in a large class of suitable functionals and the choice depends on the particular risky situation. Nevertheless in this class a functional can be studied as preference functional, that is functional (evaluating lotteries) working in every choice situation and inducing an ordering in the set of all the alternatives. Then we can see this functional enjoys classical properties as independence property and first dominance principle. Anyway to make use of a single functional is not sufficient to describe paradoxical situations that arise for instance in the Kahneman and Tversky experiment.

2 Aggregation Operators

The problem of evaluating the alternatives is an essential point of a decision problem. Usually, given the set of alternatives $\mathbf{A} = \{A_1, A_2, , A - m\}$, the evaluation of each alternative A_i is made starting from n local estimates, $a_{i1}, a_{i2}, , a_{in}$. Depending on the particular decision context, these extimates can be either:

- degrees of satisfaction of the alternative to n given criteria (*multicriteria decision problems*);
- or judgements of the n individuals or experts on the alternative (*group decision problems, expert problems*);
- or evaluations of the n possible consequences of the alternative; each consequence (is) determined by the occurrence of one of the n exhaustive and independent events (*decision making under uncertainty*);
- preference ratios of the alternative A_i to the other alternatives .

Then the first step in the choice process is to evaluate the alternative A_i by translating the n estimates $a_{i1}, a_{i2}, , a_{in}$ in a global evaluation $a_i = F(a_{i1}, a_{i2}, , a_{in})$ of A_i; so that an ordering is induced in the set of the alternatives an the best alternative can be chosen. The functional F carrying out this translation is called aggregation operator or synthesis functional. The shape of an aggregation operator depends on several elements as the nature of the alternatives, the relationship among the criteria or the experts involved, the particular choice situation and so on. In the classical maxmin method the aggregation

$$F_\wedge : (a_1, ..., a_n) \to F_\wedge(a_1, ..., a_n) = \min\{a_1, ..., a_n\} = \wedge_j a_j$$

operator is the *min* operator giving the least estimate as global evaluation of an alternative. Then the selected alternative is A_k iff $F_\wedge(a_{k_1}, ..., a_{k_n}) = \max F_\wedge(a_{i_1}, ..., a_{i_n}) = \max_i \min_j a_{ij}$.

The operator $F_\wedge$ inform us about the level at which an alternative surely verifies all the criteria or satisfies all the experts, the first *and* the second *and* *and* the last; so it is called AND operator by R.R. (Yager 1988). Then the choice of the AND operator $F_\wedge$ as aggregation operator corresponds to the preference or the need of the Decision Maker for an alternative satisfying at a good level all the criteria.

In the max max method the aggregation operator is the max operator $F_\vee$

$$F_\vee : (a_1, ..., a_n) \to F_\vee(a_1, ..., a_n) = \min\{a_1, ..., a_n\} = \vee_i a_i$$

also called OR operator by Yager (1988). The operator $F_\vee$ gives the maximum estimates as global evaluation of the alternative; so the choice of the OR operator corresponds to the need of an alternative satisfying at high level almost one criterion or expert, it doesn't matter which one.

The AND and the OR operators represent extremal situations. Usually an aggregation operator is required to be an averaging operator, that gives a global evaluation of an alternative lying between the worst and the best local estimates; this allows a compensation between the compatibilities of the alternative whit different and sometimes conflicting attributes. Most used averaging operators are the arithmetic mean $F(a_1, ..., a_n) = \sum_{i=1}^{n} \frac{1}{n} a_i$ and the geometric mean $\sqrt[n]{a_1 \cdot ... \cdot a_n}$. In the setting of the multicriteria decision problems, it can occur that the criteria are not equally important, then, for every $i = 1, , n$, and then a most used aggregation operator is the weighted arithmetic mean $F(a_1, ..., a_n) = \sum_{j=1}^{n} p_j a_j$, where p_j is the weight of importance assigned to the jth criterion and $\sum_{j=1}^{n} p_j = 1$. The weighted arithmetic mean plays a role also in the framework of decision making under uncertainty. In this context the criteria are replaced by a finite number of states of the world, $E_1, , E_n$, that are independent and exhaustive events. An alternative A is a lottery with n possible consequences $c_1, .c_n$: if the alternative A is chosen and the event E_j occurs, then the consequence c_j comes off; so the probability p_j of occurence of the event E_j is assigned as weight to the consequence c_j. Then, in the setting of the von Neumann - Morgensten Utility Theory, an alternative A is evaluated by aggregating the utilities $u(c_j)$ of its consequences by means of the weighted arithmetic mean $\sum_{i=1}^{n} p_i u(c_i)$.

We can need of an aggregation operator also in determining a local estimate of an alternative with respect a criterion as in the setting of the Analytic Hierarchy Process (A.H.P. for short), that is a multilcriteria approach to decision making, introduced by Saaty (1980). In the A.H.P. the estimate of each alternative with respect a given criterion C is built up starting from a parwise comparison matrix $A(a_{ij})$, in which the entry a_{ij} represents the preference ratio of the alternative A_i to the alternative A_j , so that $a_{ij} > 1$ means that A_i is preferred to A_j, $a_{ij} < 1$ express the reverse preference and it is $a_{ji} = 1/a_{ij}$. Then the geometric mean of the preference ratios $a_{i1}, , a_{in}$ is a very used tool to get the estimate of the alternative A_i with respect the criterion C.

2.1 Quasilinear means as weighted averaging aggregation operators

The form of an aggregation operator depends on the particular choice context or evaluation problem. Then the problem is to individuate a general form characterizing a large number of aggregation operators obeying some suitable conditions. We want to select operators affecting any operators by a vector of weights $P = (p_1, ..., p_n)$, under the assumption: $p_j \geq 0$ for every $j = 1, 2, , n$ and $\sum_{j=1}^{n} p_j = 1$. In this way we can consider either the case that a difference in importance among the criteria or experts (or a difference in likelihood among the states of the world) occurs ($p_i \neq p_j$ for some $i \neq j$) and the case of equal importance of criteria or experts ($p_1 = ... = p_n = \frac{1}{n}$). In order to point out the contribute of the weights, we use the notation $F(a_1, ..., a_n; p_1, ..., p_n)$ for the aggregation operator and we reserve the notation $F(a_1, ..., a_n)$ to the case $p_1 = ... = p_n = \frac{1}{n}$. We start from the following question: what properties does an aggregation operator have to satisfy? The minimal requirements for an aggregation operator are the following:

1. $F(a, ..., a; p_1, ..., p_n) = a$ (*idempotency or consensus property*);
2. $a_i \leq b_i, \forall i = 1, 2, ..., n \Rightarrow F(a_1, ..., a_n; p_1, ..., p_n) \leq F(b_1, ..., b_n; p_1, ..., p_n)$
   (*monotonicity in the estimates*);
3. $F(a_{i_1}, ..., a_{i_n}; p_{i_1}, ..., p_{i_n}) = F(a_1, ..., a_n; p_1, ..., p_n)$ for every permutation
   $i_1, i_2..., i_n$ of $1, 2, ..., n$ (*symmetry*)

The AND operator and the OR operator verify the properties 1, 2, 3; but if we look for an aggregation operator taking into account the separated contributions of all local estimates and the different contributions of the weights, then we also require:

4. $a_i \neq a_i', p_i > 0 \Rightarrow$
   $F(a_1, ..., a_{i-1}, a_i, a_{i+1}; p_1, ..., p_n) \neq F(a_1, ..., a_{i-1}, a_i', a_{i+1}; p_1, ..., p_n)$;
5. $a_i < a_j$ and $0 < \varepsilon < p_i \Rightarrow F(a_1, ..., a_i, ..., a_j, ...a_n; p_1, ...p_i, ..., p_j, ..., p_n) <$
   $F(a_1, ..., a_i, ..., a_j, ...a_n; p_1, ...p_i - \varepsilon, ..., p_j + \varepsilon, ..., p_n)$ (*monotonicity in the weights*);

A functional verifying the conditions 1, 2 and 4 satisfies in addition the following

6. $a_i \leq b_i, \forall i = 1, 2, ..., n$ and $a_i < b_i, p_i > 0$ for some $i \in \{1, 2, ..., n\}$
   $\Rightarrow F(a_1, ..., a_n; p_1, ..., p_n) < F(b_1, ..., b_n; p_1, ..., p_n)$ (*strictly monotonic in the estimates*);
7. $\underline{a} = F_\wedge(a_1, ..., a_n) \leq F(a_1, ..., a_n; p_1, ..., p_n) \leq \bar{a} F_\vee(a_1, ..., a_n)$ (*internality*)
   and moreover
7'. $\underline{a} \leq a_i \leq \bar{a}, p_i > 0$, for some $i \in \{1, ..., n\} \rightarrow \underline{a} < F(a_1, ..., a_n; p_1, ..., p_n) < \bar{a}$.

So the required functionals lie in between the AND and the OR operator, but no one of them is the AND or the OR operator.

The following proposition hold (see D'Apuzzo and Squillante (2002))

Proposition 2.1 *Let ϕ be a continuous, strictly monotonic function defined over a real interval. Then the quasilinear mean*

$$F(a_1, ..., a_n; p_1, ..., p_n) = \phi^{-1}\left(\sum_i p_i\phi(a_i)\right)$$

satisfies the conditions 1, 2, 3, 4, 5.

Quasi linear means also satisfy a property of associativity that, in the case n=2, is expressed by

8. $F(F(x, y; r, 1-r), z; p, 1-p) = F\left(x, F\left(y, z; \frac{p-pr}{1-pr}, \frac{1-p}{1-pr}\right); pr, 1-pr\right)$ (*associativity*).

In Aczél (1966), section 5.3.2 Aczél gives the following characterization of the quasilinear means $\phi^{-1}(p\phi(x) + (1-p)\phi(y))$.

Aczél Theorem - *Conditions 1, 2, 3, 5, 6, 7, 8 are necessary and sufficient for the functional $F(x, y; p, 1-p)$, $a \leq x, y \leq b$, $p \in [0, 1]$, to be of the form $F(x, y; p, 1-p) = \phi^{-1}(p\phi(x) + (1-p)\phi(y))$.*

For further properties and characterizations of quasilinear means see also Hardy et al. (1952), Holzer (1992).

The class of the quasilinear means provides a suitable class of aggregation operators including the arthmetic weighted means, the geometric means, the means of order p, $(\sum_i p_i a_i^p)^{\frac{1}{p}}$. The choice of the function ϕ can be made taking in account particular requirements of the decision maker. For example the request of the reciprocal condition

$$F\left(\frac{1}{a_1}, ..., \frac{1}{a_n}\right) = F\left(\frac{1}{a_1}, ..., \frac{1}{a_n}; \frac{1}{n}, ..., \frac{1}{n}\right) = \frac{1}{F(a_1, ..., a_n)}$$

for the aggregation operator is satisfied by choosing $\phi(x) = a\psi(\log x) + b$, $a \neq 0$, with ψ arbitrary continuous odd function; in particular by choosing, $\phi(x) = \log x$, we get the geometric mean. If the reciprocal condition and the homogeneity condition

$$F(\alpha a_1, ..., \alpha a_n; p_1, ..., p_n) = \alpha F(a_1, ..., a_n; p_1, ..., p_n), \quad \alpha > 0$$

are required together, then $\phi(x) = \log x$; while if the only homogeneity condition is required, then $\phi(x) = x^p$.

We can restrict ourselves to suppose that the estimates of the considered alternatives belong to the interval [h, k]; so we denote by $\Phi = \Phi_{[h,k]}$ the set of continuous and strictly monotonic functions on that interval. In the sequel we will call *quasilinear aggregation operator* any functional F_ϕ provided by

$$F_\phi(a_1, ..., a_n; p_1, ..., p_n) = \phi^{-1}\left(\sum_i p_i\phi(a_i)\right), \quad \phi \in \Phi_{[h,k]} \qquad (2)$$

ϕ is called the *generating function of F_ϕ*.

2.2 Comparing functionals F_ϕ depending on ϕ

The quasilinear aggregation operators (2) lie in between the AND and the OR operator because of the property of internality 7, but the AND or the OR operator are not quasilinear operators because of the property 7'. Nevertheless we can find quasilinear operators as much close to the operator or the operator , as we would: indeed it is well known that Hardy et al. (1952)

$$\lim_{p \to -\infty} \left(\sum_i p_i a_i^p \right)^{\frac{1}{p}} = F_\wedge(a_1, ..., a_n) \qquad \lim_{p \to +\infty} \left(\sum_i p_i a_i^p \right)^{\frac{1}{p}}$$

A more general question is: how can we vary the generating function ϕ in way as to slide the operator F_ϕ from the AND operator to the OR operator? The answer is: by means of a preorder $\trianglelefteq$ stated in the set $\Phi_{[h,k]}$ and representing the partial order $\leq$ among the quasilinear aggregation operators.

Indeed a reflexive and transitive relation $\trianglelefteq$ in $\Phi_{[h,k]}$? is stated in Basile and D'Apuzzo (1996) by setting, for ψ, ϕ, in $\Phi_{[h,k]}$ and $\omega = \psi \circ \phi^{-1}$:

$$\phi \trianglelefteq \psi \Leftrightarrow (\beta) - \begin{cases} either & ''\psi \, strictly \, increasing \, and \, \omega \, convex'' \\ or & ''\psi \, strictly \, decreasing \, and \, \omega \, concave'' \end{cases}$$

and it results

$$\phi \trianglelefteq \psi \, and \, \psi \trianglelefteq \phi \Leftrightarrow \psi \circ \phi^{-1} \, is \, linear.$$

Moreover

Proposition 2.2 *(Basile and D'Apuzzo (1996) prop. 5 and Hardy et al. (1952) p. 169). Let $\phi, \psi \in \Phi_{[h,k]}$. Then the following statements are equivalent:*

$$(\alpha) - F_\phi \leq F_\psi;$$
$$(\beta) - \phi \trianglelefteq \psi$$

Furthermore $F_\phi = F_\psi$ if and only if $\omega = \psi \circ \phi^{-1}$ is linear.

The relation $\trianglelefteq$ can checked be by means of the ratios of the second derivative to the first derivative of the generating functions in the subset Φ'' of $\Phi_{[h,k]}$ constituted by two time differentiable functions. Indeed

Proposition 2.3 *(Basile and D'Apuzzo (1996)). For $\phi, \psi \in \Phi''$, it results*

$$\phi \trianglelefteq \psi \, iff \, \phi''/\phi' \leq \psi''/\psi'.$$

As consequence from the above propositions we get:

Corollary 2.1 *Let ϕ and ψ be in Φ''. Then*

$$F_\phi \leq F_\psi \, iff \, \phi''/\phi'.$$

So the ratio ϕ''/ϕ' inform us about the closeness of the operator F_ϕ to the AND or the OR operator.

3 Generalizing the expected utility model

In the framework of Decision making under uncertainty the von Neumann - Morgensten Expected Utility Theory provides the classical decision model from both normative and descriptive point of view. Failures of this model are originated by the fact that, in many situations discrepancies between the individual and the expected behaviours have been observed (see Machina (1987)). Hence the necessity of new models able to describe either the behaviours embodied into the classical model and some classes of its systematic failures. In Section 3.2 we present the Expected Utility model and in Section 3.3 some of the paradoxical situations describing failures of the model. Then we illustrate a model proposed in D'Apuzzo and Squillante (2002), that use the quasilinear operators as main tools to generalize the expected utility model: these operators provide a class of functionals evaluating lotteries and the preorder in the set of the generating functions is devoted to describe different attitudes toward risk. We stress that also in the work of Chew (1983), quasi-linear means are used in explaining some failures of the expected utility model; but they are devoted to the representation of certainty equivalent and the generating function ϕ is the utility function of the decision maker.
We start by describing the basic elements of choice problem under uncertainty.

3.1 Notations

In the sequel we consider:

- a set **C** of outcomes, endowed with a weak order $\succeq$, that is a reflexive, transitive and complete relation on C called *preference relation*;
- a set P of all probability distributions p or lotteries on **C** obeying the following conditions: $p(c) \geq 0$ for every $c \in C, p(c) > 0$ for at most a finite number of $c \in C$ and $\sum_{c \in \mathbf{C}} p(c) = 1$;
- a set **A** of the alternatives constituted by lotteries and outcomes.

Symbols as

$$A(c_1, ..., c_n; p_1, ..., p_n), \quad A\begin{array}{|c|c|c|c|}\hline p_1 & p_2 & ... & p_n \\\hline c_1 & c_2 & ... & c_n \\\hline\end{array}$$

denote the lottery A that assigns the probability p_i to the outcome c_i in the set $\{c_1, ..., c_n\}$ and null probability to every $c \ni \{c_1, ..., c_n\}$. Let us remark that any outcome c can be regarded as a certain lottery $(c; 1)$. Let $A(c_1, ..., c_n; p_1, ..., p_n)$ and $B(z_1, ..., z_n; q_1, ..., q_n)$ be lotteries and $p \in [0, 1]$. Then the lottery

$$pA + (1 - p)B = (c_1, ..., c_n, z_1, ..., z_h; pp_1, ..., pp_n, (1 - p)q_1, ..., (1 - p)q_h),$$

is called a mixture of A and B and it is also denoted as follows

$$ApB = (A, B; p, (1 - p)).$$

The lottery ApB gives the possibility to take part on the lottery A with probability p and on lottery B with probability $(1-p)$.

We suppose that the set of the alternative **A** is closed under the operation of mixture.

To each lottery $A(c_1, ..., c_n; p_1, ..., p_n)$ in **A** is associated the function

$$F_A : c \in \{c_1, c_2, ..., c_n\} \to F_A(c) = \sum_{c_h \preceq c} p_h$$

that is called the *cumulative distribution* function of A. To the preference relation $\succeq$ in the set **C** there are naturally associated the relations of indifference $\approx$ and strict preference $\succ$ defined by

$$c \approx c' \Leftrightarrow c \succeq c' \quad and \quad c' \succeq c$$
$$c \succ c' \Leftrightarrow c \succeq c' \quad and \quad not \, c' \approx c$$

Then in **C** is defined the order topologie, a subbasis of which is given by the family of subsets $\{c \in C : c \prec a\}$, $\{c \in C : c \succ b\}$.

The preference relation $\succeq$ on **C** is separable in the sense of Debreu iff there exists a countable subset $D \subseteq C$ such that, if $c \succ c'$ then $c \succeq d \succeq c'$ for some $d \in D$.

If we assume the above separability condition for the relation $\succeq$, then the relation is representable by a real continuous function u (see Bridges and Mehta (1995)) defined over the set **C**. The function u is called *utility* function. We can suppose u is bounded and takes its values in the compact interval [h, k].

3.2 Expected Utility model and criticism

The von Neumann - Morgensten Utility Theory provides the classical model for describing and solving decision problems under uncertainty. In this model the consequences of an alternative are evaluated by means of the utility function u and an alternative $A(c_1, ..., c_n; p_1, ..., p_n)$ is evaluated by translating the utilities $u(c_i)$ of its consequences into the number

$$U(A) = \sum_i p_i u(c_i),$$

that is called the *expected utility* of A. The *Expected Utility principle* (E.U. principle for short) requires the Decision Maker selects the alternative with the greatest expected utility. Nevertheless in many situations, individuals make their choice without maximizing the expected utility. So non - expected utility models have been developped for representing individual behaviours different from that indicate by the E.U. principle. Non - additive measures structures, Choquet capacities (see Choquet (1953-54)) and empirical adjustments in the evaluations of prospects or lotteries have been useful tools in order to build non expected utility models. Among the others Kahneman and Tversky (1979), Machina (1982), Yaari (1987), Ventre (1996), indicate behavioural models for which the linearity in probabilities of the preference functional is not assumed. On the other hand, by giving up the additivity of probability measures, we have the drawback of violating some usually required properties of utility theory like dominance principles.

Another aspect of the von Neumann - Morgensten Utility Theory can be questioned: this is the role played by the utility function as unique representative of the attitude of the decision maker toward risk; indeed, the Arrow - Pratt index of risk aversion is given by the opposite of ratio of second and first derivative of the utility function. But one can argue that the utility function of the decision maker can be determined without reference to gambling situations; indeed the utility function is essentially related to the values and the tastes of the decision maker, while the risk attitude plays a role when the decision maker is faced with several lotteries (see Hansson (1997)), so the utility curve and the attitude towards risk are different and partially independent things. This suggests the attitude toward risk have to be embodied in the functional evaluating lotteries. Furthermore, it has been observed and confirmed by experimental data that a unique functional hardly represents every choice structure (see Munier (1998)).

In D'Apuzzo and Squillante (2002) the authors define a context including the standard decision scheme, preserving probabilistic structures and describing some classes of systematic failures of Expected Utility principle such as Kahneman and Tversky experiment, Allais paradox and common ratio effect. They indicate a class of functionals from which the decision maker chooses his functional for evaluating lotteries depending on the particular risky structure. The failures of Expected Utility Theory described in the next section allow us to introduce the decision model proposed in D'Apuzzo and Squillante (2002).

3.3 Kahneman and Tversky experiment and other paradoxes

In an experiment described by Kahneman and Tversky in Hardy et al. (1952) the following choice problems have been proposed to a sample of 72 people:

1. choose between the lotteries

$$A\ \begin{array}{|c|c|c|} \hline 0.33 & 0.66 & 0.01 \\ \hline \$\ 2500 & \$\ 2400 & \$\ 0 \\ \hline \end{array}\ ,\quad B\ \begin{array}{|c|c|c|} \hline 1 & 0 & 0 \\ \hline \$\ 2400 & \$\ 0 & \$\ 0 \\ \hline \end{array}$$

2. choose between the lotteries

$$C\ \begin{array}{|c|c|} \hline 0.33 & 0.67 \\ \hline \$\ 2500 & \$\ 0 \\ \hline \end{array}\ ,\quad D\ \begin{array}{|c|c|} \hline 0.34 & 0.66 \\ \hline \$\ 2400 & \$\ 0 \\ \hline \end{array}$$

It has been observed that a percentage of 82% of the subjects choose alternative B = ($ 2400; 1) in the first case and a percentage of 83% of the subjects choose alternative C in the second case.

As a consequence, at least the 65% of people choose B in 1 and C in 2. But this behaviour does not reflect the MEU principle as we are coming to see. The outcomes of the lotteries involved are the same, so it is quite natural to assume that a unique utility function for a given decision maker works in both situations; then, using the Expected utility functional U for evaluating the lotteries we get the following contradictory result:

$$B \succ A \Leftrightarrow u(2400) > 0.33u(2500) + 0.66(2400) + 0.01u(0)$$
$$\Leftrightarrow 0.34u(2400) > 0.33u(2500) + 0.01u(0)$$
$$C \succ D \Leftrightarrow 0.33u(2500) + 0.67u(0) > 0.34u(2400) + 0.66u(0)(0)$$
$$\Leftrightarrow 0.33u(2500) + 0.01u(0) > 0.34u(2400)$$

Furthermore, the majority of people exhibits aversion to risk, in the first case, and risk - seeking behaviour, in the second case: the utility function, which is the same in both cases, does not justify such a behaviour.

A similar contradiction emerges from the Allais paradox (1953) Allais (1953):

1.

A_1
0.01	0.10	0.89
$ 500,000	$ 500,000	$ 500,000

A_2
0.01	0.10	0.89
$ 0	$ 2,500,000	$ 500,000

2.

A_3
0.01	0.10	0.89
$ 500,000	$ 500,000	$ 0

A_4
0.01	0.10	0.89
$ 0	$ 2,500,000	$ 50

The majority of people chooses $A_1 = (\$500,000; 1)$ in the first case, showing to prefer a sure winning choice to a lottery having a very high possibility to win and a bit of risk. The most risky choice is preferred in the second case.

The motivation of the failure of the MEU principle resides in the fact that, in presence of the certainty, the decision maker rejects risky options; this is known as the "certainty effect". The previous examples are particular cases of the following paradox known as the "common ratio effect" (see also Schmidt (1998)).

L_1
α	$1 - \alpha$
$ X	$ 0

L_2
β	$1 - \beta$
$ Y	$ 0

L_1^*
$\gamma\alpha$	$\gamma\alpha$
$ X	$ 0

L_2^*
$\gamma\beta$	$1 - \gamma\beta$
$ Y	$ 0

where $\alpha > \beta$, $Y > X$, $\gamma \in]0, 1[$.

It has been observed that individuals tend to choose L_1 in the first couple and L_2^* in the second; that is, in the first case the lottery with higher probabiliy of winning and lower outcomes has been chosen; in the second one, at lower chance levels, the more risky lottery is preferred.

Forgetting the paradoxical result we are intersted in stressing the role of the
E.U. functional in the Kahneman and Tversky experiment and the role that
can play the quasilinear functional

$$U^* = \left(\sum_j p_j \sqrt{u_j} \right)^2$$

Suppose the utility of an outcome of the lotteries A, B, C, D, in the Kahneman
e Tversky experiment, coincides with its monetary value; then by choosing the
functional U^* for aggregating the utilities, we get the inequality:

$$U^*(A) = \$(0.33\sqrt{2500} + 0.66\sqrt{2400})^2 = \$2384, 69 < U^*(B) = \$2400$$

in according with the most used choice, while, the expected utility functional
U gives

$$U(A) = \$(0.33 \cdot 2500 + 0.66 \cdot 2400) = \$2409 > U(B) = \$2400$$

by disagreeing with the actual choice of most of the decision makers.
Hence the functional U^* used as functional for evaluating lotteries can describe
the choice of the certain lottery in the first choice problem, while it easy to
check the Expected Utility functional U represents the choice made by most
people in the second problem.
More generally, as it results

$$U^* = \left(\sum_j p_j \sqrt{u_j} \right)^2 \leq \sum_j p_j u_j = U$$

U^* can be interpreted as representing a less proclivity to risk.
The described situations suggest the expected utility functional hardly can
describe every choices made in the real life; moreover the choice of the functional for evaluating a lottery can depend on the particular risky situation.
On the other hand the attitude towards risk can only partially be embodied
in the utility function, that is more related to the values of the prizes than to
the evaluation of uncertainty: the attitude towards risk should be represented
by the shape of the functional that aggregates utilities and probabilities.
The above remarks suggest the behaviour of the decision maker could be modelled by a two steps procedure: first the decision maker expresses his or her
personal preferences over the possible outcomes, by exhibiting the shape of
the utility curve; secondly, the decision maker, faced with gambling choices,
reveals his or her own attitude toward risk by maximizing a functional of
aggregation of the utilities, that would be selected in a suitable class.

3.4 The class of the functionals U_ϕ

The decision maker evaluates lotteries by choosing every time the operator
for aggregating the utilities in a suitable class. Which class? In D'Apuzzo

and Squillante (2002) the authors look for a class of functionals allowing to represent several choice situations, enjoying a minimal set of requirements and owing an analytical representation available for computations.

A functional of the class have

1. to extends the utility function u from the set $\mathbf{C}$ of outcomes to the set $\mathbf{A}$ of the alternatives, that is to assign the utility of its unique outcome to every certain lottery;
2. to be increasing with respect to the utilities of the outcomes;
3. to give an evaluation of the lottery $A(c_1, ..., c_n; p_1, ..., p_n)$, that does not depend on which order the couples $u(c_i), p_i$ are considered;
4. to take into account the separated contributions of all the consequences, according to the related probabilities; in other words, if the value of a just one consequence changes, and its positive probability does not, then the value of the alternative changes too;
5. to be increasing with respect to the probabilities in the following sense: if the consequence c is preferred to the consequence d and the probability of c increases to the detriment of the probability of d, then the value of the alternative increases too.

The above requirements can be translated in the properties 1, 2, 3, 4, 5 of the section 1. This suggests that an alternative can be evaluated using an operator (1.1) for aggregating the utilities of its outcomes. So, taking on the range of the utility function u is the interval $[h,k]$, every function $\phi \in \Phi_{[h,k]}$ individuate a functional evaluating lotteries: this is the functional U_ϕ, which value on the alternative $A(c_1, ..., c_n; p_1, ..., p_n)$ is given by

$$u_\phi(A(c_1, ..., c_n; p_1, ..., p_n)) = F_\phi(u(c_1), ..., u(c_n); p_1, ..., p_n)$$

$$= \phi^{-1}\left(\sum_i p_i \phi(u(c_i))\right) \tag{3}$$

In the sequel U_Φ will denote the class of the functionals (3); each functional in the class is generated by a function $\phi \in \Phi = \Phi_{[h,k]}$. If we take $\phi(x) = x \ \forall x \in [h, k]$, then we get the expected utility functional U, as particular functional in the class $\mathbf{U_\Phi}$.

We can also define the functionals

$$U_\wedge(A) \le U_\phi(A) \le U_\vee(A), \quad \forall A \in \mathbf{A} \ \forall U_\phi \in \mathbf{U_\Phi}$$

From the property of internality 7 related to the quasilinear aggregation operators (2) we deduce

$$U_\wedge(A) \le U_{\phi(A)} \le U_\vee(A), \quad \forall A \in \mathbf{A} \ \forall U_\phi \in \mathbf{U_\Phi}$$

The partial order $\preceq$ in the set $\mathbf{U_\Phi}$ classifies the different attitudes toward risk. More exactly the inequalities

$$U_\phi \leq U_\psi \quad and \quad U_\phi \neq U_\psi$$

mean that the U_ϕ represents more aversion to risk than U_ψ; moreover more the functional U_ϕ is close to the max operator $U_\vee$, more proclivity to risk it represents; more the functional U_ϕ is close to the min operator $U_\wedge$, more aversion to risk it represents.

How we can represent the attitude toward risk by means of the generating function ϕ? In section 2.2 a preorder $\trianglelefteq$ is stated in the set $\Phi_{[h,k]}$ of generating functions, that inform us about the partial order $\preceq$ in the set $\mathbf{U_\Phi}$; indeed by Proposition (2.2) we get

$$U_\phi \leq U_\psi \Leftrightarrow \phi \trianglelefteq \psi \tag{4}$$

and furthermore

$$U_\phi = U_\psi \Leftrightarrow \psi \circ \phi^{-1} \, is \, linear$$

By restricting to the subset $\Phi'' \subseteq \Phi$ of the twice differentiable functions the partial order $\preceq$ in the related subset $U_{\Phi''}$ of U_Φ can be checked by the partial order among the ratios $\frac{\phi''}{\phi'}, \phi \in \Phi''$; indeed by (4) and Proposition (2.3) we get:

$$U_\phi \leq U_\psi \, iff \, \phi''/\phi' \leq \psi''/\psi'$$

So we can consider the ratio ϕ''/ϕ' as an index of propension to risk and the opposite ratio $-\phi''/\phi'$ as an index of aversion to risk.

3.5 U_ϕ as preference functional

Individuals act as if they chose different functionals for different classes of risk situation. Nevertheless we can consider the case that a unique functional U_ϕ is chosen in the class $\mathbf{U_\Phi}$ for evaluating all the alternatives of the given set $\mathbf{A}$. Then the functional U_ϕ induces in $\mathbf{A}$ a preference relation $\succeq$ defined as follows

$$A \succeq B \Leftrightarrow U_\phi(A) \geq U_\phi(B)$$

and the corresponding strict preference and indifference relations are given by

$$A \succ B \Leftrightarrow U_\phi(A) > U_\phi(B)$$
$$A \approx B \Leftrightarrow U_\phi(A) = U_\phi(B)$$

We can see the preference relation induced by the functional U_ϕ satisfies conditions the are naturally required to a preference relation. Indeed in D'Apuzzo and Squillante (2002) the following propositions are proved

Proposition 3.1 (Independence Property) $A \succ B \Leftrightarrow ApC \succ BpC \, for \, p \in$ $]0,1[$.

Proposition 3.2 (1 order stochastic dominance principle) Let $A(c_1, c_2, ..., c_n;$ $p_1, p_2, ..., p_n)$ and $B(c_1, c_2, ..., c_n; q_1, q_2, ..., q_n)$ be two lotteries, F_A and F_B the *related cumulative distributions and* **U** *the class of utility functions represent-ing the orderings in* **C** *giving* $c_1 \preceq c_2 \preceq, ..., \preceq c_n$. *Then*

$$F_A(c) \geq F_B(c) \ \forall c \in \{c_1, c_2, ..., c_n\} \Leftrightarrow U_\phi(A) \geq U_\phi(B) \ \forall u \in \mathbf{U}$$

Proposition 3.3 (ϕ - linearity)

$$U_\phi(ApB) = \phi^{-1}(p\phi()U_\phi(A) + (1-p)\phi(U_\phi(B)))$$

for every couple of alternatives A, B *and for every* $p \in [0, 1]$.

A problem is to characterize the functionals inducing the same preference re-lation in the set of the alternatives. In order to solve this problem in D'Apuzzo and Squillante (2002) the authors introduce the following concept:

"*a certainty* ϕ − *equivalent of a lottery* A *is every outcome* $\underline{c}$ *such that*
$u(\underline{c}) = U_\phi(A)$"

Moreover they consider the condition
α) for every choice of ϕ and for every lottery A in **A**, there exists in **C** a certainty ϕ-equivalent of a lottery A.
    and show the following result

Proposition 3.4 *(D'Apuzzo and Squillante 2002) Under the assumption* α) *the functionals* U_ϕ *and* U_ψ *induce the same preference relation on the alter-natives if and only if* $U_\phi = U_\psi$, *that is* $\psi = a\phi + b$, $a \neq 0$, $b \in \Re$

The condition α) is surely verified if **A** is a set of monetary lotteries and u is a continuous utility function over a real interval.

3.6 Certainty equivalent and risk attitude for monetary lotteries

Let U_ϕ be a chosen functional for evaluating monetary lotteries; then the certainty ϕ-equivalent of a monetary lottery $A = A(c_1, ..., c_n; p_1, ..., p_n)$ is the monetary amount c_ϕ) verifying the equality

$$u(c_\phi) = \phi^{-1}(\sum_{i=1}^{n} p_i\phi(u(c_i)))$$

So c_ϕ is given by

$$c_\phi = u^{-1}(\phi^{-1}(\sum_{i=1}^{n} p_i\phi(u(c_i))))$$

The *risk premium* of a monetary lottery will be given by

$$\rho = \sum_i p_i c_i - c_\phi$$

Then the attitude toward risk of the decision maker is modelled by means of the risk premium ρ in the following way:

the decision maker is risk averse if and only if $\rho > 0$,
the decision maker is risk neutral if and only if $\rho = 0$,
the decision maker is risk prone if and only if $\rho < 0$.

It is straightforward to check that if ϕ is strictly increasing, then the decision maker is risk adverse if and only if

$$\phi(u(\sum_i p_i c_i)) > \phi(c_\phi) = \sum_{i=1}^n p_i \phi(u(c_i))$$

whereas, if ϕ is strictly decreasing, then the decision maker is risk adverse iff

$$\phi(u(\sum_i p_i c_i)) < \phi(c_\phi) = \sum_{i=1}^n p_i \phi(u(c_i))$$

Hence the aversion to risk is translated into the choice of a functional U_ϕ such that $\phi \circ u$ concave and increasing, or $\phi \circ u)$ convex and decreasing.

Of course, the risk proclivity leads to $\phi \circ u)$ convex and increasing or $\phi \circ u)$ concave and decreasing.

4 Final remarks

In Kahneman and Tversky experiment a suitable choice of the function $\phi(x) = \sqrt{x}$ and, then, of the functional $U_\phi = U^*$ has allowed us to describe the behaviour of a decision maker that prefers the lottery B in the first problem of choice; nevertheless we remark that a unique functional cannot provide an interpretation for paradoxical behaviour exhibited by most decision makers in that experiment. Indeed, if we assume that the preferences expressed in both the choice problems can be described by means of the same functional U_ϕ, then we get, for an increasing ϕ

$B \succ A \Rightarrow$

$\quad \Rightarrow \phi^{-1}(\phi(u(2400))) > \phi^{-1}(0.33\phi(u(2500))) + 0.66\phi(u(2400)) + 0.01\phi(u(0))$
$\quad \Rightarrow \phi(u(2400)) > 0.33\phi(u(2500)) + 0.66\phi(u(2400)) + 0.01\phi(u(0))$
$\quad \Rightarrow 0.34\phi(u(2400)) > 0.33\phi(u(2500)) + 0.01\phi(u(0))$

$C \succ D \Rightarrow$

$\quad \Rightarrow \phi^{-1}(0.33\phi(u(2500)) + 0.67\phi(u(0))) > \phi^{-1}(0.34\phi(u(2400)) + 0.66\phi(u(0)))$
$\quad \Rightarrow 0.33\phi(u(2500)) + 0.67\phi(u(0)) > 0.34\phi(u(2400)) + 0.66\phi(u(0))$
$\quad \Rightarrow 0.33\phi(u(2500)) + 0.01\phi(u(0)) > 0.34\phi(u(2400))$

We get an analogue contradiction for ϕ strictly decreasing. The above remark suggests that some behaviours of the decision maker, like most of people in the in the case of Kahneman and Tverski, and Allais paradoxes, cannot be modelled by applying just one functional for every choice situation: the functional representing the preference depends on the gambling schemas.

It remains as an open problem to state a sharp relation between the different classes of risk options and the functionals that correspondingly represent the behaviour of the decision maker.

References

Aczél, J.: 1966, *Lectures on Functional Equations and their Application*, New York and London Academic Press.

Aczél, J. and Saaty, T.: 1983, Procedures for synthesizing ratio judgements, *Journal Math. Psycology* **27**, 93–102.

Allais, M.: 1953, Le comportment de l'homme rationnel devant le risque: critique des postulats et axiomes de l'école américaine, *Econometrica* **21**, 503–546.

Basile, L. and D'Apuzzo, L.: 1996, Ordering for classes of aggregation operators, *International Journal of Uncertainty, Fuzziness and Knowledge-Based Systems* **4.2**, 145–156.

Bridges, D. and Mehta, G.: 1995, Representation of preference ordering, *Springer-Verlag* .

Chew, S.: 1983, A generalization of the quasilinear mean with application to the measurement of income inequality and decision theory resolving the allais paradox, *Econometrica* **51**, 1065–1092.

Choquet, G.: 1953-54, Theory of capacity, *Ann. Ist. Fourier, Grenoble* **5**, 131–292.

D'Apuzzo, L. and Squillante, M.: 2002, Representation of preferences by quasi-linear means, *Annals of Mathematics and Artificial Intellingence* **35**(Nos. 1-4).

D'Apuzzo, L., Squillante, M. and Ventre, A.: 19,Aczél6690, Extending aggregation operators for multicriteria decision making, *in* J. K. M. Fedrizzi (ed.), *Multiperson Decision Making Models using Fuzzy Sets and Possibility Theory*, Kluwer Publishing Company.

deFinetti, B.: 1931, Sul concetto di media, *G.I.I.A.* **II**, 369–396.

Hansson, B.: 1997, Risk aversion as a problem of conjoint measurement, *in* G (ed.), *Decision, Probability and Utility*, Cambridge University Press.

Hardy, G., Littlewood, J. and Polya, G.: 1952, *Inequalities*, Cambridge Sity Press.

Holzer, S.: 1992, Sulla trattazione assiomatica delle medie, *Atti del Sedicesimo Convegno A.M.A.S.E.S.* .

Kahneman, D. and Tversky, A.: 1979, Prospect theory: an analysis of decision under risk, *Econometrica* **47**, 263–291.

Machina, M.: 1982, Expected utility analysis without the independence axiom, *Econometrica* **50**, 277–323.

Machina, M.: 1987, Choice under uncertainty: Problems solved and unsolved, *Economic Perspectives* **1**(1), 121–154.

Munier, B.: 1998, Two stage rationality under risk: Experimental results and perspectives, *Rivista di Matematica per le Scienze Economiche e Sociali* **21**(1-2), 3–23.

Saaty, T.: 1980, *The Analytic Hierarchy Process*, McGraw-Hill.

Schmidt, U.: 1998, A measurement of the certainty effect, *Journal of Mathematical Psycology* **42**, 32–47.

Skala, H.: 1991, Concerning ordered weighted averaging aggregation operators, *Statistical Papers* **32**, 35–44.

Ventre, A.: 1996, Decomposable expected utility, *Rivista di Matematica Univ. Parma* **5**(5), 1–11.

Yaari, M.: 1987, The dual theory of choice under risk, *Econometrica* **55**, 95–115.

Yager, R.: 1988, On ordered weighted averaging aggregation operators in multicriteria decision making, *I.E.E.E., transactions on Systems, Man, and Cybernetics* **18**(1), 183–190.

Business Competition as a Self-organizing Process: Toward an Increasing Returns-Based Microeconomic Theory

DO1

F. Buendia

D83   D23

1 Introduction

The order and relative efficiency we observe in Western economies stem from the coordination of the multiplicity of decisions made by millions of individual economic agents. Presently, there are two radically different explanations about how individuals find a solution to this extraordinarily difficult problem: *decreasing returns economics*[1] *and increasing returns economics.* The former economics assumes, among other thing, perfectly informed and rational agents; frictionless transaction; homogenous, independent, and non-improving products; hard-to-improve production factors; decreasing-returns production function; and technology as an exogenously given variable. Under these assumptions negative feedbacks become prevalent and produce a stable, unique, and predictable equilibrium, which is supposed to be reestablished smoothly and instantaneously if a disturbance takes place and to occur in all the sectors of the economy. Competition among price taking firms, avoidance of concentrated industries, and no government intervention are the main recommendations to coordinate economic activity and achieve economic efficiency.

In some sectors of the economy, such as agriculture and mining, the stabilizing forces created by negative feedback allow for perfect competition markets and the application of conventional economics. Nevertheless, most manufacturing industries in modern capitalist economies do not exhibit the peculiarities that microeconomics textbooks associate with perfect competition. It is a proven fact that most manufacturing industries in capitalist countries are served by a small number of large firms with non-negligible market share. Alfred D.

---

[1] The terms decreasing returns economics, standard economics, conventional economics are used interchangeably in this paper and refer to the kind of microeconomics theory we can find in leading graduate textbooks on microeconomics, such as Layard and Walters (1978) and Varian (1978).

Chandler is perhaps the scholar who has best been able to describe the historical importance of big business enterprises in the evolution of capitalist economies.[2] In *Strategy and Structure* (1966), *The Visible Hand* (1977), and *Scale and Scope* (1990) Chandler argues that before 1840 big corporations did not exit, so the economic activity was coordinated through the market mechanism. But by World War I the large corporation became the dominant economic institution, for it took the place of the market mechanism in the coordination of economic activities and the allocation of resources. In addition to being widespread, big firms are arranged around concentrated industrial structures exhibiting a very skewed distribution of firm sizes (Simon and Bonini 1958, Hart and Prais 1956, Hymer and Pashigian 1962, Ijiri and Simon 1964, Eatwell 1971, Vining 1976, Lucas 1978, Quandt 1970, Evans 1987). Buzzell (1981) confirms these findings and further suggests that the distribution of market shares of the leading competitors in narrowly defined product markets also follows a highly skewed pattern. This slanted market share distribution is so common that Buzzell (1981) considers it a *natural market structure*.[3] Furthermore, these slanted results may be exacerbated by the tendency of certain cases of inter-technology competition to end up in a technological monopoly. Finally, these characteristics of the business landscape usually follow a dynamic, cumulative pattern.

Fortunately, many scholars with a less conventional approach have suggested a number of important ideas to explain this tendency toward increasing polarization in business competition, but they have built their theories on a handful of factors and claim at least widespread and some times universal applicability. Some of these theories, for instance, attribute inter-firm differences to some competitive advantages related to cost reductions (Porter 1980). Other authors consider that these differences come from the efficiency of the orga-

---

[2] Chandler (1966) provides some statistics about the dominant position which the giant corporation had acquired in the American economy by 1960. In that year six hundred American corporations had annual earnings of over $10 million. These six hundred represented only 0.5 per cent of the total corporations in the United States; yet they accounted for 53 per cent of the total corporate income. Or, if we look only at industrial corporations, in 1960 the four hundred largest of these, all of which had assets of over $100 million, earned 46 per cent of all income earned before taxes in the manufacturing sector and controlled 30 per cent of all assets. Of these the one hundred largest alone accounted for 54 per cent of all profits in the manufacturing sector. With no doubt, the role of Fortune magazine's 500 largest corporations in the economy of the United States has been increasingly important in the last decades.

[3] During different periods of the history of capitalist economies, besides, we have witnessed an increasing number of mergers, alliances, joint ventures, networks of firms and other manifestation of cooperation that have exacerbated the skewness of the industrial structure of modern economic sectors.

nizational structure of the firm (cf. Minztberg (1994)) or from the strategic factors the firm possesses (Barney 1986, Dierickx and Karel 1989, Montgomery 1995). Some others believe that business success is due to well designed marketing strategies and suggest that price, distribution channels, advertising, servicing, and products should be well chosen and designed to satisfy rapidly and effectively consumers' preferences (Vandermerwe 1999). In the economic literature business competition is explained by the effort of the firm to introduce constantly innovations in the market (Schumpeter 1949, Nelson and Winter 1982). In the literature of technological change there are also some theories that have underlined the importance of qualitative improvements of products (Hirsch 1956, Arrow 1962, Rosenberg 1982). Finally, the literature on technological competition has emphasized the relevance of certain sources of increasing returns to explain technological monopolies (Arthur 1994).

As against these views, which ordinarily associate business competition with a very reduced number of variables and conceive the growth of the firm, industrial structure, and technological competition as independent levels of analysis, in this article I will argue that the world of commerce is too diverse and complex so as to be described by models based exclusively on a handful of factors explaining specific aspects of business competition. In order to move away from this decomposing approach I suggest that business competition is better characterized by a more comprehensive framework where a variety of increasing returns mechanisms combine to explain simultaneously the growth of the firm size, industrial structure, and technological competition. Although this framework is quite preliminary, it is suitable enough to capture the most important regularities that exist in a large variety of business situations across a wide range of firms competing in a large variety of industries. This business model is also more flexible, adaptable and better attuned to explaining markets shifts, greater uncertainty, complexity and turbulence that characterize business in emerging industries (specially in knowledge-based, network-based, and information-based economic sectors).

After a brief discussion on the sources of increasing returns, we integrate them in a general model of business competition. This model will provide tools and insights concerning size of the firms and skewedness of industrial structures. However, it will be far from being complete, since it will incapable to explain the path dependent, indeterminate, suboptimal, locking-in nature of technological competition under increasing returns. Because of this, in a second step, we incorporate in the general model a whole set of strong and important -yet neglected by many conventional approaches- increasing returns mechanisms, namely, reputation effects, network externalities and infrastructure effects. In sum, by using natural language and keeping conventional economics' aspiration of universal theory, the theorizing process through which this general model of business competition is constructed will gradually recognize the central role of increasing returns mechanisms in generating and sustaining dominant firms and technologies. We also discuss the potential this model has to become a revision to conventional microeconomics and be formalized as a dissipative structure.

2 The Sources of Increasing Returns

There is large number of sources of increasing returns in the economy. But those sources producing polarized outcomes in business competition are closely related to the following increasing returns mechanisms.

The Resource-Based Loop

At the end of the 1980s and beginning of the 1990s a new perspective emerged within the strategy tradition: the resource-based perspective.[4] Rooted in the old strategy concepts of corporate strengths and weaknesses, this paradigm looks at the firm as a broad and coherent set of resources, rather than in terms of its product-market positions. Originally, this idea was based on Barney (1986, 1989) notion of imperfections in markets for strategic factors. Barney argued that, when the markets for strategic factors are perfect, competitors can obtain them at will by simply purchasing them at the going market price. In these circumstances, the economic value of strategic factors will equal their marginal cost, so firms will not be able to generate above-normal performance on the basis of those factors. In contrast, firms competing in imperfectly competitive strategic factor markets may obtain above-normal economic performance by acquiring some rare assets offered in those markets.

Later on, Dierickx and Karel (1989) introduced the notion of incomplete factor markets. This notion implies that assets to implement strategies, apart of being firm specific, must be non-tradeable, -i.e., hard to acquire on the factor markets[5] -, hard-to-imitate, and nonsubstitutable, otherwise firms would realize their value through the market instead of deploying them in production activities. For this reason, strategic factors have to be created, controlled, and accumulated within the firm.

The notion of in-house creation, accumulation, and exploitation of firm-specific, hard-to-imitate, nontradeable, non-substitutable assets sheds light on two long-ago debated issues. To begin with, assets as sources of sustained

---

[4] The pioneer of this approach was Penrose (1959). Wernerfelt (1984, 1989) defined and named it. Other notable contributions are Barney (1991, 1992), Mahoney (1992), Peteraf (1993), Grant (1991), Conner (1991) review this literature.

[5] When markets for strategic factors do not exist or are incomplete, these non-marketable resources can be obtained by entering the corporate control market -i.e., buying and selling business through merger and acquisitions- or exploiting opportunities through certain forms of collaboration, such as R&D joint ventures.

competitive advantages provides the firm with the internal coherence that allows it to compete in specific product markets, differentiate itself vis-á-vis other firms, and compete across multiple lines of business. From this notion, besides, follows the implication that the levels of performance that accrue to a firm may indeed be due to its merits and efficiency in creating and exploiting its resources advantages, rather than its efforts to create imperfectly competitive conditions in a way that fails to maximize social welfare (Barney 1991). These developments, besides, have led to a number of daring theoretical propositions. First, the resource-based model has been proposed as a theory to explain acrossfirms heterogeneity, the optimal scope of the firm (Peteraf 1993), the direction and limits of diversified growth, the motivations for growth, and the relationship between diversification and performance. Furthermore, this model has been advanced as a new theory of the firm (Conner 1991) and as a central paradigm that may integrate the behavioral theory of the firm, transaction cost theory, property rights theory, agency theory, and the evolutionary theory of the firm (Mahoney 1992).

Despite these insights, the resource-based approach has some glaring weaknesses.[6] First, it lacks an explicit link between the firm's internal configuration and the industrial structure around it. Second, it attributes commercial success to strategic factors in general, but make no effort to spell out the causes of success of each specific case. Third, granted that it considers that commercial success depends exclusively on the stock of resources held by each competing firm, it implicitly assumes that product markets are strictly *ergodic*.[7] This implies that the mapping from resources to relative product market rewards

---

[6] Recently, some authors have addressed some of the resource-based approach's shortcomings. For instance, in the context of the dynamic capabilities approach, Teece, Pisano, and Shuen (1991) suggest organizational learning process as the source of strategic factors which lead to inter-firm, inter-temporal and inter-industry differences. This learning process, besides, provides the limits and direction for the growth of the firm along technological trajectories that correspond to precise "dominant designs". Central to this approach is the idea that know-how and skills are rarely embedded in plant and equipment and protected through the institution of private property. Rather, they exist in organizational routines and practices, which are developed through a long run, path-dependent learning process involving repetition and experimentation. Foss et al. (1995) believe that the resource-based view and evolutionary theory can complement each other: Nelson and Winter (1982) notion of routines can provide an evolutionary framework to explain the process of change at the industry level (selection), while in the resource-based approach, concepts like adaptation and learning are more related to the firm (heredity).

[7] For a discussion on the difference between ergodic and nonergodic markets, see Arthur (1994).

is linear and, therefore, strongly deterministic and fairly predictable.[8] Finally, in spite of its alleged emphasis on the creation and accumulation of strategic resources, this approach is unable to specify in a satisfactory manner the mechanisms whereby firms create and accumulate those strategic resources that cannot be acquired in the factor market. A way to make operational the process of creation and accumulation of resources suggested by the resource-based approach is by establishing a circular causality between market share and the firm-specific assets. Through such circular causality, as figure 1 shows, the firm's specificity and capacity to obtain extra-normal benefits which can be invested on new strategic resources become explicit. We are going to call this self-reinforcing mechanism the resource-based loop.

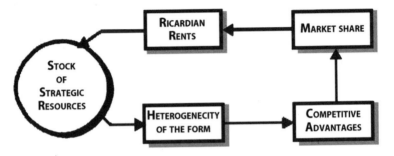

Fig. 1. The Resource-Based Loop.

Supply-side Scale Economies

The first source of increasing returns contained in the standard textbooks of microeconomic theory were those which assume constant technology and see concentrated industry structure as the result of traditional supply-side scale economies (Peltzman 1977, Carter 1978). In many cases large firms are more efficient than smaller companies because of its scale: larger corporations tend to have lower unit costs.[9] This efficiency in turn fuels further their growth. However, as Shapiro and Varian (1999) have correctly pointed out, positive feedbacks based on supply-side economies of scale usually runs into natural

---

[8] In other words, for this approach the product market and the resource market are isomorphic, that is why Wernerfelt (1984) considers them as the "two sides of the same coin". Though, as Arthur (1994) and Katz and Shapiro (1985) among others this is not always the case.

[9] At the level of inter-firm competition, scale economies may also hamper the late entry and survival of small producers.

limits. Past a certain size -they say- companies find growth difficult owing to the increasing complexity of managing a large organizational structure. From then on, negative feedback takes over. As traditional supplyside economies of scale generally become exhausted at a scale well below total market dominance, large firms, burdened with high costs, never grow to take the entire market and smaller, more nimble firms can find profitable niches. Shapiro and Varian (1999) conclude that because of this most industrial markets are oligopolies rather than monopolies.

Negative feedback generated by the difficulties of managing large organizations (scale diseconomies) indeed interrupts the growth of the firm and the level of industrial concentration. This situation, nevertheless, may be transient, because firms may be subject to other sources of increasing returns. Large firms that go through increasing returns mechanisms other than scale economies may increase their efficiency and overcome the negative aspects of overgrown organizations. Industries in which scale diseconomies are counterbalanced by other increasing returns mechanisms, then, may begin to head toward the extreme of a single winner. The increasing returns mechanisms capable to offset scale diseconomies are usually related to technological progress, so in what follows we analyze other major causes of the growth of the firm, namely, the Schumpeterian loop, cost reducing learning, learning-bydoing, learning-by-using, and demand-side increasing returns.

The Evolutionary Economics and The Schumpeterian Loop

The most widely accepted theory of technological change among neoclassical economists is Schumpeter's. In a Schumpeterian world, scale economies are present as well, but technology is not a constant. Here the creative role of the entrepreneurs allows for the introduction of new technologies capable to displacing the establish ones. Most of Schumpeter's discussion stresses the advantages of concentrated market structures involving large firms with considerable market share. According to this economist, it is more probable that the necessary scale economies in R&D to develop new technologies be achieved by a monopolist or by the few large firms of a concentrated industry. Large size firms, besides, may increase their rate of innovation by reducing the speed at which their transient rents and entrepreneurial advantage are eroded away by imitators. In the absence of patent protection large firms may exploit their innovations on a large scale over relatively short periods of time -and in this way avoid rapid imitation by competitors- by deploying their productive, marketing and financial capabilities. Large firms may also expand their rate of innovation by imitating and commercializing other firms' technologies.

Among the economists following Schumpeter's lead, Nelson and Winter (1978, 1982) stand out for having formalized and completed many of Schumpeter's original intuitions. Whereas the connection between industrial structure and innovation has been viewed by Schumpeter as going primarily from the former to the latter, in Nelson and Winter (1978, 1982) there is a reverse causal flow, too.[10] That is, there is clearly a circular causality - that is to say, a self-reinforcing mechanism between the innovations and the firm's growth. Using this source of increasing return, they describe the evolution of the concentration of industrial structure in the following terms:

Under a regime of Schumpeterian competition, temporary supranormal profits are the reward to successful innovation. To the extent that growth is keyed to profitability, successful innovators grow relative to other firm. If a firm is a successful innovator frequently enough, or if one of its innovations is dominant enough, the consequences of successful innovation may be a highly concentrated industrial structure. In this sense, a clear 'winner' may emerge from the competitive struggle (p. 525).

Further on, they conclude:

Schumpeterian competition is, like most processes we call competitive, a process that tends to produce winners and losers. Some firms track emerging technological opportunities with greater success than other firms; the former tend to prosper and grow, the latter to suffer losses and decline. Growth confers advantages that make further success more likely, while decline breeds technological obsolescence and further decline. As these processes operate through time, there is a tendency for concentration to develop even in an industry initially composed of many equal-sized firms (p. 541).

Evolutionary economists define innovation very broadly. It encompasses the introduction of new products and production processes, opening up of new markets, and acquisition of new sources of raw material. They also describe the nature of technological progress as succession of major discontinuities detached from the past and with quite transitory life span. This process of change is characteristic of certain industries, but it is not the sole kind of technological change. Technological change can also be *continuous*. That is to say, technologies improve constantly in absolute terms after their introduction. The view of technological progress as a continuing, steady accumulation of innumerable minor improvements and modifications, with only very infrequent major innovations, has two sources: (1) the accumulation of knowledge that makes possible to produce a greater volume of output from a given amount of resources and (2) the accumulation of knowledge that allows the production

---

[10] In the early literature on the relationship between technology and market structure there was no agreement on whether the direction of causation ran from concentration to R&D intensity or vice versa. The debate faded out in the late 1970s with the widespread acceptance of the view that both concentration and innovation are endogenous and should be simultaneously determined within the model (Phillips 1971, Dasgupta and Stiglitz 1980a,b, 1981, Dasgupta 1986). Nelson and Winter (1982) stand out not only for having recognized the endogenous character of innovation and market structure, but also for having pointed out and modeled the mutual causality between technical change and market structure.

of a qualitatively superior output from a give amount of resources. The former source of technological progress is result of a cost *reducing learning process*, while the second category is the result of what is known as *learning-by-doing and learning-by-using*. Given that both categories of technological progress are important determinants of the number and size of firms in a given industry, we analyze them in the next sections.

Costs Reducing Learning

An important aspect of technological change is costs reducing in nature. Porter (1980) and Henderson (1975), in the strategic field, pioneered the notion of experience curve as a source of costs reductions. In economics, Hirsch (1956) has underlined the importance of repetitive manufacturing operations as a way of reducing direct labor requirements, while Arrow (1962) has explored the consequences of learning-by-doing (measured by the cumulative gross investment, which produces a steady rate of growth in productivity) on profits, investment, and economic growth. However, the historical study on the patterns of growth and competitiveness of large corporations of Chandler (1990) is a major and detailed contribution to our understanding of the way firms grow by diminishing costs.

Large corporations, according to Chandler, along with the few challengers that subsequently enter the industry, do not compete primarily on the basis of price. Instead they compete for market share and profits through functional and strategic effectiveness. They compete functionally by improving their products, their processes of production, their marketing, their purchasing, and their labor relations. Big corporations compete strategically by moving into growing markets more rapidly and effectively than do their competitors. Such rivalry for market share and profits make more effective the enterprise's functional and strategic capabilities, which, in turn, provide the internal dynamic for continuing growth of the enterprise. In particular, it stimulates its owners and managers to expand into distant markets in its own country and then to become multinational by moving abroad. It also encourages the firm to diversify and become multiproduct by developing and introducing products in markets other than the original ones.

Manufacturing enterprises become larger owing to its investment in new operating units. It then becomes critical to explain how and why the firm became multifunctional, multiregional and multiproduct. Chandler (1990) argues that the modern industrial enterprise rarely continues to grow or maintain its competitive position over an extended period of time unless the addition of new units actually permits hierarchy to reduce costs; to improve functional efficiency in production, marketing, and purchasing; to ameliorate existing products and develop new ones; and to allocate resources to meet the challenges and opportunities of over-changing technologies and markets. Such process of growth provides this bureaucratic institution with the internal dynamic that makes it maintain its position of dominance.

Reductions in costs and efficient resource utilization result from the exploitation of economies of scale in production and distribution, scope economies (exploitation of joint production and joint distribution), and decreases of transaction costs. Economies of scale in Chandler's analysis differ from those of conventional economics. Economies of scale in Chandler's world are those that result when the increased size and efficiency of a single operating unit producing or distributing a single product reduces the unit cost of production or distribution of that product. In the older, labor-intensive industries, Chandler (1990) says, where traditional scale economies are prevalent, higher levels of output came primarily by adding more machines and more workers. In newer industries, expanded output comes by a drastic change in capital-labor ratios; that is, by improving and rearranging inputs; by using new and greatly improved machinery, furnaces, stills, and other equipment; by reorienting the processes of production within the plant; by placing the several intermediary processes employed in making a final product within a single works; and by increasing the application of energy.

The economies of joint production and distribution (scope economies) also bring significant cost reductions. Here cost advantages come from making a number of products in the same production unit from much the same raw and semifinished materials and by the same intermediate process. The increase in the number of products produced simultaneously in the same factory reduces the unit costs of each individual product. These potential costs advantages, however, cannot be fully realized unless a constant flow of materials through the plant factory is maintained to assure effective capacity utilization. If the realized volume of flow falls below capacity, then actual costs per unit rise rapidly. In the capital-intensive industries the throughput needed to maintain minimum efficient scale requires careful coordination not only of the flow of production but also of the flow of inputs from suppliers and the flow of outputs to intermediaries and final users. When manufacturer's volume attains a scale that reduces the cost of transporting, storing, and distributing products, it becomes more advantageous for the manufacturer himself to make the investment in product-specific purchasing, marketing, and distribution facilities.

Coordination cannot happen automatically. It demands the constant attention of managerial team or hierarchy. This step is done by recruiting and organizing of the managers needed to supervise functional activities pertaining to production and distribution of products; coordination and monitoring the flow of goods through the production process; and resources allocation for future production and distribution. Scale and scope economies depend, to a great extent, on knowledge, skill, experience, and teamwork of managers; that is, on the organizational human capabilities essential to exploit the potential of technological processes.

Once the investment in production and distribution is large enough to exploit fully economies of scale and scope, and once the necessary managerial hierarchy is in place, the industrial enterprise grows by acquiring or merging with enterprises. Another way to grow is by taking on units involved in the early or later stages of making products, from processing raw material to the final assembling or packing. The third way of growth is to expand geographically to distant areas. The fourth is to make new products that are related to firm's existing technologies or markets. The initial motive for the first two strategies of growth is usually defensive: to protect the firm's existing investment. As for the other two strategies, firms use their existing investments and above all their existing organizational capabilities to move into new markets and into new business.

Although the barriers to entry raised by a first mover's investment seem intimidating, challengers do appear. They enter a given industry most often when rapid demographic changes alter existing markets and when technological change creates new markets and diminishes old ones. But in those industries where scale or scope provide cost advantages, the number of players remain small and there is little turnover among the leaders. These industries quickly become and remain oligopolistic and occasionally monopolistic. It is clear, therefore, that accumulated experience in production, organization and distribution -cost reducing learning- is another factor that reduces considerably the perverse effects of negative feedback caused by scale diseconomies, otherwise firms would not have incentives to add new units to their established organizational structure.

Learning-by-doing

An important part of the literature on business competition assumes that firms compete mainly in cost-reducing competitive advantages, especially those achieved through scale economies, scope economies, and innovations in production and organizational processes. In this literature technical progress is implicitly treated as the introduction of new processes that reduce costs of producing essentially *unchanging* products. Notwithstanding, there is a category of learning known as *learning-by-doing* (Rosenberg 1982), which enhances the qualitative aspects of final products.[11]

Western industrial societies today, Rosenberg (1982) argues, enjoy a higher level of material welfare not merely because they consume larger per capita

---

[11] Rosenberg (1982) was not the first theorist in analyzing the nature and consequences of learning-by-doing: in Hirsch (1956), learning (the performance of repetitive manufacturing operations) is associated to improvements in efficiency due to constant reductions of direct labor requirements that result from cumulative output. In Arrow (1962), learning-by-doing is interpreted as an accumulation of gross investment or production capital goods. But it is to Rosenberg (1982) to whom it should be attributed the introduction of that kind of learning which allows the firm to produce constantly improving products. Learning for producing larger quantities of unchanging products to a lower cost is essentially different from learning for producing qualitatively better products.

amounts of the goods available. They have also made available improving forms of rapid transportation, instant communication, powerful energy sources, life-saving and pain-reducing medications, and other goods that were undreamed of one or two centuries ago. Therefore, ignoring product innovation and quality improvements in products is to overlook what well has been on of the most important long-term contributions of technical progress to human welfare. Many products, such as beverages, toothpaste, soap, clothing, VCRs, TV sets can be subject to improvements. Such improvements, however, are marginal when compared with the amazing rate of development that other products and technologies can reach. Automobiles, aircraft, flight simulators, computers, and nuclear reactors are very complex technologies and, as a consequence of this, have a tremendous capacity of being enhanced. Consequently, the competitive behavior of the firms that produce these technologies consists not only of the innovative acts they perform to improve production, organizational, and distribution processes, but also from the efforts to improve constantly their products.

To exclude product innovation from technical progress, especially when we are considering long historical periods, means also to neglect one of the main forces reducing the impact of negative feedback and, consequently, one of the primary propellers of the number and growth of the firm. All growing industries eventually experience a slowdown in growth as the impact of costs-reducing learning diminishes. Continued rapid growth, therefore, can only come from other sources of increasing returns such as leaning-by-doing. Ford, for example, keeps its dominant market position in the world automobile industry not only for the application of costs-reducing innovations -such as the application of mass-production to manufacture the T Model at the beginning of this century-, but also for qualitative improvements incorporated into its final products. If this company had continued producing T model cars, eventually it would have had to go out from the industry, even though it had considerably improved its original mass-production process. In fact, one of the main failures that Henry Ford committed was to have trusted heavily in his production process. Afterward, when GM started producing better and a larger variety of automobiles, Ford had to turn to product innovations and qualitative improvements of products and use them as strategic weapon to survive in the industry. Learning-by-doing seems to be overwhelmingly more powerful than scale diseconomies in the automobile industry, since for decade this increasing returns mechanism has made its companies and its level of concentration grow constantly.

Learning-by-using

With respect to a given product, Rosenberg (1982) distinguish between that kind of learning that is internal to the production process (learning-by-doing) and that which is generated as a result of subsequent use of that product (learning-by-using). The later category of learning begins only after a certain new product is used. In an economy where complex new technologies are common, there are essential aspects of learning that are a function not of the experience involved in producing a product but of its use by the final consumer.

The optimal performance of durable goods (especially complex systems of interacting components) often is achieved only after intensive and prolonged use. In the aircraft industry, for instance, the attainment of high standards of reliability is a major concern, in particular during the development stage. But it is only through extensive use of aircraft by airlines that faults are discovered and eliminated and detailed knowledge about metal fatigue, weight capacity, fuel consumption of engines, fuselage durability, minimum servicing, overhaul requirements, maintenance costs, instruction manuals, and so on is gained.

Demand-side Increasing Returns

In the economy there are increasing returns mechanisms that come from the demand side of the market, not just from supply side.[12] For the risk-averse and imperfectly informed consumer it becomes more attractive to adopt the widespread technology or product. Minimizing the risk of purchasing a defective technology or the cost of searching for an adequate one introduces a reputation or informational feedback that may produce a disproportionately high selection of the *best-selling* option.

Informational or reputation feedback occurs in the following situations. First, when the complexity of the technology or product in question is such that consumers try to reduce uncertainty by asking to previous purchasers their experience with these technologies (Arthur and Lane 1993). Second, in other situations the source of uncertainty is not the complexity of the technology, but the large quantity of options the consumers face. For instance, no person has the time to see all films or theater plays, to attend all concerts, to read all books, or to listen all recordings available in the market place (?). One is forced to choose, and the best way to do so is by confine one's attention to the best-sellers lists, which are not necessarily the best. Third, in a market where the quality or value of a product is defined on the basis of arbitrary and short-living conventions, rather than strictly on the basis of lasting objective value, consumers usually tend to follow the expert's opinion. This kind of easy-to-manipulate, reputation-driven market success is typical of markets for highly symbolic products (e.g., many art markets, fashion wear and luxury items),

---

[12] Network externalities should be considered as part of demand-side increasing returns, for they breed the growth of the firms. Network externalities, however, play a more important role at the level of inter-technology competition, so we study them in the next section.

which also will result in a disproportionately high selection of one of the options. Finally, the most preeminent and common kind of reputation effects in the economy, arise plainly as a result of a well-timed and very aggressive advertising campaign. This self-reinforcing mechanism -and the lasting market dominance that it causes- might be quite unrelated to relative added value, but it certainly might produce an excessive predilection for one of the options.

3 Technological Competition

The increasing returns mechanisms described so far go a long way to explain the way firms grow and how industrial structure evolves. Its intrinsic logic is that, when increasing returns mechanisms are present in a market and palpably perceived by an analyst, it is possible to establish a positive relationship between efficiency and skewed industrial structures. This model, however, offers only a partial explanation of the market process, for they take on a ergodic view of technological diffusion, competition, and substitution. In an ergodic markets technologies are stand-alone, relatively inexpensive to develop, and easy to appraise, use, appropriate. In a ergodic market, therefore, strategic resources markets and product markets are isomorphic and technological transition from an old to a new technology is not subject to inertial forces. However, it has been shown that in the presence of increasing returns to adoption markets can become rather tipping (Arthur 1994, Katz and Shapiro 1985, Farrell and Garth 1985). In this kind of markets competition among several comparable technologies or standards may evolve in such a way that the market share of one of the technologies increases and approaches 100 per cent, while other technologies are excluded from the market and technological substitution is subject to strong inertial forces. Two increasing returns mechanisms are the causes of these kind of situations: infrastructure effects and network externalities.

Infrastructure

Effects It is common that, as technologies are adopted, compatible complementary technologies, sub-technologies, and services, become part of their infrastructure. Infrastructure gives core technologies a self-reinforcing advantage in the sense that other less adopted technologies may lack the needed infrastructure. For instance, automobiles, to reach their highest value, require an extensive system of roads. Another automobile complement for driving gas-powered cars is fuel (gasoline), which needs to be available through drive-in gas stations, particularly along roads and highway. Additionally, "compatible" care and maintenance also require being at hand. Thus, the availability of both expertise and products for auto repair increase the value of cars.

Network Externalities

When several products have to be compatible with each other in order to
be functional, they form a network. Similarly, when several persons have to
coordinate their choices in order for those choices to be optimal, those people
are part of a network. In very general terms, network effects[13] are the advantages or disadvantages that accrue to a group of people for having made
coordinated (or simply similar) choices. Network effects can arise from physical interconnections -as in the case of telecommunication networks- or from
very intangible, though no less real, interdependencies -as in the case of the
companies and consumers forming the VCR network. Network effects can be
positive (as when many of my friends and acquaintances buy a lot of land
near my country place) or negative (as when many of my friends and acquaintances buy the very same tie I just bought). Positive network effects
may result from direct or indirect network externalities. Direct externalities
increase the added value of a spreading technology, individual skill, or social
conventions immediately and in direct proportion to its rate of diffusion. They
are typical of telecommunication technologies (the more people buy faxes the
more useful each fax will be, since there will be more people who can contact
each other using the fax) and also of tacit skills (the more people learn to
use Qwerty keyboards -or to speak English- the more my knowledge of that
particular keyboard -or language-will be useful, since the easier it will be to
find a Qwerty keyboard -or an English speaker). The basic element common
to all direct network externalities is the possibility of some sort of direct exchange or interaction between adopters. Indirect externalities, on the other
hand, have nothing to do with interactions between adopters. They work instead via the positive impact of the diffusion of a core technology or skill upon
the availability of complementary products or services (the more people buy a
Windows-compatible computer, the more software will be developed for that
computer format and the more useful Windows computers will be).[14] Just as
scale economies, learning, or reputation effects, positive network externalities

---

[13] Since our discussion does not concern general welfare considerations, we shall follow the convention of using the terms "network effect" and "network externality"
indistinctively, thus ignoring Liebowitz and Margolis' plea in favor of reserving the
latter term for those cases where there has been a clear market failure (Liebowitz
and Margolis, 1994).

[14] Some networks are subject to both direct and indirect externalities. For example,
the more people learn to speak English, the more people I can communicate
with, but also the more "third-party software" (textbooks, novels, magazines,
movies, songs, etc.) in English will be developed. The same applies to content
and/or software-intensive telecommunication technologies such as the television,
the radio and the Internet.

result in a self-reinforcing diffusion dynamic. Network effects[15], however, differ from the other self-reinforcing mechanisms in several important respects: First, while the benefits of scale economies, learning and (some) reputation effects can only be reaped at the time of purchasing the product in question, most of the benefits accruing from network externalities can be enjoyed well past the point of purchase and throughout the entire life cycle of the product. Second, network effects are considerably forward looking and less bounded and therefore more powerful than scale and learning effects. In fact, because they cast a shadow into the future, network effects can combine with reputation effects to create extremely powerful and lasting self-reinforcing dynamics in market success. Since most of the benefits accruing from network externalities can be enjoyed throughout the full life cycle of a product, new users faced with a multiplicity of competing technical options will have to make their choices not simply in function of what the majority of past purchasers have already chosen, but also in function of what the majority of future users are likely to choose. Interestingly, while very pessimistic user expectations about an overall emerging market can be self-dampening, optimistic expectations about the success of a specific technical format in a battle of standards could easily become self-fulfilling. The greater the number of people who think that a given technical option is likely to become dominant, the more new users will side with it and the more likely and pronounced the dominance will in fact become.[16] Third, while scale economies and learning can only be a source of increasing returns to adoption and while users' learning costs (or switching costs) can exclusively be a source of inertia, both reputation effects and network externalities, in contrast, can act as both strong inertial and increasing returns to adoption.

---

[15] Since our discussion does not concern general welfare considerations, we shall follow the bulk of literature in using the terms "network effect" and "network externality" indistinctively, thus ignoring Liebowitz and Margolis' plea in favor of reserving the latter term for those cases where there has been a clear market failure (Liebowitz and Margolis, 1994).

[16] Back in the early 80s, some people may have bought an IBM PC or developed software for it, on the immediate merit of what the machine offered vis-à-vis the Apple II and others. But most people who bought an IBM PC, or developed software for it, at that early stage did so because, sensing that a winner-takes-all battle of standards was looming, they naturally wanted to minimize their risk of being left with an orphan product and they figured that the IBM machine (not because it was the best possible product, but because it was backed by IBM) stood a better chance than Apple's, or any other, of becoming the dominant choice. Since the people who reasoned thus were sufficiently numerous, both among users and among software developers, they triggered a buy-and-support IBM bandwagon which (helped as well by Apple's considerable mistakes) turned their expectations into a reality.

4 A General Model of Business Competition

The idea of technological progress as a facilitator of economic growth and improved welfare was advanced long before economists became concerning with measuring its impact. It remained, however, for Schumpeter (1942) to suggest the distinction between price-taking firms and perfect competition markets and those firms and industries most favorable to rapid technological progress. In Schumpeter's view atomistic firms competing in a perfect competition industry is a suitable means for static resource allocation, but the large firm operating in concentrated markets was the *"most powerful engine of progress and ... long-run expansion of total output"* (Schumpeter 1942). Schumpeter's thesis encouraged a large body of empirical literature in the field of industrial organization. Most of this literature focused on two hypotheses associated with Schumpeter's assertion: (1) innovation increases more than proportionally with firm size and (2) innovation increases with market concentration.

The most authoritative review of the empirical evidence of the relationship between innovation and firm size and market structure is Cohen and Richard (1989). These authors observe that the empirical results on the Schumpeterian relation are accurately described as fragile. They note that the lack of robust results seems to arise in part from the inappropriate attention to the dependence of these relationships on more fundamental conditions. From their overview Cohen and Richard (1989) draw the basic methodological lesson that the omission of important and potentially correlated variables that influence innovation can lead to misleading inferences concerning firm size and concentration. *"A clear implication, Cohen and Levin (1989: 1078) conclude, is that further evaluation of the Schumpeterian hypotheses should take in the context of a more complete model of the determinants of technological progress"*.

In this paper we move beyond the Schumpeterian hypotheses and focus on a more complete model of business competition. Specifically, we have identified other fundamental determinants that affect the mutual link between firm size and market structure. These determinants -which in our analysis takes the form of increasing returns mechanisms- are usually studied as if they work independently from the other. But there are not many cases of industries where one single mechanism acts in isolation from the other sources of increasing returns. Therefore, the growth of the firm and the evolution of skewed industrial structure, more than the result of a single a self-reinforcing mechanism, are the effect of the combination of the several sources of increasing returns, which overlap and feed back upon one another.

The analysis so far done has gradually recognized the central role of increasing returns mechanism in generating and sustaining dominant firms and technologies. As depicted in figure 2, the unification of the resource-based loop, the Schumpeterian loop, scale economies, the different categories of learning, and demand-side increasing returns (reputation) -loops A, B and C, respectively, in figure 2- constitutes a simple but useful model quite capable to explain in an endogenous, dynamic way the number and growth of firms in a given industrial, and, in a wider context, the gap in economic performance which is often said to exist among economies. In the model sketched in figure 2 the positive relationship that runs from industrial structure to efficiency operates through the accumulation of rare resources, innovations, scale economies, reputation, and the different aspects of learning.

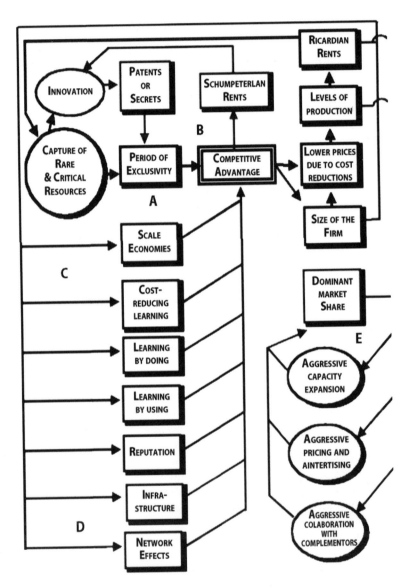

Fig. 2. Increasing Returns-Based Model of Business Competition.

This dynamics, over time, makes costs fall as learning accumulates, new technologies are developed and improved, and firm-specific factors are amassed and exploited due to output increases. As a result of this mutual causality, market share and production levels increase, price falls, profitability rises, with which relatively profitable firms expand continually while unprofitable ones contract uninterruptedly. A set of loops (D), composed of a mesh of scale economies, learning, reputation effects, infrastructure effects, and network effects, links increasing competitive advantages with increasing returns to market share. A last set of loops (E) indicates that, if increasing returns to adoption are present and considerable, market share becomes a strategic asset well worth investing on in an aggressive manner through vigorous production capacity expansion, price reductions, infrastructure development, and alliances with manufacturer of complementary technologies, products, and services.

An interesting aspect of this preliminary model, therefore, is that it offers an endogenous explanation of the number and size of firms. In contrasts with the traditional economic views -that see industrial structure (number of firms) as an exogenous variable and assume homogenous firms- and the strategic paradigms -which are focused first and foremost in explaining heterogeneity among firms within a industry-, our preliminary model recognizes that the strategies choices and acts of the firms have an effect not only on the performance and size of the firm itself, but also on the structure of market. Then, as depicted in figure 3, in the general model causality run not only from conduct to performance and from performance to the size of the firm, but also from the later to industrial structure. Technological adoption goes between conduct and performance in the chain of causality because it affects the firm's performance, but under the presence of infrastructure effects and network externalities, technological adoption does not depend on the conduct of the firm.

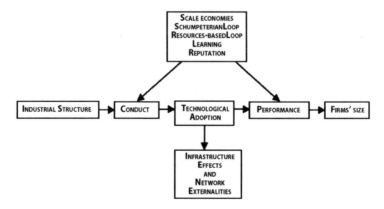

Fig. 3. Revision to the Traditional Industrial Approaches.

Obviously, other economists have suggested models where industrial structure is endogenous, but they do it by establishing a relationship between industrial structure and innovation or industrial structure and cost reductions and so on (Nelson and Winter 1982, Dasgupta and Stiglitz 1980a, Chandler 1990). In our general model, in contrast, industrial structure is caused by a combination of various increasing returns mechanism. Here, then, the combination of accumulation of resources, product innovation, scale economies, costs reducing learning, learning-by-doing, learning-by-using, or reputation enhances the performance of the firm and determine, to great extent, the level of skewness of the structure of the industry where it competes.

Another relevant aspect of the structural determinants of the number and size of firms in an industry suggested in this model is that, when one of them is exhausted, causing a slowdown in the growth of the firm, the other mechanisms may be activated, which may allow for a further period of continued rapid growth. When the firms of a given industry are capable to create and accumulate firm-specific resources, innovations, costs reducing learning, qualitative product improvements based on learning-by-doing and learning-by-using, and reputation, these firms usually use them as strategic weapon. In doing so, they are capable not only to neutralize but also to overwhelm the negative effects of complex, overgrown, hard-to-manage organizational structures that arise from their constant growth. The process can take a long period of time, but eventually the sources of increasing returns can drive the markets toward increasingly skewed industrial structures.

For instance, in the commercial aircraft industry competition principally involves considerable development costs continuous improvements in aircraft models, technology and product support, so this industry exhibits substantial scale economies, large scope for learning-by-doing, learning-by-using , and reputation effects. Because of this, the commercial aircraft industry has been characterized by an increasing skewed industrial structure. Recently, the structure of this industry, after the acquisition of McDonnell-Douglas by Boeing, was reduced to a monopoly in the United States . In the world aircraft market Boeing only competes with European Airbus. It is obvious that the merge of the two main manufacturers of the American aircraft industry should have brought about some gain in efficiency, which counterbalanced the diseconomies owing to the managing a more complex organization. Otherwise, the merge would not have taken place or would have been the result of irrational behavior.

The structure of some industries does not seem to head toward monopoly. However, over time, their level of concentration has increased substantially. The world automobile industry, for instance, in 1970 was composed of at least 40 major competitors. In 1998, with some merges and acquisitions, the number of the main manufacturer was reduced to 17 . Because of the large possibilities to accumulate cost reducing learning and the large scope for qualitative product improvements in the world automobile industry, both the number and the homogeneity of the firms competing in this industry are expected to decrease even further in the future. Here, again, benefits due to both costs reducing learning and qualitative product innovations brought about by merges and acquisitions are larger that any cost created by scale diseconomies.

5 The General Model of Business Competition as a Revision to Conventional Microeconomics

Our analysis would not be complete without a contrast between the results of our analysis and that of the standard economic theory. In offering such contrast, we hope to clarify the relevance of particular contributions of our general model and offer further systematization and order to its doctrine. For any fortuitous observer, most modern industrial sectors are clear counterexamples of the kind of industries that neoclassical theory describes. The insights generated by the dominant mode of theorizing in conventional economics have not been capable to bridge the vast gulf that separates its mechanic, atomistic approach from the real business world, because they just ignore the characteristics of most economic sectors. And in doing so, they simply assume away all sources of increasing returns. But if the assumptions of the decreasing returns economics are relaxed so as to embrace and bring together the forces causing the emergence of dominant firm, skewed industrial structures, and technological monopoly, the result is not only general model of business competition, but a rather complete increasing returns microeconomic theory that explains satisfactorily the increasing returns economy.

With little exaggeration we can assert that such increasing returns economics is a satisfactory revision to the conventional decreasing returns economics, because it de-emphasize the assumptions of competitive markets and seeks instead to understand the economic mechanisms that visibly shape the attributes of the business world. By far the most simplifying assumption of conventional economics is to take technology as given. The general model of business competition includes innovative improvements in the way of doing things. Here distribution, organizational, and production enhancements and other aspects of technological change -which are pervasive aspects of reality- are explicit.

In standard economics, the firm is a black box -which transforms unchangeable factors of production through unchangeable production functions into unchangeable outputs-, so the boundaries of the firm thus lie outside the domain of the traditional economic analysis. In the general model of business competition, the internal structure of the firm can be modified by its conduct through an accumulative process of experience and learning. The different learning regimes to which the firm may be subject shape not only the changing and complex organizational structure of the firm, but also the industrial structure where it competes.

Conventional economics also assumes that firms produce homogeneous products. This implies that products are not subject to improvements. Product homogeneity also means that products are stand-alone and independent from other products and complementary infrastructure. In reality many products are constantly improved and complement each other. This causes powerful mechanisms that explain the behavior of many firms and the structure of an important number of industries, especially those characterized by technological monopolies.

Decreasing returns economics vs. increasing return economy

Decreasing-returns Economics Assumptions	In Reality	Increasing-Return Mechanism
Independent, rational, perfectly-informed individuals	Products require special knowledge and skill to be used them appropriately	Reputation effects
	Individuals' decisions depend on other individuals' to minimize risk and information costs	Demand-side increasing returns
Products are homogeneous, stand-alone and not subject to further improvement	Products are subject to improvements	Learning-by-doing and learning-by-doing
	Products require to be interconnected to other products and compatibility to function correctly	Network effects
	Products require complementary sub-technologies	Infrastructure effects
The production function is subject to decreasing returns Inputs (K and L) cannot be enhanced Technological change is exogenous Firm is a black box Transactions are frictionless and instantaneous	Production requires large investments	Scale economies
	Production processes, marketing (distribution and advertising), and the organizational structure of the firm are driven by cumulative knowledge and skills	Cost reducing learning

The fact that individuals' decision concerning the purchase of a product depends on the decision of other individual is another distortion that conventional economics cannot handle in an appropriate way. Product complexity, indeterminate outcomes of technological competition, product abundance, etc. challenge the characterization of rationality of conventional economics. In the general model these distortion are accurately captured within the increasing returns mechanisms that, both on the supply and the demand side, are produced by economic agents seeking to reduce risk and information costs. All these results are summarized in table 1.

Finally, conventional economics provides limited prescription power, let alone prediction. Its theoretical structure erected on so narrow and shallow factual and empirical foundations provides few tools to make operational predictions and to deal with a large range of strategic management issues. Our general model, in contrast, presents an intellectual framework for explaining a large number of industrial situations at different phases of business competition.

6 Business competition as a self-organizing process

The general model suggested in this article, is a more realistic representation of the business competition process and subject to the basic notions of far-from equilibrium thermodynamics as developed by Prigogine (1976). Business competition is a dissipative structure because it is a thermodynamically open system and a self-organizing process because it develops, without central control, structure of increasing complexity from nonlinear interdependencies among its components. Such reinterpretation, however, takes a different, more elaborated path. In contrast to the typical interpretation, which considers that market coordination takes its self-organization form from innovation and the generation of new knowledge, the general model of business competition is self-organizing in character not just for the production and accumulation of innovations and knowledge, but from the complex combination and interdependence of various increasing returns mechanisms.

References

Arrow, K.: 1962, The economic implications of learning by doing, *Review of Economic Studies* **29**, 155–173.

Arthur, W.: 1994, *Increasing Returns and Path Dependence in the Economy*, The University of Michingam Press.

Arthur, W. and Lane, D.: 1993, Information contagion, *Structural Change and Economic Dynamics* **4**(1), 81–104.

Barney, J.: 1986, Strategic factor markets: Expectations, luck, and business strategy, *Management Science* **32**(10), 1231–1241.

Barney, J.: 1989, Asset stock and sustained competitive advantages, *Journal of Management* **35**(12), 1511–1513.

Barney, J.: 1991, Firm resources and sustained competitive advantages, *Journal of Management* **17**(1), 99–120.

Barney, J.: 1992, Integrating organizational behavior and strategy formulation research: a resource based analysis, *Advances in Strategic Management* **8**, 39–61.

Buzzell, R.: 1981, Are there natural market structure?, *Journal of Marketing* **45**, 42–45.

Carter, J.: 1978, Collusion, efficiency and anti-trust, *Journal of Law and Economics* pp. 435–444.

Chandler, A.: 1966, *Strategy and Structure*, Anchor Books Edition.

Chandler, A.: 1990, *Scale and Scope: Dynamics of Industrial Capitalism*, The Belknap Press of Harvard University Press.

Cohen, W. and Richard, C.: 1989, Empirical studies of innovation and market structure, *in* R. Schmalensee and R. Willing (eds), *Handbook of Industrial Organization*, North-Holland.

Conner, K.: 1991, A historical comparison of resource-based theory and five schools of thought within industrial organization economics: Do we have a new theory of the firm?, *Journal of Management* **17**(1), 121–154.

Dasgupta, P.: 1986, The theory of technological competition, *in* J. Stiglitz and M. G.F. (eds), *New Developments in the Analysis of Market Structure*, MIT Press.

Dasgupta, P. and Stiglitz, J.: 1980a, Industrial structure and the nature of innovation activity, *Economic Journal* **90**, 266–293.

Dasgupta, P. and Stiglitz, J.: 1980b, Uncertainty, industrial structure and the speed of r&d, *Bell Journal of Economics* pp. 1–28.

Dasgupta, P. and Stiglitz, J.: 1981, Entry, innovation, exit: Towards a dynamic theory of industrial structure, *European Economic Review* **15**, 137–158.

Dierickx, I. and Karel, C.: 1989, Asset stock accumulation and sustainability of competitive advantage, *Management Science* **35**(12), 1504–1511.

Eatwell, J.: 1971, Growth, profitability and size: the empirical evidence, pp. 389–421.

Evans, D.: 1987, Test of alternative theories of firm growth, *Journal of Political Economy* **95**(4), 657–674.

Farrell, J. and Garth, S.: 1985, Standardization, compatibility and innovation, *Randal Journal of Economics* **16**(1).

Foss, N., Christian, K. and Montgomery, C.: 1995, An exploration of common ground: Integrating evolutionary and strategic theories of the firm, montgomery edn.

Grant, R.: 1991, The resource-based theory of competitive advantage: Implications for strategy formulation, *California Management Review* pp. 114–135.

Hart, P. and Prais, S.: 1956, *Journal Royal Statistics Society* **A1**(19), 150–181.

Henderson, B.: 1975, The market share paradox, *The Competitive Economy*, General Learning Press, pp. 286–287.

Hirsch, W.: 1956, Firm progress ratios, *Econometrica* **24**(2), 136–143.

Hymer, S. and Pashigian, P.: 1962, Firm size and rate of growth, *Journal of Political Economics* **70**, 556–569.

Ijiri, Y. and Simon, H.: 1964, Business firm growth and size, *American Economic Review* **54**, 77–89.

Katz, M. and Shapiro, C.: 1985, Network externalities, competition and compatibility, *American Economic Review* **75**(3), 424–440.

Layard, P. and Walters, A.: 1978, *Microeconomics Theory*, McGrow-Hill.

Lucas, R.: 1978, On the size distribution of business firms, *Bell Journal of Economics* **9**, 508–523.

Mahoney, J.: 1992, Organizational economics within the conversation of strategic management, *Advances in Strategic Management* **8**, 103–155.

Minztberg, H. e. a.: 1994, *Strategy Safari: A Guided Tour through the Wilds of Strategy Management*, Simon And Schuster.

Montgomery, C.: 1995, *Resource-Based and Evolutionary Theories of the Firm: Towards a Synthesis*, Kluwer Academic Publisher.

Nelson, R. and Winter, S.: 1978, Forces generating and limiting concentration under schumpeterian competition, *Bell Journal of Economics* p. 524.

Nelson, R. and Winter, S.: 1982, An evolutionary theory of economic change, *Harward University Press* .

Peltzman, S.: 1977, The gains and losses for industrial concentration, *Journal of Law and Economics* pp. 229–263.

Penrose, E.: 1959, *The Theory of the Growth of the Firm*, Blackwell.

Peteraf, M.: 1993, The cornerstone of competitive advantage: a resource-based view, *Strategic Management Journal* **14**, 179–191.

Phillips, A.: 1971, *Technology and Market Structure: a Study of the Aircraft Industry*, Reading Mass.

Porter, M.: 1980, *Competitive Strategy*, Free Press.

Prigogine, I.: 1976, Order through fluctuations: Self-organization and social system, *Evolution and Consciousness*, Addison-Wesley.

Quandt, R.: 1970, On the size distribution of firms, *American Economic Review* **56**, 416–432.

Rosenberg, N.: 1982, *Inside the Blasck Box: Technology and Economics*, Cambridge University Press.

Schumpeter, J.: 1942, *Capitalism, Socialism, and Democracy*, Harper.

Schumpeter, J.: 1949, *Change and the Entrepreneur*, Harvard University Press.

Shapiro, C. and Varian, H.: 1999, *Information Rules*, Harvard Business School Press.

Simon, H. and Bonini, C.: 1958, The size distribution of business firms, *American Economic Review* **48**, 607–617.

Vandermerwe, S.: 1999, *Customer Capitalism: A New Business Model of Increasing Returns in New Market Spaces*, Nicholas Brealey Publishing.

Varian, H.: 1978, *Microeconomic Analysis*, W.W. Norton.

Vining, D.: 1976, Autocorrelated growth rates and the pareto law: a further analysis, *Journal of Political Economy* **8**(2), 369–380.

Wernerfelt, B.: 1984, A resource-based view of the firm, *Strategic Management Journal* **5**, 171–180.

Wernerfelt, B.: 1989, From critical resources to corporate strategy, *Journal of General Management* **14**(3), 4–12.

Part III

Empirical Works

Detecting Structural Changes in the Italian Stock Market through Complexity

G12

(Italy)

A. Abatemarco

1 Introduction

The role and effect of structural changes in the economy, economic models and data generating processes has been the subject of vivid discussions in economics for a long time. In particular, the new difficulties arising in a globalized market economy have been the main source for a return of interest in this subject.

Leaving aside the impact and effects of structural changes, we mostly concentrate on the possibility for detection as well as the recognition of main sources. With the same objective in mind, most of the researchers have been focusing on the behaviour of crucial macroeconomic variables in presence of exogenous events (Stock and Watson 1996).[1] Especially econometric models, like in the neo-keynesian approach (Muellbauer 1978), and, auto-regressive ones, like time-varying ARCH model (Evans 1991) have been developed highlighting structural instabilities which characterize economic phenomena.

In this paper, we investigate the Italian stock market[2] in order to highlight the occurrence of structural changes by the use of analytical tools mostly used in econophysics.[3]

---

[1] Stock and Watson tested the relevance of stability and the current lack of systematic evidence on it through an assessment of those parameters which are expected to be relevant in order to explain the main behavior of economic time series and whether current state-of-art adaptive forecasting models capture the instability found by stability test.

[2] The Italian stock market has been analysed considering Mibtel's time series, which consists of a weighted media of all quoted shares. In order to test results, the same analysis has been run for the MIB30.

[3] "Econophysics is an interdisciplinary field of research applying methods from physics to analyse economic systems. This field has gained increased practical

Within the "financial fragility hypothesis" (Minsky 1977), Minsky (1986) investigates the high level of instability generated by high trading volumes. The more financially fragile is a specific economic system the smaller is the shock which may induce insolvency, which force it to change radically its financial behavior. This approach seems to suit particularly what happened in the Italian stock market at the end of the nineties, where the clearest abrupt change in trading volumes has occurred in the 1997.

In order to model this idea for our purposes we have to resort to a different concept of instability, structural instability. For our purposes, a system is intended as structurally unstable whenever in consequence of a small shock ε, it undergoes a sizeable and abrupt change in its functional and parametric structure which alters "qualitative" properties of its dynamic behaviour. Endogenous factors of the system's dynamics are not limited in this case to disequilibrium dynamics but include also the structural features of the system which may change beyond certain thresholds either in consequence of the endogenous dynamics or in consequence of a perturbation. In this sense the implementation of linear analytical tools would be useless, because they do not allow to deal with the main idea behind structural instabilities by construction.

By the empirical investigation it is highlighted that structural instabilities can be detected in the Italian stock market as a result of crucial changes in the Italian tax system on returns in the capital market.[4] In particular, a similar phenomenon is present in the existing literature about "coordination failures", by which it may be well the case that specific fiscal policies cause abrupt changes in sub-optimal equilibria (Cooper 1988). In this sense, recent

---

and theoretical interest in the recent years. From a theoretical viewpoint, it offers a fresh look at existing theories in finance. Due to the increased availability of high-frequency data, the need for new tools to analyze the data has become crucial" (Vercelli 2000). Recent studies have found that many financial market time series scale as fractals and behave as chaotic systems. Much of the methodology is explicitly derived from physics, so much so that the field has been called econophysics. Since fractals and chaos have been identified primarily in the physical sciences, there has been a tendency in this literature to assume that the mechanisms leading to fractality and chaoticity in financial markets are analogous. The parallels between physics and economics cannot be carried too far, however, since the structural equations used in econometric models do not posit the same causal mechanisms.

[4] In the 1996 a fiscal reform on the taxation of Certificate of Deposits has been approved, by which fiscal charge on returns from capital passed from a time-based structure (12,5% up to 12 months, 25% up to 18 months and 30% for larger times) to the unique rate of 27%. As a result, Certificate of Deposit (CD) which had represented the most relevant way to invest up to the fiscal reform, became a non convenient investment.

studies have been developed which take into account interrelations among public and financial sector (Crowder 1999, Alfano and Salzano 1998), where nonlinear and complex tools have been implemented.

This paper is organized as follows: in section 2 the main methodology which is implemented for our purposes is discussed. In section 3, evidences about the strong impact of the reform of tax system over capital returns, especially Certificates of Deposit (CD), is pointed out adopting complex tools, as phase-space, lyapunov exponents and NN approach. Also, the need for the recognition of structural breaks in economic data for forecasting purposes is stressed in line with Stock and Watson (1996), Trývez (1995) and Andrews (1993). Section 4 concludes.

2 Detecting Structural Changes

2.1 Approaches

The idea of financial instability, and even more clearly, the synonym financial fragility, evokes the idea of a possible sizeable and abrupt change in the functional and parametric structure of the unit which forces it to change the qualitative characteristics of its dynamic behaviour.

In the economic and statistic literature, several methodologies for the recognition of structural changes have been discussed. The most part of these contributes investigate the way structural changes affect forecasting, and as a result, economic control, using various techniques such as time varying vector autoregression models (e.g.,. Webb, 1995), Markov switching models (i.e., Evans & Wachtel, 1993) and genetic algorithms (e.g., Arifovic, 1995). More specifically, Clements and Hendry (1998) analysed the role of parameter instability and structural breaks in affecting the forecast performance of autoregressive models.

In many cases, statistical inference is applied, like in the Chow test, even if the main problem in this approach is still represented by the detection of the break point where measuring, estimating and comparing both estimates to see whether they are significally different. We think that structural instabilities, as they come from changes in people's behavior, need to be analysed mainly from a qualitative point of view. In this paper, because of the non-stationarity, non linearity (Guizzardi and Paruolo 1997) and chaoticity (Section 3) of the main Italian stock index a complex methodology is applied considering particularly analytic tools recently proposed in econophysics.

In the majority of cases linearization is not enough for describing main properties of control systems. Often the linear control is realized on the way from complex models to primitive behavior. The discovery of "self-organization" in many biological, chemical, economic and physical process adds some new features to traditional conceptions of control. However, self-organization or dissipative structures can be handled in nonlinear systems with chaotic dynamics by means of small external perturbations not under usual linearity as well as normality restrictions.

Dynamical chaos is a nonlinear phenomenon in principle. Control of chaos must be based on nonlinear principles. The above-mentioned "industrial" conception of control leads to large efforts in simplifying system dynamics. The desire to reduce these efforts and to take advantage of useful properties of chaotic dynamics requires revision of this conception. A new conception of controlling chaos and structural instability must be based on the principle of conversion from simple models to complex behavior. This is not possible without detailed analyses of nonlinear phenomena. Thus, we seek to analyse stock market price evolution using methods drawn from statistical physics.

The pathology of financial instability is usually represented in terms of progressive divergence from an equilibrium having optimal, or at least desirable, properties. However this view does not capture the essential features of financial fragility and of its influence on the economy, since it ignores i) structural changes induced by financial fragility to the financial structure and ii) the behaviour of agents and of the economy as a whole. Especially in the stock market orbits in the phase space rather than equilibria with optimal properties need to be considered.

Tsay (1988) identifies two types of outliers in high instability, additive (AO) or innovative, and structural changes as level shifts (LS) and variance changes (VC). Tsay's procedure[5] is labelled as an iterative one, which treats outliers, level shifts and variance changes in a unified manner by adopting a parametric approach to describe the exogenous disturbances using as basic variable the delay time. Modification in the delay time are recognized through a continuous an iterative control of parameters. The delay time is usually considered in chaos theory, especially for the reconstruction of the phase-space in a multidimensional nonlinear framework, and, in line with Tsay's studies, in this paper, it is labelled as highly explicative parameter in structural unstable scenarios.

---

[5] In presence of outliers the observed series might be disturbed and affected by unobservable events. In this case the actually observed series $\{Y_t\}$ should be described as $Y_t = f(t) + Z_t$ where f(t) is a parametric function representing the exogenous disturbances of the original observed series Z_t such as outliers or structure changes. Tsay considers different cases about f(t), explicating this function with an indicator variable describing the occurrence of a disturbance and the lag operator so that $LZ_t = Z_{t-1}$. So the difference among the two cases above of disturbance' effects in the economy depends basically on the variation of the lag operator. In the case of a parametric change which is respected during disturbances we are in front of a additive or innovative outliers, instead in the presence of functional changes when disturbances take the floor, i.e. $Y_t = Z_t$ at one time and $Y_t = w_{LC} + Z_t$ at the time of the disturbance, we have a level shift.

2.2 Phase-space, attractor, unstable periodic orbits

In the existing literature about structural changes, test of hypothesis is usually regarded as quantitative tool, while in this paper we propose a more qualitative approach, by which the main attention moves from quantitative differences between estimated parameters at break points to attraction zones and unstable periodic orbits.

In the study of equilibrium phenomena, phase-spaces display the fundamental quantitative and qualitative information on the systems. Similarly in non-equilibrium systems there is some search for the equivalent phase-space. For example in equilibrium cases, the basic phase-space depends on the interrelationship between gross variables, like GDP, interest rate and inflation. The fundamental ideas behind non-equilibrium state phase-spaces has already been identified in a dissipative system behavior, as each variable can represent the input to lead to level shifts.

In one-dimensional variable systems the map features can be related to the Lyapunov exponent behaviors, and to description of chaotic motions. In more complicated systems, this has led to the notion of embedding dimension for measuring the number of variables necessary to define a phase-space and of delay time to define what is usually said lag time. Embedding dimension and delay time are necessary in the reconstruction of the phase-space as discussed in the well-known Takens' Theorem (Takens 1981). In addition, as we will discuss later on, they represent a qualitative description of a time series, because of their conceptual meaning in endogenous growth cycles.

In a linear context, lag time is defined through a cross-correlation analysis, while in a nonlinear and non-stationary scenario, delay time is usually defined through the method of "mutual information"[6], which is a way to determine the best delay time for plotting attractors. The idea of delay coordinates is simple. If you can only observe one variable from a system, $X(t)$, and you want to reconstruct a higher-dimensional attractor, you can consider $\{X(t), X(t+T), ..., X(t+nT)\}$ to produce a $(n+1)$-dimensional coordinate

---

[6] The method of mutual information for finding the delay T was proposed in an article by Andrew M. Fraser and Harry L. Swinney ("Independent coordinates for strange attractors from mutual information," Phys. Rev. A 33 (1986) 1134-1140). The idea is that a good choice for T is one that, given $X(t)$, provides new information with measurement X(t+T). To quote from the article, mutual information I is the answer to the question, "Given a measurement of $X(t)$, how many bits on the average can be predicted about $X(t+T)$?" $I(T)$ should be small. Practically speaking, the way this method works is to calculate $I(T)$ for a given time series. A graph of $I(T)$ starts off very high (given a measurement $X(t)$, we know as many bits as possible about $X(t+0) = X(t)$). As T is increased, $I(T)$ decreases, then usually rises again. Fraser and Swinney suggest using the first minimum in $I(T)$ to select T.

which can be plotted. It is important to choose a good value for T, the delay. If the delay is too short, then $X(t)$ is very similar to $X(t + T)$ and when plotted all of the data stays near the line X(t)=X(t+T). If the delay is too long, then coordinates are essentially independent and no information can be gained from the plot (Fraser and Swinney 1986). From a conceptual point of view, the delay time is synonymous of periodicity in endogenous cycles.

From the other side, embedding dimension are determined through the application of the "false nearest neighbour". This methodology is particularly preferred because it allows to improve the elimination of false nearest neighbours and a better visibility and comprehension of time series. Embedding dimension is usually identified in the minimum number of criteria able to explain evolutionary patterns in the phase-space. In other words, delay time and embedding dimension represent quali-quantitative parameters which allows a quali-quantitative analysis in the attractor construction. In fact, these two parameters, above all, are necessary to plot attractors whose orbits are extremely meaningful in structural change detection.

In the case of chaotic behavior, it is generally accepted the relevance of unstable periodic orbits in the attractor. In fact, UPOs represent the skeleton of the attractor, or better, orbits with a high power of attraction on the other ones. Knowledge of these orbits require a large amount of data, but in the analysis UPOs allow an optimal synthesis of the phenomenon. For this reason, in Section 3, where Mibtel's attractor is constructed and parameters investigated, "Dominant Lyapunov Exponent"[7] method is applied, which is based on divergence between unstable periodic orbits (UPOs). Obviously, to highlight the existence of an abrupt change in the structural behavior, the unique time series has been splitted in the break point, to underline different parameters which characterises the period before and after this point.

2.3 NN approach in pattern recognition

In statistics, methods to estimate trends, or to recognize patterns, are mainly based on optimization algorithms, where objective is error minimization. In neural network, instead, the whole pattern rather than sequential points are considered.

As it has been observed (Kim and Han 2000), neural networks represent the most efficient analytic tool in learning financial time series, even if more troubles have been highlighted in the generation of the prediction set. In this paper, a genetic algorithm with back-propagation is applied for pattern recognition, highlighting structural changes through functional and parameters changes in

---

[7] Wolf et al. (1985) described a general procedure to compute Lyapunov exponent eliminating locally noise, by the consideration of the skeleton of attraction (UPOs), which was presented as alternative to the Lyapunov spectrum.

the time series learning procedure.

In the last decade, financial market analysis has been often developed applying genetic algorithms and neural networks. In these studies, various types of neural networks are considered to predict accurately stock indexes and direction of their change.

One of the earliest studies (Kimoto et al. 1990) uses several learning algorithms and prediction methods for developing the Tokyo stock exchange prices index (TOPIX) prediction system. They used the modular neural network to learn relationships among various market factors. Kamijo and Tanigawa (1990) build the recurrent neural network and Ahmadi (1990) employs the back-propagation neural network with the generalized delta rule to predict the stock market.

The main reason to explain this increasing interest in neural networks is concerned with their optimal skills in nonlinearity and non-stationarity modelling in applications such as control and model-based diagnostics. However, most studies show that neural networks have some limitations in learning patterns with tremendous noise. Neural network has preeminent learning ability while it is often confronted with inconsistent and unpredictable performance for noisy data. For this reason, in the last decade, a large literature focused mainly on NN approach in pattern recognition (Kamijo and Tanigawa 1990).

In this paper, NN approach is applied for two main reasons: first of all, neural network is implemented in order to recognize the main features in the evolution of the Italian stock market and in order to support results observed through the attractor analysis. Secondly, by the application of the same neural network, implications of structural changes in forecasting activity is shown.

A back-propagation network with multiple slabs has been preferred (Fig. 1). This kind of network is characterized by the presence of hidden layers. In a neural network without hidden layers inputs are connected to the output by a link, such that the input to the output node is the sum of all the appropriately weighted inputs. Instead, hidden layers allow a transfer of nodes' outputs to other nodes in another layer through links that amplify or attenuate or inhibit such outputs through weighting factors. Each node is activated according to the input, the activation function and the bias of the node. The net input to a node in layer j is:

$$net_j = \sum w_{ji} x_i$$

where x_i is the ith input, and the output of node j is:

$$y = f(net_j) = \frac{1}{1 + e^{-(net+\phi)}}$$

where f is the activation function, and ϕ the bias (Ahmadi 1990). In particular, the neural network we apply is a back-propagation network that adds a third slab to existing hidden layers. When each slab in the hidden layer has a different activation function, it offers three ways of viewing time series.

Different activation functions applied to hidden layer slabs detect different

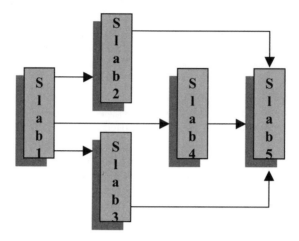

Fig. 1. Back-propagation Network with Multiple Hidden Layers.

features in a pattern processed through a network.[8] For example, a network design may use a Gaussian function on one hidden slab to detect features in the mid-range of the data set and use a Gaussian complement in another hidden slab to detect features from the upper and lower extremes of data. Thus, the output layer will get different "views of the data". Combining the two feature sets in the output layer may lead to a better prediction. Looking at pattern recognition, this neural network allows the identification of the best mix of functions, which is obviously determined by the minimum error in learning procedure. In this context, structural change can be easily highlighted through the recognition of the prevailing structure in the splitted data set considering quantitative (parameters) and qualitative aspects (functions).

3 Empirical Results

3.1 Financial Market Analysis in the phase-space

As it has been discussed above the reconstruction of the phase-space represents the crucial starting point for a qualitative analysis of the main behavior shown

---

[8] In back-propagation networks, the number of hidden neurons determines how well a problem can be learned. If you use too many, the network will tend to try to memorize the problem, and thus not generalize well later (although Calibration mitigates this effect to some extent). If you use too few, the network will generalize well but may not have enough power to learn the patterns well. Getting the right number of hidden neurons is a matter or trial and error, since there is no science to it.

by Mibtel from 1985 to 2001. The first step concerns with the delay time and embedding dimension, which is elaborated respectively by the application of the "mutual information" and "false nearest neighbour" method. Only after the identification of main parameters, the attractor can be reconstructed in the phase-space and divergence among unstable periodic orbits can be calculated. Initially, Mibtel's data have been implemented without any consideration of possible structural breaks, and as a result, the attractor in Fig. 2 is obtained.

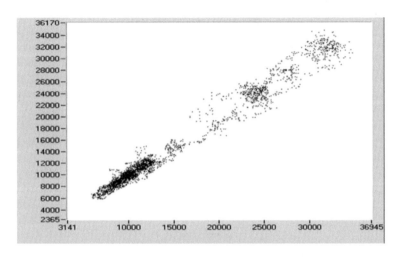

Fig. 2. Mibtel's attractor (1985-2001).

In Table 1(a), we have reported parameters described above, considering Mibtel's data from 1985 to 2001.

Tab. 1: Reconstruction of the phase-space.

a)

Mibtel 1985-2001	
Delay Time	18
Embedding Dimension	4
Lyapunov exponent	0.021

b)

Mibtel 1985-1997		Mibtel 1997-2001	
Delay Time	18	Delay Time	7
Embedding Dimension	4	Embedding Dimension	5
Lyapunov exponent (avg.)	0.037	Lyapunov exponent (avg.)	0.056

In the phase-space (Fig. 2) a structural break is clearly suggested by the radical move of the attraction zone, even if, as it will be discussed later on, do not support the idea of a new well-defined attraction zone. The analysis of the phase space has been undertaken splitting the initial time series in the break point, which is identified as starting point of the new attractor in July 1997. In Table 1(b) parameters are reported taking into account two time series independently. Even if same methods are applied for both time series, different delay times, lower in the second series, occurred. It can be easily shown that this abrupt change in the delay time leads to what Tsay (1988) called LS or better Level Shift, which is synonymous of structural break.

Other relevant information comes from the implementation of the dominant Lyapunov Exponent[9]: in the first application, with the whole time series a low divergence between UPOs is detected, which is not confirmed in the second analysis, where an abrupt increase in the exponent occurs. In econophysics this phenomenon is well known; in fact structural instabilities affect the spectral decomposition process leading to erroneous results.

Summing up, the analysis of the phase-space clearly shows the occurrence of a structural break, but it cannot be neglected that it does not allow for the identification of the new attraction zone. Indeed, from the reconstruction of the phase-space, as restricted to observations after the structural break, it is almost evident that no significant UPOs are detected. That is, there are no reason by which the new zone might be regarded as a real attraction zone.

In order to support our idea, by which the structural break occurred in the 1997 is strictly related to the abrupt increase of the trading volumes due to the reform of CD's taxation, a simple correlation analysis has been undertaken between CD and Mibtel's trading volumes from 1995 to 1998. We have found a correlation -0,88 in monthly data, which is a very high negative correlation. The impact of the reform is even clearer if we compare this result with the low positive correlation (0.12) detected in the period 1991-1995.

3.2 NN Implementation

The chaotic equation possesses many dynamic properties such as non-linearity, limit cycle oscillations, aperiodic wave forms and other dynamic behaviors,

---

[9] In practice, we cannot take into account all periodic orbits. However, only a limited number of low-period orbits may be sufficient for some purposes. Numerous recent studies confirm this hypothesis. It is shown that one can approximate attractors of dynamical models using a set of low-period orbits only. The accuracy obtained in the approximation is rather good even when the number of UPOs used is not large. Thus, the attractor of the the Lorenz model, its dimension, Lyapunov exponents and Lyapunov vectors were characterized by the UPO set in Trevisan A. et al. (1998).

and provides a useful benchmark for testing predictive techniques (Farmer 1987, Moody and Darken 1989).

In the previous section, the existence of a clear break point in the Mibtel's behavior has been shown. To confirm this last result we have applied a back-propagation neural network with multiple slabs and hidden layers usually used in pattern recognition (Ahmadi 1990). In this case, as in the previous section, the analysis is developed dividing the original time series in the break point. Two input variables are implemented. First of all, the trading volume is implemented as we detected the high correlation among it and Mibtel's price in the period 1995-1998. Secondly, considering the relevance of delay time in the error minimization process of genetic algorithms (Day and Davenport 1993, Lin 1992, Kim 1998) a lagged exponential moving average (3-months) is considered.

In Tab. 2, optimal network architecture and results are reported highlighting the strong change in pattern recognition after the break point period. It's important to precise that the optimal network architecture is not intended from a forecasting point of view, but it refers only to the learning process. From a forecasting point of view, obtained results Fig. 3 and Tab. 2 confirm significance of trading volumes for the NN's learning and highlight i) the high degree of predictability which characterizes the second period and ii) the importance of the structural break for forecasting purposes.

Tab. 2: Network's architecture and forecasting in the production set.

Mibtel 1985-1997		Mibtel 1997-2001	
NN's architecture		NN's architecture	
lin.-sine-sine-gaus.-log.		lin.-log.-lin.-gaus.-tan.	
Neurons	2-7-7-6-6	Neurons	1-5-8-8-7
NN's learning		NN's learning	
R-square	0.94	R-square	0.98
Forecasting in the prod. set		Forecasting in the prod. set	
R-square	0.45	R-square	0.88
Forec. in the prod. set 85-01			
R-square	0.37		

Indeed, NN's forecasting in the production set of the data set from 1985 to 2001 does not produce nice results.[10] As it appears in Tab. 2, despite of the learning capacity found in both two periods, the lower predictability of Mibtel in the period immediately before the break point is clearly underlined. As it would be expected in presence of a structural change, the architecture of the network turns out to be strongly different in the two reference periods. Also,

---

[10] The production set is obtained subtracting the last 10% observations in the data set. Results are not significantly different when other proportions (20,15,5) are adopted for the definition of the production set.

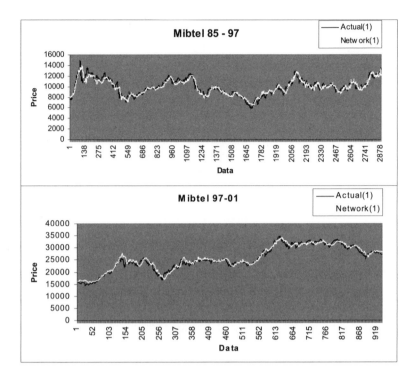

Fig. 3. Mibtel learning and forecasting results. The production set consists of the last 100 data.

if the optimal network's architecture for the first reference period (1985-1997) is applied to Mibtel 1997-01, then parameters are strongly affected (overall R-Square 0.61, R-Square in the Production Set 0.28).

Summing up, the NN Approach seems to confirm evidences from reconstruction and analysis of the phase-space, in the sense that the main behavior of the Mibtel is trongly changed after the 1997. This fact can be deduced from the failure of the same NN'architecture over the two periods and the significant increase in predictability of the Mibtel's behavior due to the consideration of the structural break discussed above.

4 Conclusions

In this paper, an analysis of the main stock index (Mibtel) of the Italian stock market has been proposed with the purpose to point out the relevance of interrelations among public and financial sector. We think that the search for structural instabilities in the financial market necessarily require a quali-quantitative approach, as this sector more than others is strictly interrelated

with other relevant economic sectors, that is, the search for structural instabilities takes place in a multi-dimensional (not univariate) space.

In the Italian financial market, nineties have represented the end of high returns from capital accumulation in bank deposits. So that, capital owners as
well as banks exploited as much as possible CDs whose highest returns were
practically guaranteed and paid choosing the best time length (note 4). When
fiscal reform on CDs occurred, capital owners began moving their capitals
from deposits to stock market and other investments. From the other side, in
entrepreneurs' plans, profits reinvestment assured in most cases higher returns
than deposits. In this context, with a large amount of available capital and
high expected profits, trading volumes increased abruptly affecting the main
characteristics of the MIBTEL's basic behavior.

Then, this analysis underlines as imperfections which dominates economic
phenomena, like in a "coordination failure" context, makes the fiscal variable,
traditionally neglected in financial market analysis, an explanatory variable to
understand and to comprehend agents' rational choices in the capital market.
This is not without any implication. Indeed, it supports the idea by which
the nature of the financial market cannot be treated with the same analytical
tools usually adopted in the general economic theory. The financial market,
instead, shows strong sensitivity to initial conditions as well as strong non-
linearities which can be handled only by the implementation of data-intensive
analyses and the logic of complex systems.

References

Ahmadi, H.: 1990, *Testability of the Arbitrage Pricing Theory by Neural Networks*,
    Proceedings of the IEEE Interantional Conference of Neural Networks.

Alfano, M. and Salzano, M.: 1998, The effect of public sector: an nn approach in
    a view of complexit, *Neural Nets - Proceedings of the 10th Italian Workshop of
    Neural Nets*, m. marinaro, r. tagliaferri edn, Springer Verlag.

Andrews, D.: 1993, Tests for parameter instability and structural change with un-
    known change point, *Econometrica* **61**.

Cooper, R.: 1988, Coordinating coordination failures in keynesian models, *Quarterly
    Journal of Economics* **103**, 441–463.

Crowder, W.J., W. M.: 1999, Are tax effects important in the long-run fisher rela-
    tionship?, *Journal of Finance* **54**(1).

Day, S. and Davenport, M.: 1993, Continuous-time temporal back-propagation with
    adaptive time delays, *IEEE trans. Neural Networks* **4**(2).

Evans, M.: 1991, Discovering the link between inflation rates and inflation uncer-
    tainty, *Journal of Money, Credit and Banking* **23**.

Farmer, D.: 1987, Predicting chaotic time series, *Ohys. Rev. Lett.* **59**.

Fraser, A. and Swinney, H.: 1986, Independent coordinates for strange attractors
    from mutual information, *Phys. Rev. Lett. A* **33**.

Guizzardi, A. and Paruolo, P.: 1997, Nonlinearità nei fondamentali dei rendimenti
    azionari italiani, *Ricerche Applicati e Metodi per la Politica Economica*, Banca
    d'Italia.

Kamijo, K.-I. and Tanigawa, T.: 1990, *Stock Price Pattern Recognition: a Recurrent Neural Network Approach*, Proceedings of the International Conference on Neural Networs, San Diego.

Kim, K.-J. and Han, I.: 2000, Genetic algorithms approach to feature discretization in artificial neural networks for the prediction of stock price index, *Expert Systems with Applications* **19**.

Kim, S.-S.: 1998, Time-delay recurrent neural network for temporal correlations and prediction, *Neurocomputing* **20**.

Lin, D.T., D. J. L. P.: 1992, Adaptive time-delay neural network for temporal correlations and prediction, *SPIE Intelligent Robots and Computer Vision XI: Biological, Neural Net, and 3-D Method.*

Minsky, H.: 1977, *A Theory of Systemic Fragility*, John Wiley and Sons.

Minsky, H.: 1986, *Stabilizing an Unstable Economy*, Yale University Press.

Moody, J. and Darken, C.: 1989, Fast learning in networks of locally-tuned processing units, *Neural Comput.* **1**(2).

Muellbauer, J., a. P. R.: 1978, Macroeconomic models with quantity rationing, *The Economic Journal* pp. 788–821.

Stock, J. and Watson, M.: 1996, Evidence on structural instability in macroeconomic time series relations, *Journal of Business and Economic Statistics* **14**.

Takens, F.: 1981, *Detecting Strange Attractors in Turbulence*, Springer-Berlin.

Trývez, F.: 1995, Level shifts, temporary changes and forecasting, *Journal of Forecasting* **14**.

Tsay, R.: 1988, Outliers, level shifts, and variance changes in time series, *Journal of Forecasting* **7**.

Vercelli, A.: 2000, Structural financial instability and cyclical fluctuations, *Structural Change and Economic Dynamics* **11**.

Wolf, A., Swift, J., Swinney, L. and Vastano, A.: 1985, Determining lyapunov exponents from a time series, *Physica D* **16**.

Heterogeneity in General Equilibrium:
The Battle of Coalitions

F. Busato, B. Chiarini[*]

D81

C78   D01

1 Introduction

An objective of the dynamic general equilibrium research program is to construct models consistent with observed fluctuations in aggregate economic variables. The new literature has developed a direction designed to assess the quantitative importance of non-Walrasian elements in a stochastic and neoclassic growth model. Phenomena such as efficiency wages, labor hoarding, taxation, production externalities and many others are some of the features, usually present in real-world economies, incorporated into the standard framework. These features force the model's equilibrium to be Pareto suboptimal. However, in accordance with many authors,[1] the incorporation of these features may improve the ability of the model to replicate adequately the set of business cycle stylized facts and, moreover, the suboptimality of the equilibrium affords a necessary rationale for countercyclical policy intervention studies.

In this paper we claim that it is useful to consider explicitly some features of the European labor market such as the union wage setting and unemployment benefits. As a factual matter, the strength of the unions in many European countries is sizeable, both in terms of ability to affect wages and employment and to influence the political economy. Moreover, the improvement in government unemployment systems that many European countries have experienced in the last decades in an environment characterized by non-competitive labor markets may well be relevant in explaining the cyclical features of the output and others aggregated real variables. To this end we should tailor the model with a monopoly union and benefits provision.

---

[*] We benefitted from discussions with John Donaldson.

[1] See Danthine and Donaldson (1990, 1995), Prescott (1998), Greenwood and Huffman (1991).

A further problem comes from the use of the decentralization scheme defined along the lines proposed by Prescott and Mehra (1980) e Brock (1982). This scheme has proved extremely convenient but, as stressed by Danthine and Donaldson (2001), it is far from real world. In a context like that described above, where dynamic trade unions are present this decentralization scheme with one-period-lived firms is not innocuous. It is inconsistent to specify a firm that will not exist in the successive period in a context with multiperiod debt, labor contracts adjustment costs, etc. Moreover, as stressed by Danthine and Donaldson, this scheme presumes that in equilibrium physical capital and shares will pay identical returns, the consumer-worker-investor being the owner of both the production inputs. Usually the firm determines its intertemporal investment plan while investors participate only in the residual claims market.

Competitive labor markets and a "passive role" of the firm are unrealistic features. The objective of this paper is to propose an alternative decentralized interpretation of one good dynamic general equilibrium representative agent's model. The fact that the model deals with multiagent environments, however, provides objective difficulties. We propose grouping them consistently according to their economic behavior in coalitions.

The paper is organized as follows. Section 2 deals with economies with heterogeneity agents. Section 3 introduces the coalition concept in macroeconomics and Section 4 describes the model with a monopoly union coalition composed by a consumer-worker and a consumer-unemployed and a firm's coalition defined as the consumer-shareholder and a delegated manager. Section 5 concludes the paper.

2 Models with Heterogeneous Agents

Many questions addressed in the dynamic general equilibrium literature require an environment with multiple and heterogeneous agents. Models with multiple agents are being used to address certain issues that are difficult to explain in the representative agent framework. These include, among other things, the cyclical behavior of factor shares of national income and the equity premium puzzle. Computation of equilibrium in this class of model is substantially more difficult than in standard representative agent models since equilibrium laws of motion become functions not only as functions of aggregate variables, but also as functions of the distributions of these variables across different types of agents.

These models can be grouped according to the criteria that give rise to heterogeneity. A first sub-set includes economies where agents face some idiosyncratic shock (productivity shocks) and where there are no markets to insure this risk. A further sub-set includes models with overlapping generations. In the latter, there exist two large groups of agent types, usually denoted as

Youngs and Olds interacting across different generations. We present a model that does not belong to the previous two.

2.1 Uninsurable Individual Risk

Consider, first, the models with uninsurable individual risk. The key assumption characterizing this class of economies is the absence of a full set of Arrow-Debreu markets. In this case the distribution of income becomes relevant, since all individuals risk cannot be perfectly insured at no cost. From the empirical perspective, this is confirmed by the existence of an insurance industry in the United States that accounts for a nontrivial share of aggregate output. Here trading arrangements only include asset holding whose returns cannot be made contingent upon the realization of individual shocks. Agents, then, trade every period, while insuring themselves against adverse realizations of stocks that will be depleted in bad times. These arrangements represent an alternative description of trading opportunities in actual economies. Differently than with a traditional representative agent scheme, here income distribution and intertemporal movement of income and wealth become critical variables to determine equilibrium patterns of the economy.

In these economies agents differ as to how they are affected by some idiosyncratic risk and in the assets (bonds and stocks) they are able to hold. More precisely, the key difference with a representative agent scheme is that the set of feasible strategies, here, is restricted. For example, consumers cannot write contracts contingent to every idiosyncratic shock, and, in some cases, consumers cannot go short in some assets. As already sketched in the introduction, these issues prevent several aggregation results from holding. This requires keeping track of agents' income distribution while computing the equilibrium. In this context, equilibrium quantities and, more importantly, prices depend on both the distribution of agents and of the aggregate shock. T echnically speaking, each agent, when solving its optimization problem, must be able to predict future prices, and hence it is necessary to use the distribution of agents and its law of motion as an input to their decision making. Furthermore, what makes the model more complicated is that the aggregate level of asset holding would not be enough to characterize each individual state, which must be known in order to predict the next period's level. Now all these considerations mean that computing a competitive equilibrium consists in finding a fixed point in the space of functions from a set of measures into itself. The key problem here is that when solving each agent's problem a measure becomes a state variable. A measure is not a standard state variable, such a productivity shock or physical capital stock, but it is a much more complex mathematical object. The derivation of its law of motion requires a lot of information to be stored in the model. These issues prevent the use of standard and cheap computation techniques, like linear-quadratic approximations, because the optimal solution sometimes hits a corner. Also other standard methods (like "discretizatio" of the state space, parameterized expectation approach, or backward solving) have several shortcomings in this context with a large number of state variables. Note that it is not possible to use an exogenous law of motion, as in the real business cycle literature for example, but it is necessary to derive the true one. This requires iteration of the problem at the individual level also.

To pin down a solution of the problem, and to derive an equilibrium, it is necessary to reduce the dimensionality of the agent's problem. The typical procedure is to simplify the economy, while moving away from the general equilibrium context. The idea is to prevent the distribution of agents affecting relative prices, and, by this end, the allocation of resources. This "trick" simplifies the problem a lot, since iteration is not required over the law of motion of the distribution. There are different ways of implementing this procedure: Imrohoroglu (1989) uses technologies that stochastically pins down the rate of return of savings, Prescott (1986, 1998) and Diaz-Giménez (1990) assumes, instead, that a government commits to a certain inflation rate that does not depend on the critical distribution.

2.2 Overlapping Generation Models

Second, consider economies with overlapping generations. Overlapping generation (OLG) models offer a natural partition of the population according to features that can be readily observed. There a lot of evidence that people's behavior differs among age groups (just think of working time). When population distribution is not modeled with respect to its attitude toward risk (as it was in the previous class of models), OLG models represent an environment in which the properties of risk sharing in the economy are assessed. Indeed, in this economy, it is usually assumed that agents live in significantly large number of periods, in order to connect the length of people's lives with the length of data collection.

Usually, the demographics of the model are kept a very simple level. It is convenient to assume that there is a maximum number of periods an agent can live in order to assume that the population has a fixed age distribution. The equilibrium of this economy is defined recursively, the state of the economy being characterized by an economy-wide shock, and by the distribution of assets holdings by agents in each age group. The typical procedure used to compute the equilibrium law of motion for this economy consists in calculating a linear quadratic approximation of a reduced form model around the steady state. More technically, Auerbach and Kotlikoff (1987) show that it is possible to reduce this problem by finding the solution of a nonlinear equation in one variable. Altig and Carlstrom (1991) used a different procedure, which can be described not as computing the exact equilibria of an approximated economy, but as an approximation to the equilibra of the original economy. The problem, however, is that it is very computer intensive, with the computations proportional to the length of the sample that is produced.

2.3 Other Types of Heterogeneity

Finally, it is useful to spend some words on other types of heterogeneity. Broadly speaking, models with heterogenous agents are being used to investigate other issues like the cyclical behavior of factor shares (e.g. Gomme and Greenwood, 1993), or the so called equity premium puzzle Standard models, like representative agent's models with time separable preferences, systematically generate a premium which is far from small. The one direction that is relevant to the heterogeneous agent class of economies is the exploration of the issue of whether the size of the premium can be accounted for by lack of markets in multiagent worlds where their endowments are not perfectly correlated. In different research Lucas (1990), Ketterer and Marcet (1989), Marcet and Singleton (1990) and Telmer (1992) have constructed models with agents where individual endowment processes are not perfectly correlated. A related paper of Danthine et al. (1992) studies the implications of the fact that stockholders bear a very large share of output uncertainty in a model with non-Walrasian features. Finally, it is natural to cast issues like asymmetric information and limited commitments into a heterogeneous agent model. For example, Marcet and Marimon (1992) have studied the set of implementable allocations in an environment where the action of an infinitely lived borrower is unobservable and there is no commitment to repay the loan. They are able to characterize and compute the optimal contract between risk neutral agents within the small country.

2.4 Heterogeneity and Bounded Rationality

Many recent economic theories emphasize the intertemporal nature of the decision faced by economic agents, while the behavioral predictions of these theories are quite often very sophisticated. Motivated by the perception and the evidence that behavior of actual economic agents is much less sophisticated that supposed by these theories, some researchers have introduced different forms of bounded rationality into macroeconomics (e.g. Sargent, 1992 or Evans and Honkapohja, 1993). It is possible to imagine that some agents face explicit costs in following sophisticated behavioral rule. The introduction of "rules of thumb" among the feasible decision rules of agents might overcome this problem. Some authors (e.g. Krussel and Smith, 1996) assume that two types of agents exist: sophisticated and unsophisticated. The former ones use what the authors call a complex rule (e.g. they solve a stochastic dynamic problem in order to derive an equilibrium pattern for consumption), while the others follow a simple rule of thumb (e.g. a state independent saving rate). An equilibrium for this economy is then one where a fraction of the agents use a simple rule, while the remaining fraction uses a complex rule. In this kind of equilibrium, the sophisticated agents are able to take advantage of their better ability to adjust consumption and investment behavior in response to shocks and changes in return to capital, but these advantages are just about equal to the cost borne by using the complicated rule.

2.5 A Simple Way of Overcoming the Heterogeneity

The need to go beyond the representative agent has led many authors to envisage some simple way to overcome the distributional difficulties without forgoing the enrichment of the model with different agents. In this respect, Cho and Rogerson (1988) provide a method of introducing heterogeneity without determining the weights on individual utilities, assuming that all families are identical and that each of them consists of two heterogeneous members. This may be accomplished for instance by a family composed of by a male and a female, an adult and a youth, a worker and an unemployed member, etc., assuming that both family members have the same strictly convex preferences for consumption. These members, whatever their nature, will always consume the same amount. Of course, distributional issues are not investigated here, and therefore we may use the standard methods to compute equilibria.

2.6 Discussion

Summarizing the current research agenda, all models with idiosyncratic shock and an absence of complete insurance possibilities are either silent on the distribution of wealth (in the sense that it must be imposed ex ante in order to solve the model numerically), or have no capital. In other words, as distributional issues become more and more important in current economic research, it is still quite complex to embed them into a general equilibrium model. The key innovation here is the development of methods able to compute equilibria in economies with capital where the distribution of wealth and income is endogenous.

3 Coalitions in Macroeconomics

3.1 Coalition and Monopoly Firm

Coalitions in macroeconomics are phenomena related to the existence of a monopoly power or to property right.

Two antithetic views exist about the effects of coalitions and thus monopoly power, over an economic system.

The first one is denoted as the classical view. The view that monopoly power impedes economic progress and leads to economic efficiencies is not new. This dates back at least to Adam Smith who stressed how monopoly provided protections for groups in the short run, while served to support negligence, profusion and malversation of the group with that monopoly power in the long run. Alfred Marshall had a quite similar perspective. He considered free enterprise, and not monopoly power, as the true engine of economic efficiency and progress. As stressed in Parente and Prescott (1999), this classical view commands little respect today. This could be because of the lack of a plausible theoretical mechanism by which monopolies impede economic progress and lead to significant inefficiencies within the economy. There exist, however, some theoretical contributions depicting some mechanisms by which monopoly leads to inefficiencies. One mechanism consists in creating a gap between the marginal rates of substitution and transformations (see the well known contribution of Harberger (1954)); a second one, proposed by Laitner (1982) stresses the role of capitalization of monopoly rents over physical capital accumulation. Notice, however, that Harberger (1954) estimates this inefficiency loss to only one-tenth of one percent of GDP. In addition, some years later Kemrschen (1966), Bergson (1973), and Cowling and Mueller (1978) found this effect as large as 5 percent of output. In other words, the inefficiencies arising from these two mechanisms are quite small, at most a few percent of the GDP.

This view is in sharp contrast with the Shumpeterian perspective that monopolies foster economic progress and developments. Innovations require large and non-firm specific investment, and monopoly profits are required to finance these investments. This intuition is captured in the theory of endogenous growth of Romer (1990), Grossman and Helpman (1991), and Aghion and Howitt (1992). It can be accepted that the adoption of better technologies requires large firm specific factors and factor-specific investment, but it is disputable, however, that such investments require monopoly rents to induce individuals to undertake them.

More recently, Parente and Prescott (1999) provide more theoretical underpinnings for the classical view that monopolies impede economic progress and lead to significantly large inefficiencies. Their view is, in their own words, *"that technology is the lever to riches, and that all countries would be rich if they just applied this lever"*. They explain the fact that poor countries do not use better technologies because they have protected monopoly rights, which are coalitions on the supply side. More precisely, the monopoly rights allow a group in each industry to be the sole supplier of its labor services to all firms using a particular production progress. The coalition has the right to dictate work practicing and its member wages. These monopoly rights are protected via regulations, making it costly for a group of potential adopters to enter the industry with a superior technology. They show that eliminating monopoly rights increases the GDP by roughly a factor or 3 without any other increase in inputs; what is even more notable is the fact that this occurs even if the strength of the protection is modest.

There exist some issues of PP approach that deserve more attention. A coalition, as defined in the PP paper, is not a legitimate agent (like a consumer, for example), but it is akin to an institution preventing the introduction of a new technology when it can offset the coalition's monopoly power. The PP coalition operates mechanically, in the sense that its choices do not depend on members' preferences.

The membership rule is interesting, too. Membership is derived as the final step of a backward induction procedure, at the beginning of which is the entry choice of a firm. In this context membership affects entry decision quite significantly, without taking into account the aggregate and the households welfare. Thus, we can argue that the model depicts a Pareto improvable economy.

Notice, moreover, that the model is static in the sense of not considering capital accumulation. Since there is no saving, current consumption coincides with current income. Incorporating an intertemporal decision might improve upon the actual allocation.

In addition, even though the model specifies the existence of two types of agents (farm worker households and industry worker households) a subgame perfect equilibrium is characterized by the existence of just one type. This is interesting, since it implies that their coalition is made of individuals of the same type (e.g. a coalition made of N industry worker households).

3.2 Coalition and Monopoly Union

The context where agent differences are crucial is the labor market. Among the key features of many European economies is the existence of trade unions, therefore, of workers who join these organizations and workers who are not members. The monopoly character of the unions generates externalities with the unemployment phenomenon. At any point in time, the state of the economy is therefore characterized by how agents are positioned across levels of asset holding and shocks (both individual and aggregate). However, unlike the standard model, agents are also positioned across markets (unionized and non-unionized) and status (employed-insiders and unemployed-outsiders), skills (capital-intensive market sector and labor-intensive underground sectors).[2] Heterogeneity in the labor market should be recomposed, however, into the family. Many European countries have a high degree of institutionalization of the traditional family model. This is a situation where different generations and labor-type components are brought together in the same household. This has the advantage of offering everyone a sort of protection and, therefore, points out the risk sharing aspect played by the family (See the papers in Gallie and Paugam (2000) and the works quoted therein).

This task has been undertaken in a recent paper by Chiarini and Piselli (2000), augmenting the labor market with a static rent seeking utility function for the union. In that model, the authors adopt a monopoly union model to unilaterally set the employment (or equivalently, the wage level), subject to the firm's labor demand curve. Moreover, they assume that unemployment insurance exists by specifying a guaranteed income flow to each unemployed worker. The presence of unions generates heterogeneity, which the authors solve according to Cho and Rogerson (1988) family labor supply model, assuming identical

---

[2] The latter aspect has been developed in a dynamic general equilibrium framework by Busato and Chiarini (2002).

families with two members, employed vs. unemployed, but with identical preferences for consumption. The problem with this framework is that in order to preserve a coherence between the trade union objective and the objective of the consumer-worker, the authors use a simple linear utility function for the trade union preferences making consistent the specification with the family objective.

In the labor market, a coalition is related to the monopoly power of unions who care for their consumer-insider and recognize the outcomes of its policy. The coalition has the right to indicate wages to its worker-consumer members, taking into account the consequences for the consumer-unemployed component of the family and the relative income for the family. The monopoly power is "protected" by union membership.

We show below that this is made operative in the model by adding a state equation for a post-entry closed-shop model of membership. For an utilitarian union, membership is crucial for its monopoly power, and this leads the union to be concerned with the sum of utilities of current and future members. In a context where membership is conditioned upon employment, the union internalizes the costs of its claims, including also employment.

4 A Theoretical Model

There exist two Coalitions, one on the labor side (the *Labor Coalition*, LC), and the other on the firm side (the *Firms's Coalition*, FC). The LC is made of a Consumer-Worker and a Consumer-Unemployed, while the FC is composed by a Consumer-Shareholder, and a Delegated Manager.[3] The context of the analysis is a stochastic dynamic general equilibrium model, where the LC chooses labor supply, n_t^s, the worker and the unemployed consumption flows, c_t^w and c_t^u, and by this end, it pins down next period membership, m_{t+1}. The FC chooses, then, labor demand, n_t^d, investment in physical capital, i_t, in assets, z_{t+1}, and the shareholder and the manager consumption flows, c_t^s and c_t^m.

The next two subsections focus with more details on the decision problem of both composite agents. Precisely, section A analyzes LC behavior, while section B details FC optimization problem.

4.1 The Labor Coalition

The labor coalition problem is the following:

---

[3] A related model is that of Parente and Prescott (1999), where they introduce a Coalition into a General Equilibrium Model, but in the production side.

$$U(m_0, B_0) = \max_{n_t, z_t} E \sum_{t=0}^{\infty} \beta^t \left(n_t u(c_t^w, 1 - n_t) + (m_t - n_t) u(c_t^u) \right)$$

$$m_{t+1} = \nu n_t - \alpha m_t + (n_t - n_{t-1})$$

$$c_t^w = w_t n_t - \varphi \tau_t$$

$$c_t^u = B_t$$

$$w_t = f_2(k_t, n_t) \lambda_t$$

$$B_{t+1} = \rho_\varepsilon B_t + \varepsilon_t$$

$$\varepsilon_t \cong iid(0, \sigma_\varepsilon)$$

where n_t denotes the number of current employees, m_{t+1} is the number of the next period member, B_t denotes an exogenous and stochastic unemployment benefit, c_t^w and c_t^u denote the worker and the unemployment consumption flows, n_t worker labor supply, and wt the wage income. Finally, $\beta \in (0, 1)$ represents the LC intertemporal discount factor. The unemployment benefits are financed via lump-sum taxation, which is partially paid by consumer workers (with share $\varphi \tau$, where $\varphi \in (0, 1)$ and $\tau_t = B_t(m_t - n_t)$).

Unlike Kidd and Ostwald (1987) membership rule, where new employees join the union (a *post-entry closed-shop* model) $m_{t+1} = n_t$, our difference equation says that membership tomorrow is determined by the existing stock of employment and the change of employment today. A portion of the new employees join the union. We assume that the remaining portion of new employees as a constant. For instance, one may think that, in each period, a constant portion of employment is addressed to the public sector. Since this share of consumption is sufficiently small in our model, we can abstract from considering it explicitly.

This membership rule is crucial because it leads the trade union to take care of both current and future members. In other word, when the union maximizes its utility function it considers the full family income, given the risk sharing procedure.[4] In this sense our formulation differs from Parente and Prescott (1999) where membership assumes a strategic flavor, since it affects adoption of a superior technology by a firm in order to enter a market. However, our labor coalition, as in Parente and Prescott's framework, has monopoly power and this power is protected by the membership rule.

Finally, the post-entry closed shop model may be made less stringent, assuming a more general formulation. However, this generalization of the membership scheme is complicated because it involves a richer heterogeneity.

Summarizing, the state variables for this problem are m_t and B_t, while the controls are n_t and c_t^w. Note that in this context, even if the consumer-worker does not undertake any saving decisions, his consumption choice is still in-

---

[4] However, the treatment of union membership may be inadequate and further effort should be addressed to this crucial issue.

tertemporal in some sense, since current employment determines next period membership, which in turn shifts labor and therefore consumption over time. Consumption behavior is still characterized by the LC Euler Equation. Note that this is a Monopolistic Coalition, since it incorporates into its information set, as a constraint, the FC labor demand schedule.

4.2 The Danthine-Donaldson Decentralization Scheme

To specify the firm's coalition, we use first a decentralization scheme of Danthine and Donaldson (2001) where the firm is split into two components. In this framework, the firm's owner is a shareholder who delegates the investment and hiring decisions to a manager. This point is crucial because the manager is an employee who receives a wage from the shareholder. Danthine and Donaldson introduce as an incentive issue the fact that managers behave in their own best interest, given the remuneration scheme provided for them by shareholders.

In this scheme the representative shareholder solves the following problem,

$$V^s(z_0, k_0, \lambda_0) = \max E \sum_{t=0}^{\infty} \beta^t u(c_t^s, 1 - n_t)$$

$$c_t^s + q_t^e z_{t+1} \leq z_t(q_t^e + d_t) + w_t n_t$$

c_t^s is the shareholder consumption flow, q_t denotes equity price and d_t is the dividend stream. The shareholder is assumed to maximize the above utility function selecting z_{t+1} and n_t.

The Firm manager maximizes the following general function,

$$V^m(k_0, \lambda_0) = \max E \sum_{t=0}^{\infty} \beta^t \nu(c_t^m)$$

$$0 \leq c_t^m \leq g^m(CF_t)$$
$$d_t + g^m(CF_t) \leq CF_t$$
$$k_{t+1} = (1 - \Omega)k_t + i_t$$
$$CF_t = f(k_t, n_t)\lambda_t - w_t n_t - i_t - (1 - \phi)\tau_t$$

where c_t^m is the manager consumption flow, $g^m(CF_t)$ represents the manager remuneration policy, CF_t is the cash flow, and it is the investment in physical capital stock. Next, $\lambda_t f(k_t, n_t)$ is a well behaved production function, where k_t is the stock of capital, n_t is the labor demand, and λ_t is a productivity shock. Finally, $(1 - \varphi) \cdot \tau_t$ is the share of social contributions charged on the manager.

4.3 The Firms' Coalition

Given this decentralization scheme, the firms' coalition is assumed to solve the following problem:

$$V_0^c(k_0, \lambda_0) = \max E \sum_{t=0}^{\infty} \beta^t [\nu(c_t^m) + \mu h(c_t^s)]$$

$$0 \leq c_t^m \leq g_t^m(CF_t)$$
$$c_t^s + q_t^e z_{t+1} = z_t(q_t^e + d_t)$$
$$d_t + g^m(CF_t) \leq CF_t$$
$$k_{t+1} = (1 - \Omega)k_t + i_t$$
$$CF_t = f(k_t, n_t)\lambda_t - w_t n_t - i_t - (1 - \phi)\tau_t$$
$$\lambda_{t+1} = \rho_\lambda \lambda_t + \xi_t$$
$$\xi_t \cong iid(0, \sigma_\varepsilon)$$

The state variables are z_t and k_t, while the controls are c_t^m, c_t^s, z_{t+1}, i_t. Labor services are chosen by the Labor Coalition.

4.4 The Income Distribution Battle

The figure depicts the distribution mechanism at work in a unionized labor market and compares it with a competitive allocation. In Figure 1, the num-

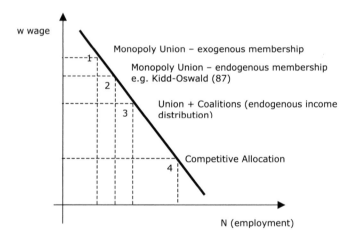

Fig. 1. Labor Demand

bers on the labor demand schedule refer to the different equilibria. Precisely, the equilibria are represented by a standard monopoly union model in partial equilibrium (n.1), which provides the highest monopoly negative externality, and by a Kidd-Oswald partial equilibrium union model (n.2), in which the outcome is mitigated by the endogeneity of the closed shop membership rule. A further improvement is obtained by casting the latter model into a general equilibrium framework with coalitions. This equilibrium (n.3) is achieved by considering a further mitigation of the monopoly power provided by the tax financing channel. In this context, a union not only takes care of the unemployed, as well as in the previous case, but now it also realizes that the financing cost of the unemployment benefits is charged to both the agents: LC and FC. In other words, a part of the benefit bill, $(1 - \varphi) \cdot B_t \cdot (n_t - m_t)$, is paid by the Firm Coalition (FC), while the remaining part, $\varphi B_t(n_t - m_t)$, is paid by the remaining employees. This implies that both the Coalitions incorporate this information and thus reconsider their strategies.

4.5 The Value Function Comparison

Danthine and Donaldson show that when a delegate manager is defined in the decentralization scheme, the equilibrium corresponds to a Pareto optimal allocation of resources, i.e. to a behavior of the standard neoclassical model, although only if the contract has a very specific form. That is only if the manager contract has a linear form (a linear relationship with the firm's profits or cash flow). However, this is incompatible with Pareto optimum if the relationship between shareholders and manager is determined by a competitive wage income for the former whereas the latter receives only the remainder. Our idea is that, with a coalition arrangement, we may make consistent the income distribution between managers and shareholders with a different form for the manager's contract and a different resources allocation.

5 Conclusions

This paper tackles two issues of dynamic general equilibrium models. First, the need to incorporate some real world features which may improve the ability of the model to replicate the stylized facts. Second, to abandon Prescott Mehra's decentralization scheme and to consider a different dynamic role for the firm behavior, following Danthine and Donaldson (2001). These issues require a model that is able to deal with heterogeneity. We set out a coalition model for the union member-worker-consumer and for the shareholder-firm's delegated manager. This setup should improve some results yielded by the decentralization scheme set out by Danthine and Donaldson and reduce the externalities produced by the monopoly union. In particular, they show that when the remuneration policy of the manager is not linear, the equilibrium will not be Pareto Optimal. We think it could be possible that a Coalition of this kind could *improve upon* that allocation.

The idea is that, comparing the steady state distribution of our model with that of Danthine and Donaldson, and with the standard model, our model could explain why in Europe production is more capital intensive. That should happen in our model since employment is higher, and thus the marginal productivity of capital and labor is larger. Finally, the suboptimality of an economy with a monopoly union (a feature that is present in European countries) should turn out to be reduced with a labor coalition. In this case, the union's goals are formulated over a larger constraint than is recognized by the single agent specification described in the labor market partial equilibrium models. In this setup the union must internalize the costs of its policy, providing higher employment levels than would occur in a standard monopoly union model.

References

Aghion, P. and Howitt, P.: 1992, A model of growth through creative destruction, *Econometrica* **60**, 323–351.

Altig, D. and Carlstrom, C.: 1991, Inflation, personal taxes and real output: A dynamic analysis, *Journal of Money, Credit and Banking* **23**, 547–571.

Auerbach, A. and Kotlikoff, L.: 1987, *Dynamic Fiscal Policy*, Cmbridge University Press.

Bergson, A.: 1973, On monopoly welfare losses, *American Economic Review* **63**, 853–870.

Brock, W.: 1982, Asset prices in a production economy, *in* J. McCall (ed.), *The Economics of Uncertainty*, University of Chicago Press.

Busato, F. and Chiarini, B.: 2002, Market and underground activities in a two-sector dynaic equilibrium model, *Forthcoming Economnic Theory* .

Chiarini, B. and Piselli, P.: 2000, Aggregate fluctuations in a uniionized labor market, *Working Paper 2 Univ. of Naples Parthenope, ISE, http: economia.uninav.it/ise/wp.htm* .

Cho, J.-O. and Rogerson, R.: 1988, Family labor suplly and aggregate fluctuations, *Journal of Monetary Economics* **21**, 233–245.

Cowling, K. and Mueller, D.: 1978, The social costs of monopoly power, *Economic Journal* **88**, 727–748.

Danthine, J. and Donaldson, J.: 1990, Efficiency wages and the business cycle puzzle, *European Economic Review* **34**, 1275–1301.

Danthine, J. and Donaldson, J.: 1995, Comuting equilibria of nonoptimal economies, *in* T. Cooley (ed.), *Frontiers of Business Cycle Research*, Princeton University Press, pp. 65–97.

Danthine, J.-P. and Donaldson, J.: 2001, *Decentralizing the Stochastic Growth Model*, Columbia University.

Danthine, J.-P., Donaldson, J. and Mehra: 1992, The equity premium and the allocation of income risks, *Journal of Economic Dynamics and Control* **16**, 509–532.

Diaz-Giménez, J.: 1990, Business cycle fluctuations and the cost of insurance in computable general equilibrium hetergogenous agent economies, *Working Paper Universidad Carlos III de Madrid* .

Gallie, D. and Paugam, S.: 2000, *Welfare Regimes and the Experience of Unemployment in Europe*, Oxford University Press.

Greenwood, J. and Huffman, G.: 1991, Tax analysis in a real business cycle model: One measuring harberger triangles and okun gaps, *Journal of Monetary Economics* **27**, 167–190.

Grossman, G. and Helpman, E.: 1991, *Innovation and Growth in the Global Economy*, MIT Press.

Harberger, A.: 1954, Monopoly and resource allocation, *American Economic Review, Papers and Proceedings* **44**, 77–87.

Imrohoroglu, A.: 1989, The cost of business cycles with indivisibilities and liquidity constraints, *Journal of Political Economy* **97**, 1364–1383.

Kidd, D. and Ostwald, A.: 1987, A dynamic model of trade union behavior, *Economica* **55**, 355–365.

Laitner, J.: 1982, Monopoly and long-run capital accumulation, *Bell Journl of Economics* **13**, 143–157.

Lucas, D.: 1990, *Estimating the Equity Premium with Undiversifiable Income Risk and Short Sales Constraints*, Northwestern University.

Marcet, A. and Marimon, R.: 1992, Communication, commitment and growth, *Journal of Economic Theory* **58**, 219–249.

Marcet, A. and Singleton, K.: 1990, Equilibrium assets prices and savings of heterogenous agents in the presence of portfolio constraints, *mimeo* .

Parente, S. and Prescott, E.: 1999, Monopoly rights: A barrier to riches, *American Economic Review* **89**, 1216–1233.

Prescott, E.: 1986, Theory ahead of business cycle measurement, *Carnegie Rochester Conference Series on Public Policy* **25**, 11–44.

Prescott, E.: 1998, Business cycle research: Methods and problems, *Federal Reserve Bank of Minneapolis Working Paper* (590).

Prescott, E. and Mehra, R.: 1980, Recursive competing equilibrium: the case of homogenous households, *Econometrica* **40**, 1356–1379.

Romer, P.: 1990, Endogenous technological change, *Journal of Political Economy* **98**, 71–102.

Telmer, C.: 1992, Asset pricing puzzles and incomplete markets, *Working Paper Queens University* .

181-86

L25 E32

Firms' Size Distribution and Growth Rates as Determinants of Business Fluctuations

D. Delli Gatti, C. Di Guilmi, E. Gaffeo, M. Gallegati, G. Giulioni, A. Palestrini

Since the pioneering work of Gibrat (1931), it has been clear that - holding the "law of proportional effect" (LPE) - the distribution of firms' size must be right skew ("Gibrat's law" in its weak form). As a matter of fact, Gibrat went even further, claiming that such distribution must be log-normal (strong form of "Gibrat's law"). In a nutshell, the argument goes as follows. The size of a firm in period t can be defined as the size in period t-1 times the (gross) rate of growth. Taking the logs of both sides of this definition and solving recursively, it is easy to see that the log of the size in period t is equal to the log of the initial size (in period 0) plus the sum of the (net) growth rates experienced in the past, i.e. from period 1 to period t. Assuming that the (net) growth rates are independently normally distributed, the distribution of the log of firms' size in period t tends to the log-normal distribution. It took more than twenty years to realize that the log-normal was not the only asymptotic distribution consistent with Gibrat's law (Simon 1955, Ijiri and Simon 1977). In fact, minor modifications in the random growth model at the basis of the Gibrat's law - for instance, allowing growth rates to be independent on average (Lee 1998) - results in a skewed distribution of firms' size of the Yule or of the Pareto (or "power law") types. Furthermore, the weak version of Gibrat's law can yield a power law distribution for firms' size also if the distribution is characterized by time-reversal symmetry, i.e. the joint probability distribution for two consecutive years is symmetric in its arguments, $P_{t,t+1}(x_t, x_{t+1}) = P_{t,t+1}(x_{t+1}, x_t)$ (Fujiwara et al. 2003). Hence, power laws and Gibrat's law are not necessarily inconsistent. These theoretical results have been confirmed in recent empirical work. The exploitation of commercially available large data sets for both the U.S. and other industrialized countries has allowed to show that firm sizes are likely to be distributed as a Pareto distribution, instead of a log-normal one (Axtell 2001, Gaffeo et al. 2003). As already emphasized in Axtell (2001), the road to a proper understanding of industrial dynamics necessarily passes through the building of models where this stylized fact - i.e. scale invariance of firms' size distributions - is coupled with results reported in e.g. Stanley (1996) and Amaral (1997), showing that the growth rates of firms' output follows a Laplace distribution. Moreover, such an endeavor is urged on by the fact that mainstream macroeconomics, where the analysis of the aggregate is reduced to that of a single "representative" agent completly insulated from any type of interactions not mediated by prices, is unable by construction to explain any scaling behavior (Reed 2004). To overcome this fatal flaw the literature has followed two lines of research. The first one is a-theoretical and focuses only on the statistical properties of the link between the distribution of the level of activity - or firms' size - and that of the rates of change (Amaral et al. 1998). The second line of research - which we follow here as well - emphasizes non-price interactions among economic agents (Bottazzi and Secchi 2003, Delli Gatti et al. 2004). In this piece we report on simulations from a model based on a multi-agent network of interacting firms, which is able to generate contemporaneously the two stylized facts mentioned above, and many others. In our work the origin of aggregate business fluctuations - which is the most important single problem in macroeconomics - can be traced back to the ever changing configuration of this network of heterogeneous interacting firms. Interestingly, simulations' outcomes can be justified from a purely statistical viewpoint. Elsewhere we have made use of statistical theorems regarding transformations between random variables to show that the difference of two exponential distributions follows a Laplace distribution. Given that the logarithm of a power law follows an exponential distribution, this finding yields that *growth rates are Laplace distributed because of the log transformation of the power law of firms' size*. Moreover, the above result holds in a more general context in which the size in period t is not independent, as one would expect in reality, of the size in t-1 (Kirman 1992). The model consists of only two markets: goods and credit. In order to simplify the analysis as much as possible, we assume that output is supply driven, i.e. firms can sell all the output they produce. In each period, there is a "large" (but, due to the entry-exit process, far from constant) number of firms N, indexed by $i = 1, .., N$, which differ according to their financial conditions. The financial robustness of a firm is proxied by the so-called equity ratio, i.e. the ratio of its equity base or net worth (A_{it}) to the capital stock (K_{it}), $a_{it} = A_{it}/K_{it}$. Since firms sell their output at an uncertain price they may go bankrupt. Bankruptcy occurs if net worth at time t becomes negative, i.e. if the individual price falls below a critical threshold. The probability of bankruptcy turns out to be an increasing function of the interest rate and the capital stock, and a decreasing function of the equity base inherited from the past. In this setting, the problem of the firm consists in maximizing its expected profits net of bankruptcy costs. The optimal capital stock turns out to be a decreasing function of the interest rate and an increasing function of the equity ratio. Output follows the evolution over time of the capital stock, which in turn is determined by investment. Firms can raise funds only on the credit market. For the sake of simplicity we assume that many heterogeneous firms interact with the banking sector (as an aggregate). As to demand, investment is financed by means of retained earnings and by new debt: Therefore the demand for credit of each firm is a function of the interest rate and financial robustness. In order to determine the supply of credit and its allocation to each firm, we assume that there is a risk coefficient α - i.e. a threshold ratio of bank's equity to credit extended - that the bank tries to target, either because of a strategy of risk management or as a consequence of prudential regulation on the part of the monetary authorities. Therefore the aggregate supply of credit turns out to be approximately a multiple $(1/\alpha)$ of bank's equity. Credit has to be allotted to the heterogeneous firms. We assume that each firm obtains a portion of total credit equal to its relative size, i.e. the ratio of the individual capital stock to the aggregate capital stock: highly capitalized (i.e. collateralized, in economics jargon) borrowers have a higher credit supply, and *vice-versa*. The rate of interest charged to each firm is determined in equilibrium when the demand for credit is equal to the credit extended by the bank to that firm.

Object	Distribution	Empirical estimates	Simulation outcomes
Firms size distribution	Power law	$\hat{\imath} = 1.16\pm 0.03$	$\mu = 1.11\pm 0.11$
Rates of variation for cumulative output	Weibull	Expansions: $\beta = 1.34\pm 0.14; \acute{a} = 0.13\pm 0.04$ Recessions: $\hat{a} = 1.24\pm 0.12; \acute{a} = 0.15\pm 0.04$	Expansions: $\hat{a} = 1.24\pm 0.08; \acute{a} = 0.03\pm 0.00$ Recessions: $\hat{a} = 1.11\pm 0.07; \acute{a} = 0.02\pm 0.00$
Exits of firms by age	Exponential	$0.01 \square \grave{e} \square 0.01$	$\theta = 0.01\pm 0.00$
Profits distribution	Power law	$0.7 \square \hat{\imath} \square 1.2$	$\mu = 1.27 \pm 0.13$
Bad debt	Stretched exp.	$\beta = 0.77 \pm 0.18$	$\beta = 0.7654\pm 0.018$
Shifts over business cycle phases	Power law	Expansions: $\hat{\imath} = 1.84\pm 0.05$ Recessions: $\hat{\imath} = 1.73 \pm 0.06$	Expansions: $\hat{\imath} \square 1.94$ Recessions: $\hat{\imath} \square 1.53$
GDP autocorrelation	–	$\square 0.93$	$\square 0.84$
GDP standard deviation	–	$\square 2.8\%$	$\square 2.9\%$

Table 1. Comparisons of characteristic parameters between empirical estimates and outcomes from simulations of the financial fragility model. Sources for empirical estimates are Gaffeo et al. (2003), Kirman (1992), Okuyama et al. (1999), Bottazzi et al. (2001). Notation in column three is ì Pareto exponent; â: Weibull shape parameter; á: Weibull scale parameter; è: exponential distribution parameter.

The equilibrium interest rate is generally decreasing with the firm's and the bank's equity. Investment and output therefore are generally increasing with the bank's and the firm's net worth. The bank's equity base, which is the only determinant of total credit supply, increases with the bank's profits, which are affected, among other things, by firms' bankruptcy. When a firm goes bankrupt, i.e. its net worth becomes negative because of a huge loss, the bank has a "bad debt". This is the root of a potential *domino* effect: the bankruptcy of a firm today is the source of the potential bankruptcies of other firms tomorrow via its impact on the bank's equity. Besides the two stylized facts discussed above, namely i) a power law distribution for firms' size and ii) a Laplace distribution for firms' growth rates, by simulating our model we are able to replicate a large number of other empirically observed facts, as table 1 shows. It is worthy to note that results are quite robust as we changed the values of structural parameters and the initial number of firms N. The distribution of firms' size (in terms of capital stock) is characterized by persistent heterogeneity and tends to a power law (Fig. 1). Note that if the distribution is skewed, small idiosyncratic shocks may generate aggregate large fluctuations. The distribution of firms' size is characterized by time reversal symmetry (or "detailed balance") for consecutive years, i.e. the joint distribution is approximately invariant as we exchange values between t and t-1 (Fig.2). The distribution of firms' growth rates is approximated by a tent-shaped curve (Laplace distribution) (Fig.3). In agreement with results in Lee (1998), the simulated data highlights a tight correspondence between the distribution of firms' growth rates and the one of aggregate output. For instance, cumulative rates of change of simulated aggregate output follow a Weibull distribution, which is the same distribution observed for real data (Di Guilmi et al. 2004).

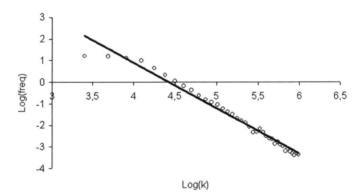

Fig. 1. Log-log plot of firms' size (by capital stock) as derived from simulations of the financial fragility model. The solid line is the OLS regression line through the data, with slope 1.11 0.11.

The empirical analysis returns striking similarities between the distributions of personal income and firm's operating revenues. Both are Pareto distributed with an exponent close to 1, and both show a time-reversal property (Fujiwara et al. 2003). Interestingly enough, our model is capable to replicate

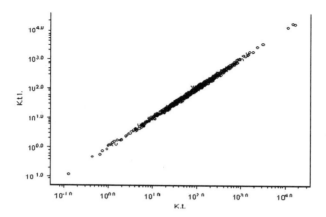

Fig. 2. Joint distribution of firms' capital at time t and time t-1. The time reversal property holds if the data points settled down on the 45 line, which is exactly what we observe here.

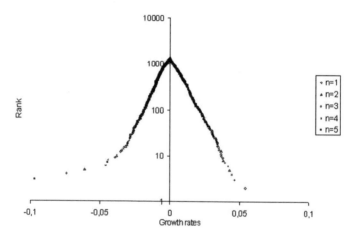

Fig. 3. Laplace plot of simulated firms' growth rates. Rates are grouped in five bins (indicated with n) according to the rank of firms' size.

these facts with a remarkably high degree of statistical precision. Good results have been obtained also for the distribution of outgoing firms sorted by age, which from simulations turns out to be exponential, and for the distribution of "bad debt" which is stretched exponential (Delli Gatti et al. 2004). A final result regards the shifts of firms' size distribution over the business cycle. From our simulations it emerges that during periods of expansion, the distribution of the "artificial" firms' sizes shifts to the right, maintaining the same slope coefficient, while recessions are associated with movements in the opposite direction (shift of the curve toward the origin). Moreover, during downturns the scaling exponent (as estimated by the regression line in the log-log plane) decreases. This shift reveals that upturns increase scaling in the distribution, i.e. concentration goes up; while during contractions firms are more evenly distributed. This is precisely what has been observed in the real world (Gaffeo et al. 2003, Gabaix 2004).

References

Amaral, L., Buldyrev, S., Havlin, S., Salinger, M. and Stanley, H.: 1998, *Phys. Rev. Lett.* **80**, 1385.
Amaral, L. e. a.: 1997, *J. Phys. I* **7**, 621.
Axtell, R.: 2001, *Science* **293**(1818).
Bottazzi, G., Dosi, G., Lippi, M. and Pammolli, F., R. M.: 2001, *Int. J. Ind. Organization* **19**, 1161.
Bottazzi, G. and Secchi, A.: 2003, *8th WEHIA International Conference* .
Delli Gatti, D., Di Guilmi, C. and Gallegati, M.: 2004, *Working Paper* .
Di Guilmi, C., Gaffeo, E. and Gallegati, M.: 2004, *Working Paper* .
Fujiwara, Y., Souma, W., Aoyama, H., Kaizoji, T. and Aoki, M.: 2003, *Physica A* **321**, 598.
Gabaix, X.: 2004, *mimeo* .
Gaffeo, E., Gallegati, M. and Palestrini, A.: 2003, *Physica A* **324**, 117.
Gibrat, R.: 1931, *Les inégalités conomiques; applications: aux inégalits des richesses, à la concentration des entreprises, aux populations des villes, aux statistiques des familles, etc., d'une loi nouvelle, la loi de l'effet proportionnel*, Librarie du Recueil Sirey, Paris.
Ijiri, Y. and Simon, H.: 1977, *Skew Distributions and the Sizes of Business Firms*, North-Hooland.
Kirman, A.: 1992, Whom or what does the representative individual represent, *Journal of Economic Perspectives* **6**, 117–136.
Lee, Y. e. a.: 1998, *Phys. Rev. Lett.* **81**, 3275.
Okuyama, K., Takayasu, M. and Takayasu, H.: 1999, *Physica A* **269**, 125.
Reed, W.: 2004, *www.math.uvic.ca/faculty/reed/dPIN.pdf* .
Simon, H.: 1955, *Biometrika* **42**, 425.
Stanley, M. e. a.: 1996, *Nature* **379**, 804.

Dynamically Sustainable Economic Equilibria as Self-Organized Atomic Structures

Y. Yegorov

C6?

1 Introduction

The facts from real economic world provide us with lots of examples when some trend develops in an unpredictable way and converges to an equilibrium (if any) which was not initially expected. The first group of examples is related to finance. The index NASDAQ has dropped to less than a half of its value two years ago. The euro since its launch in 1999 has lost 20-30 % of its value without significant drop in fundamentals. The second example is transition. Now it becomes clear that nobody would launch a transition in Russia in 1991 if there would be a rational expectation of that kind of equilibrium that now takes place. However, examples of China and Poland show that it is not a unique possible equilibrium. Clearly, there exists a multiplicity of equilibria and path dependency. Also history matters, in the sense that all dynamics on the way of equilibrium emergence is important. The third example is globalization. Declining of transport costs and opening the barriers for trade normally do not bring Pareto improvement. There always exist some groups that suffer from this process. If globalization takes place in a sequential way, different of multiple final equilibria can emerge.

These examples pose serious problems to the equilibrium concepts which dominate contemporary economic theory. The traditional concept of equilibrium in economics often lacks the property of dynamic sustainability, in the sense that there might be no process leading to its emergence. On contrast, equilibria in physics and other natural sciences emerge as natural outcomes of some dynamics and bear the property of stability with respect to small perturbations. On one hand, rational behaviour is quite consistent with absence of dynamics, and this criticism can easily be misregarded be economic theorists. On the other hand, economic theory often faces multiplicity of equilibria and without dynamics cannot distinguish which of them is more stable and can be more often observed in practice.

The present paper tries to fill this gap by using analogy with physics, where all complex and stable structures can dynamically emerge from initially separated

atoms. All particles in physics interact with each other but not uniformly. All
stable structures in physics emerge from the decline of field intensity around
particle with distance from it. Some economic models tried to use this "gravity
principle" *ad hoc*, but there are not sufficient micro-economic foundations in
its support. These structures in physics are named molecules or N-body systems, while in economics they naturally correspond to firms, groups and even
countries. The analogy is that all these structures are composed of elements
(atoms in physics and agents in economics) and are relatively stable. The difference is that atoms are irrational and obey laws of nature while agents are
fully or partly rational and maximize some internal objectives. The gap can
be closed by imposing some information structure, which makes agents not
so rational at some stages and thus more similar to atoms. The principle of
local interaction in economics makes it possible to derive structures similar
to physics. The local interaction in real world can be supported by transport
costs. The process of globalization diminishes there relative value, but not
everywhere: costs in internet are so low that it makes no difference whether
to copy a file from 100 or 10000 km away. On the other hand, the Big Mac
index does not equalize across countries since it does not make sense for any
individual to travel from Rome to Budapest for 250 Euro to save on Big Mac
menu just 2 Euro.

Another mechanism is non-uniform information spread and non-symmetric
access to information. Here space may be completely different, and neighbours in this space may be located far from each other in geographical space.
Investors are likely to be heterogeneous in their access to information at least
at the time of its receiving.[1] This may explain inefficiency of some financial
markets and justify the reason why their performance might not be well captured by equilibrium fully rational models. While micro-economists normally
assume full information available to all agents, in labor economics, for example, agents are often involved in search process, which does not assume full
information and reminds more behaviour of an atom. If atom meets another
atom, they may join in a molecule given that potential energy is minimized
by such a structure. Similarly, if two agents form a production function which
creates a surplus given the same individual inputs due to scale effects, they
normally join a group. While game theorists are interested more in how the
surplus is to be shared, the fact of a possibility of its creation in particular
pairs represents a not less interesting issue. This is how match between worker

---

[1] Mantegna and Stanley (2000) show a plot for autocorrelation function for S&
P 500 index of NY Stock Exchange, with the time lag about 20 minutes before
the first zero. It means that those investors who can receive information quicker
can profit from that, and thus market is not efficient. For some developing stock
markets autocorrelation function does not vanish for several days, and this opens
a possibility of chartist behaviour.

and vacancy, or male and female can occur. No one would object that such matches are rarely optimal and that path dependence plays an important role. Although discussion about theoretical foundations of modelling are quite important, it makes sense to consider some simple examples in order to see details. The paper studies the dynamics of group formation given that different shapes of production function are possible. It is shown that different types of equilibria with respect to stability can emerge. For simplicity, competition of only two technologies is studied, but some results can be generalized. The study of dynamical procedure of group emergence from atomized individuals opens important economic questions. For dynamics to be consistent, there should be no conflict between individual and group interests. With concave technologies, a group is neutral towards new joining individual if all its members get the income equal to their marginal productivity at the moment of joining this group. If we have ex ante identical agents, they are different ex post, and this difference depends only on historical randomness: the temporal sequence of joining a group. In the presence of scale technologies, more complicated phenomena can be observed. Group may no longer tolerate individual freedom of agents to shift across them, as these contradicts group interests independently on the principle of output sharing. It is also shown that different equilibria are selected in a dynamic process when we have different historical sequence of group emergence.

The applications include not only emergence of a firm or group. It is possible to go further and to predict an optimal size of a country, when parameters of structural interaction across agents are known.

The structure of the paper is as follows. Section 2 describes the basic ideas related to atoms in physics in application to economic models. Section 3 describes the procedure of group emergence as a process similar to chemical reaction or crystallization. The elements of these self-organized groups formally obey economic laws, but the dynamics of the process depends on the shape of production technologies. Interesting questions related to a possibility of conflict between individual and group interests, as well as multiplicity of equilibria and path dependency are also discussed. Section 4 describes an emergence of such stable spatial structures as countries. The paper ends with conclusions.

2 Economic Activity from Atomic Perspective

Atomic society. The idea of atomic society has probably inspired the creators of classical microeconomic theory. A large group of identical agents with identical preferences got together at the market place to exchange goods. How it is close to the concept of monoatomic gas. Atoms may also have different speeds, like agents can have different initial endowments. From this point on, the laws governing the interaction, differ. Now let us look to what extent further analogies with natural sciences can be potentially exploited. We know from chemistry, that atoms are not identical and that they can form molecules. Further, collection of molecules form different substances, and they can be in different states: solid, liquid, in form of gas and plasma. The transition across states depends on temperature, pressure, concentration, etc.

What similar phenomena can be observed in economics? Individuals which are usually called "agents" in economic literature resemble atoms. Families, or households, can be viewed as simple molecules. But this social structure does not have only economic background. The history of family formation was studied by F.Engels in his "History of emergence of family, private property and state". This is quite a descriptive paper, without any formulae, but it captures the self-organizing property and dynamics based on Hehel's laws of dialectics. It has significant analogy with the processes in natural sciences. What is slightly ignored is the principle of rationality.

Rationality principle. We have to admit that human beings have much more rational component in their behaviour than animals and thus evolutionary laws have to be formulated taking this into account. On the other hand, as it was recently discovered by antropologists and experimental economists (Henrich and Boyd 2001), the economic model of rational Homo Economicus is not supported in any of fifteen experimentally studied small societies. Experiments show that people are more cooperative than it is suggested by modern game theory. Pure rationality and individualism is not sufficient to model the typical pattern of agents' interaction in real societies. McClintock (1978) has represented 8 basic social orientations as 8 vectors of Rose of Winds. According to him, altruism is another direction orthogonal to pure individualism. Adding care about social utility into agents' preferences would allow to describe much richer pattern of possible social interactions that is done currently according to pure individualistic preferences, considered by neoclassical economists. It is possible to go further and to argue whether the principle of rationality which forms one of the core principles of neoclassical economics is correct. For example, Simon (1978) proposes the theory of incomplete rationality, which was also supported by some results in experimental economics. Rejection of more neoclassical principles leads to institutional economics (see, for example, (Oleynik 2000)). But institutionalism has its own problems (for example, it does not allow for heavy use of mathematical models), and I do not want to depart too heavily from neoclassical mainstream. Rationality can be kept but incomplete or asymmetric information can change behaviour of agents completely. In neoclassical models incomplete information is widely used, but it is assumed that agents are aware of all probability distributions. But one can easily find plenty of examples when uncertainty is fundamental, so that no idea about probability distribution can be obtained.[2]

---

[2] Think about the following examples: probability to be employed after having interview, probability that dollar will gain against euro tomorrow, etc. Smart

Dynamic approach. Like in physical problems, the dynamic approach to evolution of a system suggests some initial conditions, dynamics and convergence to a set of attracting points, which only in some special cases might be a unique equilibrium.[3] Assume that initially there is a set of separated individuals. If production technologies are such that cooperation is beneficial, people meet each other and form a group. Note that if they are pure egoists, bargaining over split of a surplus might take too much energy. In evolutionary perspective, those groups are more successful where no bargaining is taking place and surplus is shared on mutually recognized agreement, sometimes equally, sometimes in proportion of productivities, sometimes to maximize the joint utility.

Effects from globalization. By globalization we will understand endogenous integration of previously separated markets. Market structures can change over time, and globalization usually undermines the role of local monopolists by bringing competition to their market. While local monopolists might try to block it since they can loose profits, the process is generally beneficial for consumers. Objectively it is driven by the decline in relative transport costs as well as elimination of other trade barriers. The process of globalization is not necessarily Pareto improving, and this is the reason of political debates about this issue. It may be argued that if all firms would remain small then globablization will increase competition. But the existence of transnational corporations growing on scale economies can leads to destruction of small local firms, with decline in competition and deadweight loss in social efficiency. As Hayek mentions (cited from (Oleynik 2000)), economic analysis should concentrate on explanation on non-planned results of human activity. Studying globalization would require dynamic approach since it is self-emerging transformation of market structures.

In physics, the system dynamics is usually generated from micro processes in itself. Postulating dynamics in economics is not a step forward; it is just a creation of school alternative to one postulating equilibrium. It is necessary to find what interactions can generate dynamics. The internal logical

---

agents can estimate these probabilities based on statistical methods, but they never can do it about their individual component of risk, and the estimates will be pretty heterogeneous. That is why even rational agents often behave with a rule of thumb if they face fundamental uncertainties.

[3] By strange reason, existence of equilibrium forms one of hard core principles of neo-classics. It would sound strange if some branch of physics studying equilibrium processes would separate completely from other branch, studying dynamics. All physicists understand that both situations are possible, and one need to distinguish what is more important in particular case. Most part of equilibria in physics are asymptotically stable states of dynamic system, and the relative change of the system during reasonable time interval can be neglected.

strength of neoclassical economics[4] is based on the fact that full rationality kills dynamics. It is similar to ancient paradox about Ahilles being unable to approach turtle. A possibility of infinite reiteration of the process "I know that they know that I know..." leads to study of fixed points instead of dynamics. Bounded rationality is a formal way to limit the deepness of iterations and to derive differential equation leading to dynamics. But there are some other realistic components which lead to self-organization of economic structures. Scale economics, spatial structure and transport costs can lead to multiplicity of equilibria and self-emergence of stable economic structures, while dynamics can be generated by fundamental uncertainty and lead to self-organization and path dependency in this environment. Some examples will be considered in subsequent models.

We observe that relatively few firms consist of one self-employed individual or family, although we should not ignore this type of economic activity which can be optimal for certain professions. The question how groups of particular size are formed is an interesting question (see (Yamishita and Onuchi 2000, Yegorov 2001a)) studied in the next section.

3 Self-Organized Economic Groups

3.1 Motivation

There are many phenomena in economic and social life which exhibit such properties as multiplicity of equilibria, path dependency and critical dependence on parameters (?). They can be better modeled with the tools of self-organizing systems, which make strong use of non-linearities and explicit models of system structure. The paper (Yegorov 2001a) studies the emergence of self-organized groups and competition among them. It focuses on theoretical description of the underlying processes. The special attention is devoted to the case when a particular part of society is decomposed into two or more groups and these groups compete for their members.

Practical applications can be discovered in quite different areas of economic and social life. Allen (2000) mentions that "the concept of a coalition provides a general way to model various economic institutions such as firms, countries, cities, customs unions, and so on". The path of the exchange rate of euro to dollar reminds more strategic game for the share in world's savings rather than random walk. Social life includes a lot of examples of intolerance between opposing parties or religious groups, which include the elements of "dishonest competition": spreading false information, punishing party members who are about to shift to opposition.

---

[4] In its current state; as any science it should evolve.

3.2 Paper Structure

The paper (Yegorov 2001a) is organized as follows. First, different types of equilibrium split in "honest competition" are studied. The role of technology is important.[5] Technology of production depends on group size and can be of decreasing-returns-to-scale (DRS), increasing-returns-to-scale (IRS) or IRS-DRS type. While the first case always leads to a unique equilibrium split, in the last two cases there is normally a multiplicity of equilibria, with part of them being stable and part - unstable.

The second part of the paper derives possible productivity paths under some assumptions about interactions within a group. This gives rise to a socially optimal group size, which takes place when an average productivity of group member is maximized. The environment where each group can reach its optimal size without any damage to other group does not bear any conflict of interests. This is likely to happen on initial stage of group formation, when there are still many free members who did not join any group.

The third part is devoted to types of competition between groups. In the case of "honest competition" at any point of time each group member has a free choice to change her group. When group productivity is of DRS type, such a principle is consistent with internal group goals: the "last" member always has minimal productivity. However, in the presence of IRS multiplicity of equilibria naturally emerges, and different groups may have conflicting interests about which of them is to be chosen.

The competition of self-organized groups depends on history, and thus is path-dependent. Initially there is a population of individuals. They meet each other and start working in a group. Every individual has a freedom to join and exit any group at any period of time. The growth of a group continues until the average productivity of its members is growing. In this case a dynamic process of self-organization is self-consistent, and there is no contradiction between individual and group goals.

There is an analogy between group formation in described sense and the process of crystallization in physics. When new particles arrives to the neighbourhood of crystall structure, it interacts with it and join the structure if average potential energy declines. It means that structure is more efficient in this state. This is how stable structures emerge from chaotic sequence of microscopic processes (Kaufman 1993). Clearly, for studying economic processes one need to find the cases when efficiency of a system is higher that the sum of efficiencies of its separate parts.

A crucial part of the analysis is how productivity depends on group size. There are at least two arguments in support of its IRS-DRS shape, that is, for small

---

[5] Beth Allen (2000) also mentions the increasing role of technology issues in economic theory.

size, group exhibits increasing returns to scale which later are replaced by decreasing returns. If the shape is of pure DRS type, there is no problem about equilibrium existence in competition across groups, but there is a problem of individual incentives at the growth stage, since it is both socially and individually optimal to have groups of the smallest size with one individual.

The second argument is based on an example. Consider an intellectual interdisciplinary group doing brainstorming activity. It is assumed that every couple of individuals can generate a new idea with some probability. Also, each member of a group has a veto right which is used on average with a certain probability. Thus, the number of generated ideas is roughly proportional to the square of group size, while only a fraction of them proportional to a negative exponent will survive. Thus, the group production function is of IRS-DRS type, with a unique maximum for average productivity.

When the total population of agents is much larger than an optimal group size, society splits into many groups of optimal size (with an exception of 1 or 2, since population size may not be exactly divisible on the optimal integer related to group size). This equilibrium is consistent with the freedom of individual choice. More interesting case arises when the total number of agents is between the number necessary for creation of 1 and 2 groups of optimal size. If 2 groups start to grow symmetrically, the equal split corresponds to suboptimal allocation of human resources. Every group is interested in capturing an agent from the rival group and is willing to pay him more than the average productivity of his group. This model may explain a stylized fact about existence of head hunting phenomenon across firms.

Assume now the environment of asymmetric technologies and asymmetric growth. A potentially more productive group based on new technology may not even break even if it emerged later, since the rival group may have a strategic interest to block its growth at the initial stage. When its average productivity is still smaller than one of a larger group which already exploits its DRS part of technology, there may be little individual incentive to join this new group unless one knows than many agents will shift later. Old group may strategically block and postpone the emergence of socially optimal allocation of resources.

There are more other interesting phenomena that can be studied in this framework. Now we turn to another example, which shows the importance of spatial structure.

4 Emergence of Countries

This model is written in a static form,[6] in order to show how field can generate structure. It is also a story about group formation, and the goal is to find an optimal group size, which is a country in this case. While spatial structure was not important for group formation, is a core of any country.[7] Spatial structure has its own topology coming from a natural relation between area and distance.

When one deals with too many elements, it makes sense to use the concept of continuous space and to work with densities. Physicists and geographers usually do it, but economists almost do not use this technique. Consider an interesting question of politico-economical geography. Are the borders of the countries only a result of the previous history, or there is some internal economic force which makes the existing political structures stable or unstable? Papers by Alesina and Spolaore (1997, 1996) touch similar questions, but in a different manner. There also exists literature on gravity models, but it deals more with international trade intensity rather then estimation of direct costs for a particular country. Just to remind, gravity model was copied from physics, with the assumption that potential of interaction of different parts is proportional to their masses and inversely proportional to the distances between them. This idea will not be employed here, because there is no obvious microeconomic reason under this assumption. Instead, very intuitive ideas, connected with the country size, population density, transportation costs will be used for defining an optimal structure (Yegorov 2001b).

4.1 The Properties of Geographical Space

In this model the philosophy of two-dimensional geographical space with its properties will be used. Economists are used to ignore these properties in most cases, and even when they consider them, usually see no big difference between distance in preferences and geographical distance. Thus, I want to remind some of the properties of geographical space which comes without discussion in any classical model in physics and geography.

1. The space has an Euclidean metric and two-dimensional measure, which has the sense of area and can be measured in square kilometers, basing on any geographical map.
2. Population is distributed heterogeneously across this space, and is immobile in the first approximation. Thus the population density function is determined and should be taken as given.

---

[6] Dynamic version of the model can also be written but then we naturally move from economics to the theory of wars.

[7] In German, land and state are given by the same word.

3. The space is covered by a dense network of roads. Without big error, one may assume that the distance between any two points can be determined as Euclidean distance. Transport costs of communication is proportional to this distance.

5 The Assumptions about Country Structure

In order to be able to talk about an optimal country size (with respect to any criteria) one should first define some essential characteristics of a country. Usually a country has a central power, which provides public goods and some control over the integrity of the country. The following formal assumptions will be made.

1. Any country has a symmetric geometric shape, with the capital located in the center. The government is located in the center and has a fixed cost of running independently of the size or population of the country.
2. The population of each country is distributed across space with uniform density.
3. Any citizen has to communicate with the center, but the communication cost is subsidized by the central power.
4. The government has to devote resources to the protection of the country's border. Efficient protection included some border guards, duties and is assumed to be proportional to the length of the border.
5. The land area of the country can be considered as a capital, bringing some rent. Further it will be assumed that this rent is proportional to the territory, independently on human resources. (One may think that the country's output is related to the mineral resources that its own. Alternatively, it may come from farming.)

6 The Main Results of the Model

Consider a country in a form of a square with the side a.[8] For simplicity, the population is assumed to be distributed homogeneously with density ?. The unit transport costs are t. There are two potential regimes - dictatorship and democracy, which differ in their objective functions. Dictator will maximize his profit, i.e. country's surplus, while democracy will care about medium voter and thus will tend to maximize per capita surplus.

The revenue is assumed to be proportional to the territory: $TR = \alpha a^2$. The total cost of running a country has several components:

---

[8] The result is easily extended for any shape, for example, circle or hexagon.

a) communication costs - the number of citizens multiplied to the average distance to the center and unit transport cost; here it is $CC = ct\rho a^3$, where $c = const$ is a certain integral, which can be calculated exactly and which may differ depending on the country shape;
b) costs of protecting borders (military, customs, etc), which is proportional to the length of borderline, $BC = 4a$ (we can put coefficient, but better we make normalization of the cost of protecting 1 km of border to be 1, and all other costs are calculated in these terms);
c) cost of having government; is can be thought as fixed cost to have a king or parliament, for rather big country it is relatively small, and we will neglect it in further discussions.

The optimal policies can be derived for both regimes.

Dictatorship. The profit function of a dictator is revenue from holding a country minus costs of running it and is given by the formula

$$\Pi = \alpha a^2 - 4a - ct\rho a^3 \tag{1}$$

It is given by a cubic function with a negative coefficient for the cubic term and positive for the quadratic. Thus, to have too big country is always unprofitable. The condition, necessary for maximum, $d\Pi/da = 0$, gives two roots. The lower corresponds to a minimum, and the bigger - to maximum. Thus, the optimal country size is given by the formula

$$a^* = \frac{\alpha + \sqrt{\alpha^2 - 12ct\rho}}{3ct\rho} \tag{2}$$

Democracy. In the case of democracy the objective is the profit per capita $\pi = \Pi/N$, where $N = \rho a^2$, and is given by

$$\pi = -cta + \frac{\alpha}{\rho} - \frac{4}{\rho a} \tag{3}$$

Thus, the optimal size is $a^* = 2/\sqrt{ct\rho}$. For democracy also the partial derivatives of country size with respect to t and ? are negative. However, the optimal corresponding population size does not depend on density. Thus, for given transportation costs two democracies might easily have different territories, but equal population sizes.

The model can be exploited further, but the main goal here was to show that optimal spatial structures can also emerge in economics. If we consider co-existence of different countries, clearly path dependency may take place. A border region between two countries can be unstable or even form a separate state; this was often observed in history.

7 Summary

1. Real economic world shows a lot of examples of deterministic dynamics, self-organization and path dependency, phenomena that cannot be ex-

plained within equilibrium paradigm that dominates contemporary economic theory. There are also many neoclassical models with multiplicity of
equilibria, and the selection of real one often requires dynamic approach.

2. It makes sense to trace the development of physical science that was quite
successful in explaining reality. Moreover, it came with theories explaining complex phenomena not only on qualitative but also on quantitative
basis. The main principles of classical physics include atomic structure
and the concept of field interaction, which makes all particles asymmetric
depending on their relative spatial location. Such a system evolves in time
and can form stable spatial structures. Evolution of physical system can
be traced from any initial point in time (snapshot). Only in some particular cases it can be treated as steady state, or equilibrium. The laws
governing dynamics are internal for the system.

3. Dynamics in economics cannot emerge if all agents are fully rational, however bounded rationality or fundamental uncertainty which limits the possibility of agents to make infinite number of iterations can do it. For example, search models, typical in labor economics, can be examples of such
dynamic systems. A firm can be an analogy of growing crystall, which
matches with atoms-workers and either accept them or not. One of the
models studied in paper is related to dynamic process of group formation.
For non-DRS production technology of a group, there exists a multiplicity
of equilibria and path dependency can take place.

4. Another model is related to optimal country size and country formation.
Here the spatial structure plays an explicit role, since agents are asymmetric depending how far from the capital they live. Historical emergence of a
country can be similar to the process of crystallization. A bigger kingdom
could emerge from several smaller and be stable, only if this structure is
optimal for all its participants. While territory gives the resources, transport costs and the length of border represent expenses. Depending on the
population density and transport costs, smaller or larger country can be
optimal for a given historical moment.

References

Alesina, A. and Spolaore, E.: 1996, International conflict, defense spending and the
size of countries, *Nber Workink Papers* (5694).

Alesina, A. and Spolaore, E.: 1997, On the number and size of nations, *Quarterly
Journal of Economics* **112**(4), 1027–1056.

Allen, B.: 2000, The future of microeconomic theory, *Journal of Economic Perspectives* .

Henrich, J. and Boyd, R.: 2001, Cooperation, reciprocity and punishment in fifteen
small-scale societies, *Santa Fe WP 01-01-007* .

Kaufman, S.: 1993, *The Origin of Order: Self-Organization and Selection in Evolution*, Oxford University Press.

Mantegna, R. and Stanley, H.: 2000, *An Introduction to Econphysics. Correlation and Complexity in Finance*, Cambridge University Press.

McClintock, C.: 1978, Social values: Their definition, measurement and development, *Journal of Research and Development in Education* **12**, 121–137.

Oleynik, A.: 2000, *Institutional Economics*.

Simon, H.: 1978, Rationality as process and as product of thought, *American Economic Review* **68**(2).

Yamishita, T. and Onuchi, A.: 2000, Effect of information on cooperative behavior in group formation with social dilemma, *Proc. of the 4th Japan - Australian Joint Workshop* pp. 193–200.

Yegorov, Y.: 2001a, Competition of self-organized groups, *Mimeo* .

Yegorov, Y.: 2001b, Gravity model, *Mimeo* .

Statistical Economics on Multi-Variable Layered Networks

T. Erez*, M. Hohnisch**, S. Solomon***

1 Introduction

Statistical Mechanics provides a universal framework to model and analyze large systems with interacting components, even beyond the traditional realm of physics. Many techniques of Statistical Mechanics are applied today in diverse areas of scientific research, such as biology, sociology and economics (Stauffer 2004). A decade ago, the economist (Grandmont 1992) coined the term *Statistical Economics*, pointing to the analogy between large economic systems and large physical systems, and suggested that large economic systems can be appropriately modeled using techniques developed in Statistical Mechanics (Brock and Durlauf 2004).

For Statistical Economics to benefit from the vast knowledge that accumulated in Statistical Mechanics, it is crucial to establish which structures are shared by physical and economic systems, and which are essentially different. Economic systems, like physical systems, involve local interactions of both attractive and repulsive type. To formalize such interactions, a Boltzmann-Gibbs measure derived from a Hamiltonian function is an appropriate formal object. However, a proper interpretation of the Hamiltonian is still an open issue in economics. While in the present paper we work within the Hamiltonian formalism, the ideas herein apply also to dynamical systems (Malcai et al. 2002, Shnerb et al. 2000) that do not admit an energy function, i.e. the interactions may be asymmetric.

* Tom thanks "SARA Computing and Networking Services" for generously providing machine time for the simulations.

** M.H. gratefully acknowledges financial support from DFG grant TR120/12-1.

*** The research of S.S. was supported in part by a grant from the Israeli Science Foundation.

The authors thank Prof. Dietrich Stauffer for advice and help.

The locality of the interactions raises the issue of the structure of the underlying network. In physics, a regular lattice is often an adequate approximation of the graph structure underlying the interaction in the real world. In contrast, economic dynamics involve social networks, for which a regular graph topology is usually a very rough and often unjustifiable approximation. Scale-free graphs are presumably more appropriate, yet empirical evidence on the actual structure of communication and social networks is only beginning to emerge (Nowak and Vallacher 1998). For theoretical and empirical results in this emerging field we refer the reader to Albert and Barabasi (2002), Cohen et al. (2003).

Lately agent-based economic models have been introduced that take into account the inhomogeneous character of the various agent variables . However, the connections/ interactions between the agents were usually represented by a single network. In the present paper we address a different aspect of economic systems: their multi-layered structure (Figure 1).

Isolating the economic interactions of one type (e.g. wealth exchange) from the wider economic context of the agents' interactions (e.g. exchange of convictions, preferences, expectations, risk attitudes, assets etc.) is often unrealistic. In general, individual economic decisions result from an interplay of such distinct variables. In fact, it is a pillar of classical economics that diverse individual variables interrelatedly determine decisions. Yet, such systems have found so far little attention in Statistical Economics models[1].

In the present paper we aim at formulating a general framework for modeling economic systems, where each agent is characterized by multiple variables of distinct nature. Each type of variable constitutes a layer with a particular graph structure, with only the set of nodes (agents) common to all layers. In addition to local interaction of neighboring variables within a layer, variables associated with the same agent in different layers interact. This introduces coupling between the layers, which qualitatively changes the dynamical pattern of every layer. We call a system with the above properties a "Solomon Network" (SN) [2].

At first glance, the dynamics of each layer in a SN may look similar to a single variable system in some external field provided by the rest of the variables. Yet, SN models are unique in the sense that the interaction between layers is bi-directional, allowing for feedback between each layer and its "external" field. The dramatic effect that this feedback can have on the system

---

[1] Multi-layered models of a different nature were considered in other areas of physics-inspired research, like neural networks (Ruck et al. 1990) and opinion formation (Schulze n.d.).

[2] This nomenclature has been introduced by Dietrich Stauffer with reference to the biblical dilemma of an agent being "claimed" by (i.e. is part of) different social networks.

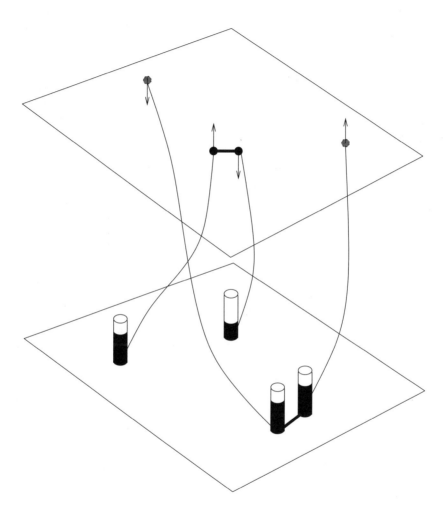

Fig. 1. A schematic representation of the Solomon Network architecture. Each agent is represented by two variables, one on each layer, connected by a curved line, while thick lines represent nearest-neighbor relations on each layer. Not all the intra-layer neighbors of the agents are depicted. Two elements are of special interest: the variables on each layer are of a different type, and the neighbors of an agent on one layer are not her neighbors on the other layer.

behavior is demonstrated already at the level of the simplest model described below. This is a step toward substituting the usual closed system and stationary/quenched environment paradigm with economics models that provide a wider and interactive (and reactive) representation of the environment.

The topology of the coupling between the layers in a SN is formally characterized by the mapping between the nodes of the different layers. In physical systems the graph structure is often formalizing physical proximity, and therefore if a physical system would be under investigation, we would expect such a mapping to be isometric (preserving distance). In contrast, social networks formalize communication links rather than physical proximity. Therefore, preserving distance is not a natural property of a mapping between different social networks. It may well be the case that an agent's reference group for a certain social or economic interaction is entirely different from her reference group for another type of interaction. For example, we may think of a scenario where, for certain people, consumption and saving patterns are formed by comparing themselves to people who live in their residential neighborhood, while their expectation of the general state of the market is formed through discussions with their colleagues at work. These two reference groups may be totally distinct, or have any degree of correlation (overlap). In general, the graph structures associated with different layers may differ: for example, a random graph may be coupled with a regular graph. Moreover, one may extend the above definition of SN to include cases in which the site correspondence between the layers is not one-to-one (e.g. people that do not go to work, or people who work in more then one place).

As a first step toward an understanding of such models and the properties of corresponding economic systems, we formulate in Section 2 a simple model with only two layers. In section 3 we discuss the theoretically expected properties of the model and in section 4 we study the model by using Monte Carlo simulations. We return to the general paradigm and discuss its possible ramifications in Section 5.

2 The model

Let A denote a set consisting of N economic agents. Each agent $i \in A$ is characterized by two random variables. First, the variable X_i represents the agent's saving ratio, i.e. the proportion of the individual budget which is saved, rather than consumed. Each variable X_i takes values in the set $\mathcal{S}_x = \{1, 2, \ldots, Q\}$ with some natural number Q. To interpret X_i as a savings ratio, one considers $\frac{1}{Q}X_i$ rather than X_i.

Second, the variable S_j represents the agent's expectation about the prospects of the economy. For simplicity, we allow only two individual states, called "optimism" and "pessimism". Accordingly, each variable S_j takes values in the set $\mathcal{S}_s = \{-1, 1\}$, and we arbitrarily interpret 1 as "optimism", and -1 as "pessimism".

Thus we define two layers for the model consisting respectively of the variables $(X_i)_{i \in A}$ and $(S_j)_{j \in A}$. Both layers are modeled as spin systems with nearest-neighbor interaction, with respect to the graph structure underlying each layer. In addition, there is interaction between those pairs of variables from different layers, which correspond to the same agent. Thereby the two spin-fields are coupled.

In the present simple SN model, we confine ourselves to one-dimensional layers with periodic boundary conditions (chains). Thus, the agent i's neighbors in the X-layer are $(i+1) \bmod N$ and $(i-1) \bmod N$. The neighborhood relation on the S-layer is specified through a permutation r of the elements of A. More precisely, the agent i is represented on the layer S by the site $r(i)$. Accordingly, the two variables associated with agent $i \in A$ are X_i and $S_{r(i)}$. The neighbors of $r(i)$ in S are $(r(i)+1) \bmod N$ and $(r(i)-1) \bmod N$. Thus the agent i interacts directly with four agents: $i+1$, $i-1$, $r^{-1}(r(i)+1)$, $r^{-1}(r(i)-1)$. Note that the interaction with the first pair is of a different nature (and in fact parametrized by different variables) than the interaction with the other pair. Note also that in this model we have chosen a one-to-one, totally random correspondence between the layers.

We denote by $\mathcal{S} = \{-1, 1\} \times \{1, 2, \ldots, Q\}$ the individual spin-space of the composite system. A configuration assigns to each agent $i \in A$ values from $\mathcal{S}$. The configuration space, denoted as usual by $\mathcal{S}^A$, consists of $(2Q)^N$ configurations.

The dynamics is defined by introducing the Hamiltonian function H that assigns to each configuration $\omega \in \mathcal{S}^A$ some real number $H(\omega)$, such that the probability of ω is given by the Boltzmann distribution associated with H

$$Pr(\omega) = 1/Z_T \exp(-H(\omega)/T). \tag{1}$$

with T denoting the temperature parameter of the Boltzmann distribution, and Z_T being the normalizing constant given by $Z_T = \sum_{\omega \in \mathcal{S}^A} \exp(-H(\omega)/T)$. The ratio H/T measures the relative strength of the social interaction of the system against other random perturbations. For $T = 0$ the peer pressure is absolute, and basically the individual has no freedom. for $T = \infty$, there is no influence between any of the variables and all states of the system are equally probable.

In our model, there are three components of interaction: 1) the nearest-neighbor interaction among different agents on the X-layer, 2) the nearest-neighbor interaction among different agents on the S-layer, and 3) interaction between the variables corresponding to the same agent in the two layers.

The term in the Hamiltonian representing the interaction within the X-layer is specified as

$$H_X(\omega) = J_x \sum_{<i,j>_x} (X_i(\omega) - X_j(\omega))^2. \tag{2}$$

with $<i, j>_x$ denoting the summation over pairs of nearest neighbors according to the X-layer topology. The basic economic content of this specification is the notion of herding behavior (Kindleberger 1978, Bikhchandani and Sharma 2000). That notion stands in economics for a variety of effects where market actors, such as stock traders, consumers, managers etc., tend to align their opinions and/or actions with those in their social neighborhood. In our case, if the current state X_i of the agent i is very different from the typical opinions X_j of its neighbors j, Eq. 2 indicates a strong energy preference for the next moves to bring X_i and X_j closer. This specification is in accordance with experimental results from social psychology (Nowak and Vallacher 1998, Festinger 1954, Lewenstein et al. 1993) suggesting that the likelihood of re-alignment of one's own actions and beliefs (i.e. the saving behavior, in the present model) with those observed in the reference group, will increase with the perceived difference in those actions and beliefs. In physics, a Hamiltonian of the above type have been used, for instance, in the Blume-Capel model (Blume 1966, Capel 1966, 1967a,b).

A similar herding behavior is observed for the agents' expectations: the expectations of the individuals, with respect to the future market behavior, will tend to conform with the opinion of their social surrounding. Thus the interaction between the agents' expectations has a similar form as Eq. 2. Since we use a rougher characterization of expectations (-1 corresponds to a pessimist view, and $+1$ corresponds to an optimist view), the interaction on the S-layer reduces to the classical Ising-model Hamiltonian:

$$H_S(\omega) = J_s \sum_{<i,j>_S} (S_i(\omega) - S_j(\omega))^2. \tag{3}$$

If $Q = 2$, the X-layer is also an Ising chain, and the model reduces to a classical Ising model on a peculiar SN graph structure. This special case was discussed in Malarz (2003). However, a key property of the SN framework is, in our view, the distinct character of the respective layers, both in terms of the spin-space and the underlying graph structure.

To complete the definition of the system, one has to specify the interaction between variables corresponding to the same agent in the two layers, i.e. X_i and $S_{r(i)}$. This interaction expresses the prominent economic behavioral regularity that an optimistic agent is likely to save less than a pessimistic agent (Davidson 1991). Thus we introduce a term that couples the variables corresponding to the same agent:

$$H_C(\omega) = J_c \sum_i (X_i(\omega) - C(S_{r(i)}(\omega)))^2. \tag{4}$$

The function $C(\cdot)$ goes from $\mathcal{S}_s$ to the real numbers, with $C(-1) > C(1)$. Obviously, when $J_c = 0$, the system breaks down to two independent chains.

Finally, the Hamiltonian of the system is obtained by adding the three components:

$$H(\omega) = H_X(\omega) + H_S(\omega) + H_C(\omega). \tag{5}$$

Since (cf. Eq. 1) the parameters of the model appear dynamically in the combination H/T, we will often consider the coupling parameters J as constants and study the behavior of the system under the variation of T. Thus in the following we use the parameter $\beta = 1/T$ as a measure of interaction-to-noise ratio in the economic system.

In the next two sections we will discuss this system from the theoretical and respectively simulation point of view.

3 Discussion of the Expected Model Properties

For complete characterization of the phases of the model, one may have to perform numerical simulations of the type we present in the next section. However, the experience accumulated in the last 30 years in Statistical Mechanics can be used to extract quite a number of predictions and intuitions about the model, and especially its herding (order-disorder transition) properties.

While the SN model was not studied before, the properties of each layer in separate are covered by rigorous general theorems (Stanley 1971). To understand the import of the theorems let us start with the behavior of the decoupled layers at T=0. In this case, both layers are in a "ground state", i.e. the state of minimal energy.

The case of the S layer is easier to analyze. The minimal energy is realized for $S_i = S_0$ $\forall i$, with $S_0 = \pm 1$. In general, for dimensions larger then one, there exists a **critical value** $T = T_c$ such that for the entire range $T < T_c$ the system remains ordered. Indeed, for $T_c > T > 0$, the configurations are not exactly uniform, but the S_i's across the entire system remain "herded" around one of the values $+1$ or -1. The degree of herding of each configuration ω is measured by the magnetization M defined as the average of the $S_i(\omega)$ over the entire range $i \in A$:

$$M = \sum_i S_i/N \tag{6}$$

The transition at T_c between the ordered ($M \neq 0$) and disordered ($M = 0$) phases is called , following the Statistical Mechanics conventions, a Phase Transition. In the present article we will use interchangeably the words "magnetization" and "herding" to denote M.

Interestingly enough, in one-dimensional systems the order-disorder phase transition is absent ($T_c = 0$) (Stanley 1971). Thus, theory predicts the absence of herding in the absence of coupling between the "expectations" layer and the "savings/consumption" layer of our model. In fact, rigorous theorems insure that ANY system with local interactions in one dimension is in the disordered phase for any $T > 0$. Thus, even the coupled system will not present herding, as long as the two layers have a roughly similar metric (i.e. $|r(i) - i| << N$ $\forall i$). Only when the two layers have significantly different neighborhood assignments a herding phase can emerge at finite T. This is because such a system would not be amenable to the format of a one-dimensional model with local interactions. Moreover, the transition between the herding and disordered phase will have a character that is not necessarily the one characteristic to any of the higher dimension Ising (or Blume -Capel) models. The Mote Carlo simulations we report in the next section confirm these predictions.

In higher dimensions each of the layers, when taken independently, may display quite different critical parameters $T_c^X \neq T_c^S$. As one brings the layers "in contact" by making them interact, the composite system might preserve two independent phase transitions (if the inter-layer interaction is weak) or change its behavior qualitatively.

One may ask how relevant is the phase transition analysis for an actual system. After all, it is *a priori* probable that the parameters of the system realized in nature are far from the critical ones. Thus the system would spend its entire life span in just one phase and ignore the other. The answer is that it falls upon the shoulders of the modeler to identify the interactions and parameters that DO matter qualitatively in the real system. Modeling interactions that do not matter is of course useless (nobody would model the current financial markets in terms of the issue of whether the dollar is or not going to be devalued by 100% during the current trading day or whether the side of the road on which the cars drive would spontaneously flip). Thus pessimism and optimism, and in general the values that the dynamical variables can take, should be and are usually chosen such as to reflect operative possibilities so that the system may very well be in either phase.

Given that a phase transition (say herding-disorder) exists, one may wonder whether establishing its type (universality class) in detail is of interest in economics. The difference between a discontinuous (first order) phase transition and a continuous one may give precious indications on whether to expect large fluctuations or rather a plain collapse. Even if the transition is continuous, it is often important to know which of the layers has the dominating role in triggering it.

4 Monte Carlo Study of the Model

We simulated the above-defined model using standard Monte Carlo simulation methods (Metropolis et al. 1953). In particular, we update the agents' state in a random order. Each Monte Carlo Step (MCS) is composed of $\check{N}$ such random selections. In each computational step, after an agent i is chosen at random, we run a Heat-Bath algorithm Landau and Binder (2000) to generate the next state. The new values for the selected X_i and S_i are sampled according to the Boltzmann distribution (Eq. 1) with respect to the potential H (cf. Eq. 5): given a particular configuration of the system $\omega \in S^A$, let us denote $\omega_{x,s}^i$ the configuration of the system which is identical to ω, except for the variables associated with agent i, where $X_i = x$ and $S_{r(i)} = s$. The probability to move from ω to $\omega_{x,s}$ is given by the following equation:

$$P(x,s) = 1/Z_T^i \exp(-H(\omega_{x,s}^i)/T) \tag{7}$$

where $Z_T^i = \sum_{(x,s)\in\mathcal{S}} \exp(-H(\omega_{x,s}^i)/T)$ i.e. the sum over all possible values for X_i and $S_{r(i)}$.

In the present investigation, we simulated a system with $N = 10^6$ agents and $Q = 10$ saving ratios. Our simulations around the T_c consisted of $6.4*10^5$ MCS, and the results were averaged over the last $3.2*10^5$ MCS. Less iterations were needed for the T ranges outside the critical slowing-down zone, where $2*10^4$ MCS were sufficient, and the results were averaged over the last 10^4 MCS in that case. Unless stated otherwise, simulations were run with $J_s = J_x = J_c = \frac{1}{3}$, $C(-1) = 8$ and $C(1) = 3$. The initial conditions were set to either the ordered configuration ($S_j = -1$ and $X_i = 8$) or to a totally random one. We obtained the randomly generated permutations r by mapping every X-layer site to a S-layer site chosen from the entire lattice with equal probability.

We found a phase transition occurring at a critical value of approximately $T_c = 2.79$. Both layers become ordered below T_c. Figures 2 and 3 depict the herding of each of the two layer as a function of T. The functional dependence of the herding M on T close to T_c appears to be: (cf. Figures 2b and 3b)

$$M \propto 1/log(T_c - T). \tag{8}$$

In contrast, Malarz (2003) measured the critical exponent β of the SN model with two Ising layers to be $1/2$ (i.e. in the Ising universality class). Therefore this feature of the model is attributed to the coupling of two layers carrying different dynamics, and not merely a result of the particular topology.

The two ordered states ($M < 0$ and $M > 0$) for $T < T_c$ can be called "pessimistic economy" and "optimistic economy" respectively. The transition between them is a first order one similar to the transition when crossing the line of zero magnetic field $H = 0$ below the critical Ising temperature. Thus our model is capable of capturing empirical results describing dramatic swings in the market mood (Hohnisch et al. n.d.). Moreover the model predicts that in the herding phase, the transition between an optimistic and pessimistic mood in the S-layer induces a transition between the "saving" and "spending" modes in the X-layer.

A variable of major interest for economics is the empirical distribution of the X-layer, since it characterizes the aggregate saving in the economy. Figure 4 depict empirical distributions of the X-layer at different T's. The distribution is symmetric above T_c, i.e. in the disordered state. Below T_c, the distribution is skewed, reflecting symmetry breaking in the herded state. If $C(-1)$ and $C(1)$ are further apart, the empirical distribution of the X-layer for $T > T_c$ becomes bimodal (Figure 5).

In accordance with the theoretical prediction, no phase transition was found in simulations where $r(\cdot)$ was the identity permutation (results not shown), since the system is essentially one-dimensional. Also, when the layers are defined on similar lattices (as is the case in our simulations), one may construct the r-transformation to be bound (i.e. $|r(i) - i| < C_0 \; \forall i$). In this

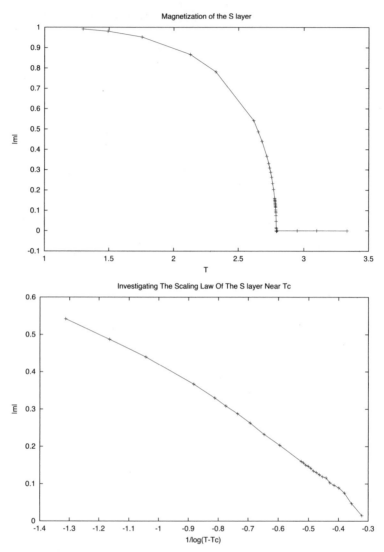

Fig. 2. Herding of the expectations as a function of T. Figure 2a displays the main feature of the model: as opposed to the behavior of the separate expectations and savings layers, the composite system present 2 distinct phases: one without herding $M = 0$ for $T > Tc$ and one with $M > 0$ for $T < T_c$ Figure 2b demonstrates the dramatic nature of the vanishing of the herding M of the expectations as one approaches T_c by showing that $M \propto 1/log(T_c - T)$, i.e. all the derivatives are infinite at the vanishing point.

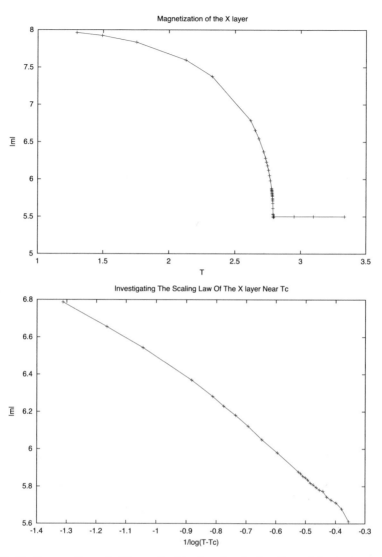

Fig. 3. Similar results as in Figure 2, this time for the herding of the savings ratios. Since X_i ranges between 1 and 10, 5.5 is the average value in the unordered phase.

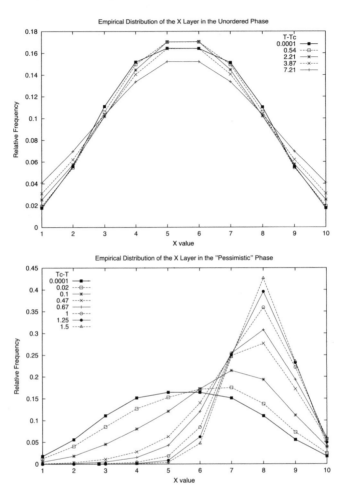

Fig. 4. Empirical distribution of individual saving ratios (X_i) at different values of T. Figure 4a depicts the distribution of X_i's at various T's in the non-herding phase. At $T = \infty$, the distribution is uniform (not shown). Note how all distributions are symmetric in the non-herding phase. Figure 4b depicts the empirical distribution of X_i at various values of T in the herding phase. In the particular shown case, the herding pattern is in the "saving" mode and the distribution is skewed towards high X_i values. Not shown, is the corresponding distribution of the S-layer which was in the herding "pessimistic" phase.

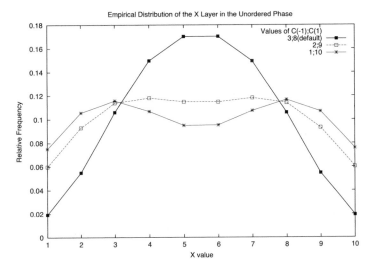

Fig. 5. Empirical distribution of individual savings (X_i) in the unordered phase for different values of $C(\cdot)$. If $C(1)$ and $C(-1)$ are far enough from each other, a bimodal distribution emerges, since most X_i are in correlation with $S_{r(i)}$, and the S variables are distributed equally between 1 and -1 at the unordered phase.

case as well, no ordered phase emerges (results not shown). According to the theory, the ordered phase shrinks to $T = 0$ as one lowers $J_c \to 0$ (Figure 6).

In order to connect the model to the actual economic reality, one can calibrate the model by comparing it to empirically measurable data. In particular one can measure the size of the various groups as defined by their expectations and saving patterns. From this, one can infer by inverse engineering the realistic values for the coupling constants in the model. We studied the relation between the sizes of the groups and the values of the J's as described below. In the "pessimistic" phase, the agents $i \in A$ with $s_{r(i)} = -1$ and $x_i \in \{6, \ldots, 10\}$ constitutes the majority. In contrast, we can arbitrarily define three different minority groups. First, the set of agents with $s_{r(i)} = 1$ and $x_i \in \{6, \ldots, 10\}$ is called S-minority; second, the set of agents with $s_{r(i)} = -1$ and $x_i \in \{1, \ldots, 5\}$ is called X-minority; and the set of agents with $s_{r(i)} = 1$ and $x_i \in \{1, \ldots, 5\}$ is called SX-minority. The values chosen for the coupling constants J determine the balance between the different minority groups. Figure 7 shows the distribution of the different minority groups for various ratios of the interaction constants. If a certain interaction constant increases, the proportion of the corresponding minority group will decline for every $T < T_c$. For example, when $J_s = 0.6$ and $J_x = 0.2$, the X-minority group is downsized considerably (Figure 7). This is because every agent "prefers" conforming to its neighbors on the S-layer (i.e. having the same S value), even at the "price" of non-conformity with its neighbors on the X-layer (i.e. having a different

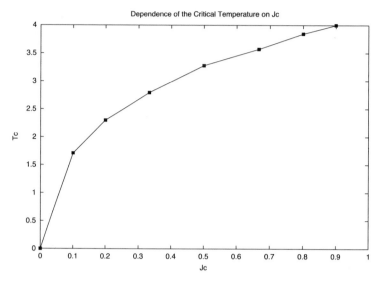

Fig. 6. Dependence of the T_c on J_c. J_x and J_s are both held fixed at a value of $\frac{1}{3}$. As J_c vanishes the system effectively decouples into two independent one-dimensional chains, and T_c approaches 0.

X value). Also, this figure shows certain symmetry of the J's. Both layers respond equally to increased preference, at least in the aspect of minority ratios - the same preference imbalance results in the same bias in the distribution between minority groups.

5 Conclusions and Outlook

In the present paper we have presented one of the simplest instances of an application of the SN framework to economic systems modeling. Already at this level one obtains interesting results, underlying the importance of the coupling of the various types of economic variables in determining the order-disorder dynamics of the global system.

Using representative agents, population averages or differential equations governing the global (macro-economic) system variables, one might have guessed that by coupling weakly two types of economic variables that do not present herding the resulting system will be in the disordered phase, i.e. the coupled system would behave somewhat as the average of the respective behaviors of its components. Instead, using theoretical and simulation tools adapted from Statistical Mechanics one finds that the coupling of two disordered economic variables has a dramatic herding effect on both variables. This shows the importance of the further study of SN models in uncovering the subtle effects of feedback in systems with multiple economic variables.

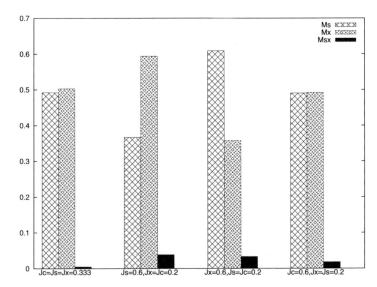

Fig. 7. Comparing ratios of various minority groups, out of the total number of agents not in the majority group, at different values of coupling parameters. Note that for each set of bars, the ratios sum to 1. The effect of increasing the relative importance of one layer over the other is symmetric. When $J_x = J_s$, the minority groups are symmetrical independently of J_c.

The study of SN models can be developed in quite a few directions. First, instead of the completely random mapping $r(i)$ between the positions of the nodes in different layers, one may consider less extreme alternatives: after all, there is often some correlation between the work place of people and their residence districts. For instance, one may consider mappings in which for a significant number of of i's one has $r(i) = i$, or mappings which preserve the topology of the neighborhoods but not their metric. This might elucidate which properties of the SN model can be traced to the mere coupling between layers (and thus possibly detectable by standard macro-economic methods), and which are a result of the particular inter-layer projection afforded by the SN framework.

Second, one should consider inhomogeneous layers, e.g. scale-free or small-world, and study projections $r(i)$ of different tyes (e.g. preserving rank or not etc.). Of course the various layers may differ in their properties, such as their scaling exponent, clustering coefficient or K-core structure (Shalit n.d.).

The SN modeling framework can also be extended to include global feedback schemes, which are particularly relevant in economic applications (Bornholdt and Wagner 2002). We intend to pursue this direction of research elsewhere (Erez et al. n.d.).

To make contact with reality, one should find and use the parameter values that represent faithfully and realistically the empirics of the modeled economic phenomenon. For example, by looking at relative sizes of the herding groups with respect to various variables, one may receive hints as to the relative strength of the couplings governing each variable. This would require the use of cross-correlational micro-data. Such data exists, for instance, for savings and consumer confidence (Kemsley et al. 1980).

In summary, we believe that the framework of Solomon Networks addresses a key property of large economic systems - the cross-interaction between the dynamics of economic variables of different types. Further investigation of such models may shed light on the mechanisms governing economic dynamics, and increase our understanding of the complex system called Economy.

References

Albert, R. and Barabasi, A.: 2002, *Reviews of Modern Physics* **74**(1), 47.

Bikhchandani, S. and Sharma, S.: 2000, Herd behavior in financial markets: A review, *IMF Working Paper* (WP/00/48).

Blume, M.: 1966, *Phys. Rev.* **141**, 517.

Bornholdt, S. and Wagner, F.: 2002, *Physica A* **316**, 453–468.

Brock, W. and Durlauf, S.: 2004, Identification of binary choice models with social interactions, *SSRI Worling Paper* (2004-02).

Capel, H.: 1966, *Physica* **32**, 96.

Capel, H.: 1967a, *Physica* **33**, 295.

Capel, H.: 1967b, *Physica* **37**, 423.

Cohen, R., Rozenfeld, A., Schwartz, N., ben Avraham, D. and Havlin, S.: 2003, *Lecture Notes in Physics* **625**(23).

Davidson, P.: 1991, *Journal of Economic Perspectives* **5**(1), 129–143.

Erez, T., Hohnisch, M. and Solomon, S.: n.d., *(in progress)* .

Festinger, L.: 1954, *Human Relations* **7**, 117.

Grandmont, J.-M.: 1992, *Journal of Economic Theory* **57**, 1–35.

Hohnisch, M., Pittnauer, S., Solomon, S. and Stauffer, D.: n.d., Socioeconomic interaction and swings in business confidence indicators.

Kemsley, W., Redpath, R. and Holmes, M.: 1980, *Family Expenditure Survey Handbook*, Her Majesty's Stationery Office.

Kindleberger, C.: 1978, *Manias, Panics and Crashes*, Basic Books.

Landau, D. and Binder, K.: 2000, *A Guide to Monte Carlo Simulations in StatisticalPhysics*, Cambridge University Press.

Lewenstein, M., Nowak, A. and Latane, B.: 1993, Statistical mechanics of social impact, *Phys. Rev. A* **45**, 703–716.

Malarz, K.: 2003, *Int. J. Mod. Phys. C* **14**, 561.

Malcai, O., Biham, O., Richmond, P. and Solomon, S.: 2002, *Phys. Rev. E* **66**.

Metropolis, N., Rosenbluth, A., Rosenbluth, M., Teller, A. and Teller, E.: 1953, *J. Chem. Phys.* **21**, 1087.

Nowak, A. and Vallacher, R.: 1998, *Dynamical social psychology*, Guilford Press.

Ruck, D., Rogers, S., Kabrisky, M., Oxley, M. and Suter, B.: 1990, *IEEE Trans. On Neural Networks* **1**(4), 296–298.

Schulze, C.: n.d., *Int. J. Mod. Phys. C* (upcoming (cond-mat/0312342)).

Shalit, A.: n.d., *(in progress)* .

Shnerb, N., Louzoun, Y., Bettelheim, E. and Solomon, S.: 2000, *Proc. Natl. Acad. Sci.* **97**(19), 10322–10324.

Stanley, H.: 1971, *Introduction to Phase Transitions and Critical Phenomena*, Clarendon Press.

Stauffer, D.: 2004, *Physica A* **336**(1).